Scottish Nationalism

Scottish Nationalism

H. J. HANHAM

HARVARD UNIVERSITY PRESS
Cambridge, Massachusetts
1969

SBN 674 79580 6

Contents

Introduction   *page* 9

1. The Scottishness of Scottish Society   15

2. The Problem of Anglicization   33

3. The Scottish System of Government   50

4. The Beginnings of Modern Nationalism   64

5. Home Rule All Round   91

6. The Fundamentalists   119

7. The Rise and Fall of Literary Nationalism   146

8. The Scottish National Party   163

9. The Lion Clamant   181

*Statement of Aim and Policy of the Scottish National
Party, December 1946*   213

Scottish Nationalist Vote at General Elections   231

A Note on Sources   232

Index   241

Introduction

Nationalism is one of the most powerful forces in the modern world. The creation of new nation states was accepted as one of the war aims by the victorious allies during the First World War. The League of Nations sanctified the independent nation state as the appropriate form of government to replace the empires of the past. The League's governing body was a parliament of the nations and its mandates to the powers administering the former colonies of Germany were designed to lead to the eventual development of nation states in those colonies. The legitimacy of the national quest for independence was again recognized by the Atlantic Charter and the Charter of the United Nations. And since 1945 a host of new nation states have come into being, some of them, like Samoa and the Cook Islands, little more than dots on the map.

Modern nationalism has not merely been legitimized by the comity of nations. It has proved itself a force of extraordinary power. At the outbreak of the First World War it destroyed the solidarity of the European working-class movement. It was the main force that kept the combatants going in two world wars. It destroyed the Austrian Empire, it destroyed the British Empire, and it has on several occasions very nearly destroyed the Soviet Empire as well. For it has divided international communism just as it divided workers' movements before the First World War. National sentiment may be crushed for the moment—as it was seemingly crushed in 1968 in Czechoslovakia and in Biafra—but it has a habit of cropping up again. International opinion sympathizes with the small nation struggling for its freedom. And international relations are habitually dominated by national rivalries. There have always been those—whether international do-gooders or international communists—who have wished to put an end to national rivalries and national diversities and

9

to fit the world into some straitjacket of their own devising, but so far the forces of nationalism have been much too strong for them.

The varieties of national self-expression are almost unlimited. There are nations like the Irish and the Magyars which have retained a national identity based on ethnic distinctions during hundreds of years of subjection to imperial powers. There are nations like the Swiss which are the creation of geography rather than of race or language. There are nations like Liberia and the United States which have been artificially constructed. And most of the post-war states of Africa are still trying to work out a viable basis for national self-expression. In Europe the normal basis for nationalism is the historic nation—the nation which enjoyed some degree of autonomy during the Middle Ages. European nationalism is, therefore, in a sense always backward-looking, always adverting to past glories, always apparently more conscious of the past than of the present. It is the English or the Scottish or the French or the Italian inheritance of which men are proud, not the untidy country one sees from the passing motor-car. It is national historians and those who write or sing about the past who have created nations, and for this reason literary men and poets often rank as national heroes alongside states-men and warriors. Indeed, in all national movements the role of the writer is a vital one, because it is to him that the nation looks to give it all the trappings which the Romantic Movement taught Europe to expect of a nation: a glorious past, a distinctive culture, a national language.

The Union between Scotland and England, which began with a union of the crowns when James VI of Scotland became James I of England in 1603, and became a formal incorporating union in 1707, was one of those artificial creations that arose from time to time in Europe as a result of dynastic alliances. It was not popular at the time either in England or in Scotland. And like those other dynastic crea-tions, the union of Holland and Belgium, the union of Sweden and Norway, and the great Hapsburg empires, it has required a dual system of government to make it work at all. Scottish institutions remain for the most part distinct from those of England, and had the Scottish estates been left in being it is possible to imagine them on many occasions doing what the Norwegian estates did in 1905, when they formally declared the independence of Norway from Sweden. The economic advantages of the Union have, however, until recently always seemed so great that it was scarcely worthwhile to break the link with England. Indeed, during the Victorian age Scotland enjoyed a prosperity so great by comparison with that of the past that unionist sentiment seemed likely to destroy Scottish national self-consciousness altogether. But though Scotland had no Mazzini, no Kossuth, no O'Connell, no Parnell, popular nationalism was always a force to be reckoned with in Scotland. There was even a Scottish equivalent of the Gaelic national movement in Ireland, whose slogan 'No language, no nation' influenced a whole generation of writers, a few of whom wrote in Gaelic, but most of whom wrote in Lowland Scots, which they set out to turn into an up-to-date literary language which might be used as a satisfactory substitute for English. And from the First World War onwards there has always been a Scottish nationalist political movement in being.

What held back the creation of a national movement in Scotland after the decline of mid-Victorian prosperity was the promise of a substantial measure of devolution within the United Kingdom. After 1885 there was a separate Secretary for Scotland, and after 1888 the Scottish Liberals at least were committed to the creation of a Scottish parliament and a Scottish administration as well. But Scottish devolution, and the Welsh devolution that was to accompany it—along with Home Rule for Ireland collectively known as Home Rule All Round—was held up by English resistance to Irish nationalism. It was 1913 before legislation to provide for the creation of a Scottish system of government could be thought about at all seriously, and war broke out before anything had been done. By the time the war was over the Irish had taken matters into their own hands and the Liberal party had broken up. Home Rule All Round was just as much a Labour party policy as a Liberal one, but the Labour party did not have a majority in parliament until 1945, and it was then much too preoccupied with problems of post-war reconstruction to spare the time and energy required to prepare a measure of Scottish and Welsh Home Rule. The best that could be done for Scotland during the inter-war and post-war years was to permit a wide measure of administrative devolution from Whitehall to Edinburgh.

The nationalist movement of the inter-war years was the creation of two distinct groups—those who were political nationalists in the traditional sense and wanted Scottish independence, and those whose hopes of Home Rule had been disappointed, and who would have been satisfied by the creation of some sort of regional parliament for

11

Scotland. Scottish nationalism has, therefore, always tended to speak with different voices. But of the support of the Scottish people for some measure of Home Rule there has never been any doubt. Rudimentary opinion polls conducted in the 1920s and 1930s showed almost exactly the same findings as have opinion polls since 1945. Rather more than 60 per cent of the people of Scotland favour a large measure of Home Rule, and a substantial body are in favour of independence. Certainly, by the standards of national movements in other countries, there is ample basis on which to build an independent Scotland.

Yet the fortunes of the nationalists have been very uncertain. By choosing to contest parliamentary elections piecemeal rather than to build up an overwhelming power outside the ordinary political system, nationalism has been exposed to all the frustrations which beset any small political party in a first-past-the-post electoral system. The motives which decide voting behaviour at elections are complex, and changes of party allegiance occur on a large scale only when the wind of change is blowing unusually strongly. But the winds of politics are notoriously fickle—'The wind bloweth where it listeth,' as Lord Salisbury once commented on some election results—and nationalist movements in Scotland have often found the contesting of elections a dispiriting task. There was a burst of nationalist fervour at the end of the 1920s and in the early 1930s, there was another one at the end of the 1940s and the beginning of the 1950s, and there has been another one since 1964. But in between there was little interest in the nationalist message. Nobody can say for sure just why the wind seemed to drop and the first two nationalist revivals to lose their impetus. Nobody can say whether or not the same thing will happen again. What is clear is that the scale of these nationalist revivals has changed. The first one was very small indeed by the standards of modern democracy, and flourished chiefly outside the mainstream of politics. The second revival took the form of a covenant movement which secured the backing of something like two million people for a measure of Home Rule (not independence). The third revival has taken the form of a massive campaign at parliamentary and municipal elections which must lead to the capture of the majority of the Scottish seats in parliament or it will be a failure.

Introduction

II

This book is the outcome of a series of chance conversations. One of these led me to write an article for the Canadian *International Journal* on Scottish nationalism today. Another led me to contemplate expanding that article into a book during the short interval between the end of the university examination period in Edinburgh in July 1968 and my departure for Harvard at the beginning of September. My object has been to explain how Scottish nationalism has developed over the past hundred years, and to give an account of the position as I see it today. I have not given much space to expositions of the nationalist point of view, such as Professor H. J. Paton's *The Claim of Scotland* (London, 1968). Nor have I gone into the history of Scotland in any depth. On that there are a number of useful books, including two good recent ones, William Ferguson's *Scotland: 1689 to the Present* (Edinburgh, 1968) and James G. Kellas's *Modern Scotland: the Nation since 1870* (London, 1968).

Lest my own standpoint be misunderstood in Scotland, let me say at the outset that though in general terms I am sympathetic to Scottish nationalism, my sympathies are derived more from having been born and educated in a small independent country, New Zealand, than from such family connections with Scotland as I have. Before moving to Scotland in 1963, where I was for five years Professor of Politics in the University of Edinburgh, I lived and worked in England. I have also spent a good deal of time during the past twelve years looking at newly independent nation states, beginning in the Federal Republic of Germany and gradually extending my range to most parts of Africa and the Middle East. By the time this book appears I shall be a Professor of History at Harvard University in the United States. I hope, therefore, that I have some of the virtues as well as the limitations of the outsider who loves Scotland, but does not quite belong to it.

Those who have read his distinguished book, *The Democratic Intellect: Scotland and her Universities in the Nineteenth Century*, will understand how fortunate I have been to be able to rely on the constant help and friendship of my Edinburgh colleague Dr. George Elder Davie. He has read the whole book, and the later chapters are to a large extent the result of a joint exploration of the ideas of the Scottish National Party. I have also had the good fortune to be able to draw on the work of a number of other friends. My historical awareness owes much to Dr. Nicholas Phillipson's unpublished Cambridge Ph.D. thesis on *The Scottish Whigs and the Reform of the Court of Session, 1785–1830*. Colin Lindsay supplied me with much valuable material about the Scottish Trades Union Congress, whose history he is writing. Dr. Barry Smith of the Australian National University helped me to track down some Australian Scottish nationalists. Dr. James Kellas of Glasgow allowed me to use his unpublished London Ph.D. thesis, *The Liberal Party in Scotland, 1885–1895*. David Murison, editor of the Scottish National Dictionary, supplied me with nationalist literature and patiently answered questions. To all of them I am most grateful. Chapter Two draws freely on my paper on 'Mid-Century Scottish Nationalism: Romantic and Radical' published in *Ideas and Institutions of Victorian Britain: Essays in Honour of George Kitson Clark*, edited by Robert Robson and published by G. Bell & Sons in 1967. Chapter Six makes use of material from my article on 'The Creation of the Scottish Office, 1881–87', published in the *Juridical Review* in 1965. Some of the themes discussed are also treated in 'The Scottish Nation Faces the Post-Imperial World', *International Journal*, XXIII (1968), pp. 570–84. For permission to use the papers of the Scottish Liberal Association I am indebted to the Scottish Liberal Party. For typing the whole manuscript in record time I am also most grateful to my secretary in Edinburgh, Miss K. U. Brown. The proofs were read with a vigilant eye by Professor Douglas Young during a visit to Harvard.

CHAPTER ONE

The Scottishness of Scottish Society

I

Scotland has possessed all the characteristics of a distinct nation since the twelfth century. Today the Scots have their own national church, their own national education system, their own national legal system, their own national banking system, their own national system of central and local government, their own national way of speaking English—even their own Scottish Trades Union Congress. As a result, Scotland is a state within the wider state of the United Kingdom of Great Britain and Northern Ireland, a state with its own characteristic pattern of life, which is in many ways quite different from that of England.

In origin the Scots are by no means a homogeneous people. In 1961 numbering 5,179,000, the people of Scotland are the product of many migrations. The best known of the early inhabitants of what is today Scotland were the Picts, whose stone monuments are still to be found scattered about certain parts of modern Scotland. The term Scot was applied at first to a group of Irish invaders and was only gradually extended to cover the whole population of Scotland. The Lowlands were partially occupied by Anglo-Saxons of various sorts, in the course of the great migration which also took the Anglo-Saxons to England, and then by the great Anglo-Norman families who dominated the history of medieval Scotland. The Western Isles, Shetland and Caithness long formed part of the Kingdom of Norway and were populated by Scandinavians, among them the founder of the great Macleod clan. The assimilation of these very different groups took a very long time, but by the end of the Middle Ages the country had settled down into two distinct cultural patterns. The Highlands, speaking Gaelic, were predominantly Celtic in culture in spite of their Scandinavian links. The Lowlands, speaking 'Inglis', were predominantly Anglo-Saxon in culture, though they had close connections with France. The two cultures were mutually hostile and as time went on Celtic Scotland was increasingly on the defensive.

The modern population pattern of Scotland was established during a period of population explosion which lasted from the end of the eighteenth century until towards the end of the nineteenth. Until the middle of the eighteenth century the people of Scotland were almost equally distributed to the north and south of the River Tay. But from then onwards the balance steadily shifted from north to south. In the nineteenth century what is now called the 'Central Belt' became a great hold-all for migrants from the Highlands, from the Lowlands north of the Tay, from the Borders, and from Ireland, north and south. Glasgow became the biggest Highland settlement in Scotland, with its own social centre, the Highlanders' Institute. And the West of Scotland became one of the major centres for Irish settlement during the great migration from Ireland, with industrial towns like Motherwell and Wishaw largely peopled by Irishmen.

Just what this big build-up of population meant can be seen clearly in the movement of the census figures. In 1801 Scotland was still a small country with a total population of only 1,608,420.[1] Of this population 748,165 lived north of the Tay and 860,255 lived to the south of it. The four big Scottish towns were still of a manageable size—Glasgow with 108,000 people, Edinburgh with 82,600, Dundee with 26,000 and Aberdeen with 27,000. Fifty years later the picture had changed remarkably. The total population had grown to 2,889,000. The population of the industrial county of Lanarkshire had grown from 147,700 to 530,200, and two of the four big towns were now becoming very big indeed, Glasgow with 345,000 people and Edinburgh with 194,000, as against the more modest increase of Dundee to 79,000 and of Aberdeen to 72,000. But Scotland's population was still growing fast. By the beginning of the twentieth century Scotland was one of the most thickly populated countries in Europe, with 4,472,000 people, the vast majority in the big towns or in the industrial Central Belt that now stretched almost unbroken from Greenock to Dundee. In the twentieth century, however, because of emigration, the rate of population increase has fallen off, and the pattern established by the beginning of the twentieth century has remained virtually unchanged.

The population explosion had a very different psychological effect

[1] For a useful summary of the population statistics see J. G. Kyd, 'Scotland's Population', *Scottish Historical Review*, 28 (1949), 97–107.

in Scotland from that of the similar change which took place in England. Eighteenth-century Scotland had been predominantly a rural and traditional society which lived close to the land. Its folk culture, whether Anglo-Saxon or Celtic, was strong, and its most characteristic poetry was that of the village poet Robert Burns. Moreover, the Scots were an emotional people, deeply rooted to their traditions, as many a Scottish sea captain or engineer in distant lands still demonstrates when in his cups. They were willing to accept with a certain pride that, in the words of one proud Glasgow commentator, Scotland, once 'the poorest country in Christendom', had become 'one of the richest countries in the world'.[1] But though they liked the thought that Scotland was now a great nation they found it hard to adjust emotionally to what this meant for life in Scotland itself. Two factors made adjustment particularly difficult: the fact that the population explosion was accompanied by large-scale emigration to countries furth of Scotland, which significantly changed the balance of Scottish population, and the social structure of the new Scotland.

Table 1. NET LOSS OF POPULATION, 1901–61

Years	Scotland net loss between censuses	Scotland percentage of population lost	England and Wales net loss between censuses (*if any*)	England and Wales percentage of population lost
1901–11	254,000	5·7	501,000	1·5
1911–21	239,000	5·0	620,000	1·7
1921–31	392,000	8·0	172,000	0·5
1931–51	220,000	4·5	*gain* 745,000	+ 1·8
1951–61	254,000	4·9	n.a.	n.a.

Emigration played a decisive part in the shaping of Scottish attitudes. Not only was the scale remarkable—as Table 1 shows it has continued unabated in the twentieth century—but it was proportionately greater from Celtic Scotland than from the Lowlands, and until the middle of the nineteenth century much of it was brought about by the clearance of people from Highland estates. The clearances not only created a profound impression all over Scotland, where they were widely resented as a deliberate attack on the traditional values of

[1] *Memoirs and Portraits of One Hundred Glasgow Men* (Glasgow, 1886), vol. I, p. xi.

Scottish society: they intensified the characteristically Scottish melancholy at the passing of the old ways, and paradoxically helped to create for the first time among the Lowland Scots a sort of vicarious identity with their Highland compatriots. Lowland hatred for Highlanders and their depredations now gave way readily to admiration for the qualities of a defeated and dispersed people. The cult of the Highlands, which had been largely created by Sir Walter Scott, found a permanent place in Scottish popular culture. Displaced Highlanders created county and clan societies in every Lowland city and Gaelic-speaking churches and chapels. And in time each Lowland town had its own Highland games. Emigration from the Highlands at last meant a rapprochement between the two cultures of Scotland, though there was still to be another clash in the 1880s.

Emigration also led to the creation of new Scotlands across the world. Many of the Scots who went abroad, and particularly the Highland Scots, went as communities determined so far as possible to stick together in the wilderness to which they were going. As a result parts of Canada and New Zealand, and to a lesser extent of Australia and the United States, became little Scotlands tied by nostalgia to the homeland. Continued emigration and a two-way stream of visitors made for continued human contact. Scots in Scotland no longer felt that they were alone in the world. Specifically Scottish newspapers and magazines, such as the *Scottish American*, now appeared in all parts of the world, Caledonian and St. Andrew's and Burns societies were strong outside Scotland before they really took root in Scotland itself, and there was a loose federation of Scottish Presbyterian churches strung out across the globe, many of them engaged in missionary endeavour.

In the Lowlands the combination of emigration from Scotland, of internal migration and of immigration from Ireland meant that the character of the urban population quite early in the nineteenth century became very different from what most Scots thought of as the national norm. Aberdeen alone of the big towns continued to recruit its newcomers largely from its own hinterland. Elsewhere the population was more mixed. This created considerable cultural problems. For a long time Highlanders and Lowlanders were cut off from one another by differences of language and tradition, and the monoglot Gaelic speaker remained a feature of Glasgow society down to the beginning of the twentieth century. Assimilation came easily enough when education became general, but for a time there was a sort of duality about Scottish city life, the Highlanders tending to keep very much to themselves. More important were the effects of Irish immigration. There had long been considerable contact between the West of Scotland and the Presbyterian communities of the North of Ireland, but the new Irish immigrants were as often Catholics as Protestants. And even the Protestants brought with them a religious bellicosity which was unfamiliar to most Scots. Just how many Irish settled permanently in Scotland is not clear, because there has always been a good deal of seasonal labour migration from Ireland and because many Irish immigrants were birds of passage who subsequently settled in the United States, England or other parts of the British Empire. But it seems likely that somewhere about one-quarter of the population of modern Scotland has a large measure of nineteenth-century Irish blood in its veins, though the largest number of Irish-born people in Scotland was recorded in 1881 when there were 219,000 of them: just under 6 per cent. The main increase in the Irish proportion of the population occurred as a result of the high birth-rate of Irish immigrants already in Scotland coupled with Scottish emigration rather than as a consequence of direct migration.

The Irish brought with them a clannishness of their own and, in the case of the Roman Catholics, an almost claustrophobic devotion to their church which had been bred by persecution and by the peculiar features of life in the Irish countryside. Both Catholic and Protestant Irish soon set up their own network of social and political organizations and churches, and Irish processions became for a time a dangerous source of disorder until they were put down by the police. Irish organizations were probably at their peak during the 1880s when the Irish Home Rule movement dominated British national politics, but every phase of Irish political activity has been reflected in Scotland, down to the present soporific politics of the Republic of Ireland. The Orange Lodges, the I.R.A., Sinn Fein, and a multitude of other Irish organizations, once strong in Scotland, are now little more than survivals kept alive largely by recent immigrants. When after I had given a lecture in the West of Scotland in 1965 a Catholic newspaper carried a headline reading 'Nationalism of Irish is Dead, says Professor', there were those who feared that my windows would be broken. But, as I had expected, nothing happened. Those who still scrawl 'Kick the Pope' (and less printable remarks) on walls are now only a reminder of past rancour.

What happened to the Irish Roman Catholics in Scotland is parti-

19

cularly interesting. The only religious census ever taken in Britain, that of 1851, showed that 33,377 people attended morning services in Catholic churches in Scotland, 15,999 attended afternoon services and 11,268 evening services, on census Sunday, most of them in the West of Scotland.[1] In 1873 an independent inquiry put the number of Catholics in Scotland at about 300,000, or just under 9 per cent of the population.[2] Today the *Catholic Directory* figure is 825,000 (just under 16 per cent of the population) as against 1,233,808 members of the Church of Scotland. But these figures need to be broken down before sense can be made of them. The most important thing about them is that the overall figures conceal the fact that the Catholic Irish came to a Scotland with its own strong Catholic tradition. In parts of the Highlands, notably in the islands of Barra, South Uist, Eigg and Canna, and in Lochaber and Morar, the Reformation never took root, with the result that there has been a continuous tradition of Catholic life through the centuries. These Catholic communities traditionally produced recruits for the priesthood who were sent to be trained at the various Scotch colleges abroad and furnished parish priests and bishops for the Catholic congregations in the towns. As a result, the Catholic hierarchy was predominantly Scottish in character, and was determined not to be swamped by the immigrant Irish and their priests. The story of the Catholic church in Scotland is, therefore, the story of the fight of the native Scottish clergy to retain control over their own church—if you will, one of the earliest struggles of Scottish nationalism against domination from outside. The important thing is that the native Scots won their battle.[3] Many Catholic priests, like the present Archbishop Scanlan of Glasgow, have Irish names, but the great majority of them are Scots born and educated, and many, like the late Archbishop Campbell, belong to the old Scots Highland tradition which led from a Catholic school in Scotland to the Scots College in Rome.

One outcome of this conflict between Irish and Scots within the Catholic church was a search for common ground. This has increas-

---

[1] These were high figures, as there were only 41,040 seats in Catholic churches: Census of Great Britain, 1851, *Religious Worship, and Education, Scotland* [1764], p. 2. H.C. (1854) LIX, 315.

[2] James Johnston, *The Ecclesiastical and Religious Statistics of Scotland* . . . (Glasgow, 1874).

[3] J. E. Handley, *The Irish in Modern Scotland* (Cork, 1947), pp. 51–92, and V. A. McClelland, 'The Irish Clergy . . .', *Catholic Historical Review*, LIII (1967–68), 1–27, 229–50.

ingly been found in the twentieth century in the development of a common loyalty to the concept of a new, culturally distinctive, Scotland. Catholics of Irish origin whose families were long committed to Irish Home Rule, transfer their sympathies readily to the idea of Home Rule for Scotland. As the historical sense seems to be more highly developed among Catholics in Scotland than among Presbyterians, this sympathy finds an outlet in devotion to historical studies (reflected in the *Innes Review,* one of the best of Scottish learned journals) and in an attempt to foster among schoolchildren an awareness of the Catholic past of Scotland. The Scottish War of Independence, it is rightly pointed out, was fought by Catholics, and the two national heroes of medieval Scotland, Wallace and Bruce (both Catholics!) become a link between Catholic and Presbyterian Scotland because they are admired equally by Catholic and Presbyterian alike. Catholic Irish nationalists, as a result, have found it natural to support the various forms of Scottish nationalism. The *Scottish Catholic Herald* in 1950 was already giving a sympathetic coverage to the Covenant movement,[1] and in the 1960s Catholics of Irish origin have readily supported the Scottish National Party, though they are not very active in it.

The movements of population, and the industrialization that fostered them, did much to change the social structure of Scotland. The industries that made Scotland a great industrial power in the nineteenth century were nearly all labour-intensive—coal, iron, shipping, shipbuilding, jute and cotton. Consequently, there was a vast demand for relatively unskilled labour and comparatively little demand for the armies of clerks and technicians which a newer generation of industrial enterprises makes use of. As a result, Glasgow, Dundee, and the towns of Western Scotland developed a pattern of life rather like that of Liverpool, with merchant princes and great manufacturers, and the professional men who worked with and for them at the top, but below them a great gulf until the vast mass of the urban working population was encountered. These Scottish towns were, therefore, essentially two-class towns: there was a wealthy upper-middle class at the top and a relatively unskilled working class at the bottom. This in turn meant that there was a rough parallel between life in the industrial towns and life in Edinburgh, for Edinburgh had long had a French-style pattern of living with an *haute bourgeoisie* of lawyers,

---

[1] S. B. Chrimes, ed., *The General Election in Glasgow: February, 1950* (Glasgow, 1950), p. 135.

churchmen, merchants, professors, bankers and manufacturers in old-style industries like brewing and printing, elevated high above a working population devoted almost entirely to catering for their needs. Scotland, in short, possessed the sort of social structure in which the lower-middle classes, and in particular the shopkeepers, were a force only in the smaller towns. And almost inevitably, the result was a pattern of urban overcrowding, chiefly in high tenement blocks whose construction was facilitated by the provisions of the Scottish land law which made the erection of high tenement blocks relatively profitable. Glasgow acquired middle-class suburbs towards the end of the nineteenth century as it became increasingly a commercial rather than an industrial town. But suburban life never took hold in Scotland as it did in England and America.

The weakness of the Scottish middle class, and above all, the lack of a rapidly growing lower-middle class, created social and political problems. There was no large popular base for a Conservative party preaching Tory democracy. The Conservative party, indeed, had long been very much the party of the landed aristocracy, the professional classes and the church. There was very little sense of community responsibility for local amenities—they had to be provided from above by wealthy benefactors or not at all. Trade unionism struck deep roots when it really got going in the eighties, but it found itself both strengthened and hampered, as in parts of the continent of Europe, by the fact that it was expected to provide a complete range of community leadership—social clubs, communal outings, newspapers, town councillors, parliamentary candidates, social and economic policies—even churches! As a result, the big unions became increasingly bureaucratic and tended to be absorbed into the wider framework of United Kingdom trade unionism. Moreover, the unions were hampered by the narrow vision of their members. They placed excessive emphasis on small savings in expenditure and committed themselves in time to municipal housing schemes which simply had the effect of perpetuating the overcrowded, often soulless, working-class tenement life of the nineteenth century in twentieth-century tenements but little better than the buildings they replaced.

The main problem created by the peculiar character of Scottish society was, however, a more serious one. There was very little opportunity for vertical mobility—for rising in the world—in Scotland, except by becoming a schoolmaster, a minor government official or a shopkeeper. The exceptionally able—the bright boy noticed at school and 'forced' like a hothouse plant by his schoolmasters, might make a great career in medicine, the church, the law or the public service. But both very able men and those who had more modest middle-class ambitions often preferred to seek a career abroad—in England, the Empire, or America.

The general level of incomes has always been lower in Scotland than in England. Moreover, there has been a marked tendency for Scots to accept overcrowded housing as a norm.[1] During the First World War 47·9 per cent of the population of Scotland lived in one- or two-roomed houses as against 7·1 per cent in England. The 1918 Royal Commission on Housing pointed out that if English norms had been applied to Scotland no fewer than 45·1 per cent of the population—over two million people—would have been classed as living in overcrowded, and hence unsatisfactory, conditions. This was as much a matter of social choice as of the level of incomes. The majority of urban Scots seem positively to have preferred living in tenement buildings, which they regarded as an essential feature of Scottish life. Moreover, tenements had advantages: they were well built and relatively warm and weatherproof, they enabled their tenants to live close to their work, they had good big rooms, even if there were only one or two of them—often rooms big enough, indeed, to be sublet to several families—and they were fairly easy to look after, and fairly safe from burglary. In addition, Scots workers were notoriously unwilling to pay more than token rents or to take on the responsibilities of private-house ownership. When government policy made it no longer profitable for private enterprise to continue to build tenements after the First World War, the state stepped in and did its best to perpetuate this Scottish tradition by subsidizing cheap tenement houses erected and owned by local authorities. Where these new tenements differed from the old was in their number of rooms. By 1931 the proportion of people living in one- or two-room houses was down to 44 per cent and by 1951 it was down to 29·7 per cent, though in Glasgow and Dundee the figures were much worse—55·4 per cent in Glasgow in 1931 and 41·5 per cent in 1951, 56·2 per cent in Dundee in 1931 and 39·4 per cent in 1951. The Scots pattern of housing none the less remained quite different from that of the English.

Of the spreading suburbs of English middle- and working-class

[1] R. H. Campbell, *Scotland since 1707: the Rise of an Industrial Society* (Oxford, 1965), is particularly good on housing. The details given here are taken from this book.

affluence little was to be seen in Scotland until very recent years. The social structure and patterns of housing have both made it much more difficult for Scots living in the big towns to obtain a house and garden of their own than it is for them to get them outside Scotland. The artisan who wished to move up in the world, the engineer trained at the bench, the baker, the bus driver, the nurse, even the doctor from a working-class home, have all found it easier to get a house of their own and to move into the comfortable ranks of the lower-middle classes in England or overseas rather than in Scotland. As a result the Scottish middle classes for the most part live outside Scotland. The resident middle classes until quite recent years appear to have expanded simply in proportion to the overall increase in population.

The first signs that there was at last to be a Scottish middle class—as distinct from a French-style *haute bourgeoisie*—did not appear until the 1950s. Then at last the suburban housing estates began to spread round Edinburgh and Glasgow and new middle-class suburbia began to be created in the New Towns of East Kilbride and Glenrothes—to which has subsequently been added the New Town of Cumbernauld. But even now the new middle classes are not secure. The overwhelming majority of Scottish housing is still utility working-class housing built by local authorities to standards of comfort inferior to those of England (partly because house-building is more expensive). The demand for private houses, except in Edinburgh, is fluctuating and uncertain, and there is still a marked shortage of 'executive housing' for the managerial and technical staffs of new industries. The great value of the new middle classes has been that they have been ready to adopt new ideas and new values, and it is no accident that the Scottish National Party has flourished most in the new middle-class suburbia, and notably in the New Towns.

II

A diverse industrial society like modern Scotland must be held together by myth as well as by politics and social pressures. And Scotland has plenty of myths. What makes them specifically Scottish is that they nearly all point to the fact that Scotland possesses distinctive national characteristics and values that distinguish Scotland from all other countries. By contrast the myths that used to point towards a united Britain—the myths of the Rule Britannia era—have lost much of their force. There is still a widespread belief in the monarchy and in the virtues of parliamentary government and the welfare state, but in this respect Scotland does not seem so very different from Australia or New Zealand which are independent and self-governing.

The dominant myths of contemporary Scotland are the continuity and distinctiveness of Scottish culture, the unique character of Scottish democracy, and the capacity of the Scots to run their own affairs better than they are at present run from Whitehall.

With the myths of Scottish culture this book is largely concerned. Suffice it here to say that there has since the eighteenth century been in Scotland a cultural conflict between those who look to the Scotland of Wallace and Bruce and Burns for their concepts, and those who look to a mixed Anglo-Scottish culture in which Magna Carta, Shakespeare and the English parliamentary tradition are fused with Scottish tradition to form a single culture which is distinctively British (i.e. *not* English). Those on each side of this conflict have, whatever they may think, been arguing for something quite distinctive from English cultural tradition. For England, having a strong cultural tradition of its own, is for the most part prepared to ignore the Scottish tradition altogether, just as it is for the most part prepared to ignore the American tradition.

'Scottish democracy' is a theme which constantly recurs in Scottish conversation, whether it concerns Scottish education, Scottish social values, or Scottish religion. Indeed, a correspondence recently appeared in *The Scotsman* in which much was made of 'the pure democracy of the ancient clan system of government'.[1] The basis of the belief in Scottish democracy is to be found in the arrangements made for the government of the Scottish church in *The First Book of Discipline* and other fundamental documents of the sixteenth and seventeenth centuries. There is to be found a system of church government based on an educated theocracy of ministers and elders, which was intended to replace the old pre-Reformation system and to make a break with the aristocratic organization of society common to medieval church and state. Within the church all ministers were to be equal and each presbytery was to be represented at regular gatherings of the church parliament, the General Assembly. To back up this system parochial schools were to be established throughout the country in order to produce an educated laity capable of reading the Bible and

[1] Macneil of Barra in *The Scotsman*, 15th August 1968.

devotional works, while the Universities were to provide all education beyond the parochial school level. As a result, where the parochial school system worked well, it was usual for the able boy to be taken away from tending the plough to be trained at the University, usually for the church or for medicine. In theory, at least, the Scottish system was thus an extremely open one in which the career was open to the talents. In practice it never worked quite so well as this, partly because the school system was weaker in some places than in others (notably in the Highlands), mainly because the system failed to cope with the rapid urbanization of the late eighteenth and early nineteenth century. Both churches and schools were much too middle class in tone to make much impact on the new urban masses (particularly in Catholic districts) with the result that even in country districts, like that which forms the subject of John Galt's great work, *Annals of the Parish*, 'Scottish democracy' soon broke down in practice. Scottish society remained less formal in its manners than English society, so that Queen Victoria got a pleasant sense of coming into effective contact with ordinary people when she was in Scotland. But the urban proletariat was no less cut off from the established sectors of society than elsewhere in Europe. Indeed, Scottish poverty was in many ways worse than English poverty, because Scottish standards of poor relief were long less generous than those of England.

The attempt to re-establish the tradition of Scottish democracy has been an important feature of the post-1872 Scottish education system and of the (largely unsuccessful) attempts of the Scottish churches and Scottish lawyers to persuade the mass of the Scottish people that they have their interests at heart. The myth of Scottish democracy has become almost entirely divorced from its presbyterian roots and is now preached by Catholics as well as Presbyterians. Scots going to England take with them a presupposition that they will find things different there, which they do, because England is a rather more complex society than is Scotland. Scots are thereupon prone to attribute the differences which they see to the contrast between Scottish democracy and English social stratification. But usually what they are really talking about are the differences between the social customs of England and Scotland, rather than structural differences between the two societies. To the outsider, Scotland, with its aristocracy still largely in being and the gracious living of its big town houses (the ladies still leave the dining-room before the port is circulated), with the workers tucked away in their tenements out of sight, often seems

26

much more of a traditional society than does that of England. It is the sense of social hierarchy that the outsider notices, not the native democracy. The rich man may swap cigarettes and stories with his chauffeur, but both men know their place and stick to it. Scottish democracy may be a powerful force as a myth, but it is a myth based on style, not on the absence of income or class differentiations.

The belief that Scots can manage the affairs of Scotland better than any outsider is a natural one, though it assorts ill with the concept of a United Kingdom. It is held by Scots of all classes and of all shades of political belief. A survey in Glasgow–Craigton before the recent upswing in support for the Scottish National Party showed that 44 per cent of those asked what changes were needed in Scotland wanted some sort of Scottish parliament, government or council, 8 per cent wanted to keep Scottish money in Scotland, 28 per cent wanted more say in running their own affairs, 10 per cent wanted more Scottish M.P.s, 5 per cent had other solutions in mind, and only 5 per cent didn't know what sort of change should be made.[1] It was a Conservative M.P. giving the Tory view of Scotland who wrote that

> Most of us . . . have a strong desire to see many more decisions on Scottish matters made by Scotsmen in Scotland. . . . I believe we should turn our energies to bringing government at all levels nearer the people. . . . We should have televising of Scottish business at Westminster. . . . Scottish Conservatives have never regarded the process of devolution as complete. . . . The sole criterion must be the good of Scotland, and we are patriots no less than anyone else in Scottish politics. . . .[2]

Gradually, step by step, the Scots have succeeded in pushing the United Kingdom parliament into giving them a separate Scottish Office staffed by Scottish ministers and (very largely) by Scottish civil servants to handle the affairs of Scotland and to advocate the needs of Scotland within the United Kingdom government. Parallel with the development of the Scottish Office, there has been a marked consolidation of organized groups in Scotland which has arisen from the growing sense of national unity that has prevailed since the First World War. The main divisive force in Scottish society—the existence of three large Presbyterian Churches side by side—came to an end

---

[1] Ian Budge and D. W. Urwin, *Scottish Political Behaviour: a Case Study in British Homogeneity* (London, 1966), p. 128.
[2] George Younger in *The Scotsman*, 15th December 1967.

after the final union of 1929. This produced a single national Church of Scotland capable of taking an overall view not merely of Scottish questions but of international questions as well. On the industrial front a series of experimental bodies were replaced after the Second World War by the highly influential and efficient Scottish Council (Development and Industry), which can speak for employers and employees alike. This has acted as a promoter and spokesman of industry on the grand scale, which is all the more remarkable because the Scottish Council has to work with employers' organizations and trade unions that are United Kingdom based. Similar developments have occurred in many other fields, and even the Congregational churches, once militantly independent, have formed a highly organized Union with full-time officers capable of negotiating with their opposite numbers in government, in the churches, and furth of Scotland.[1] Yet the process is by no means complete, and patriotic Scots have a long list of organizations which they think should be put under Scottish management—headed by the Scottish universities.

One thing of which the Scots have no reason to complain is English governmental interference. It is true that much of the welfare state is largely organized on a United Kingdom basis, but this is simply to ensure uniformity of standards in the administration of unemployment relief, welfare payments, pensions and the like. But the United Kingdom parliament prefers to leave Scottish matters so far as possible to be settled between the Scottish members and the Scottish ministers. English M.P.s may sometimes have to be pressed into service on Scottish committees to preserve the government majority which is customary on all parliamentary committees, but they rarely take an active part in the proceedings. The great weakness of the system has, indeed, been that it has encouraged the illusion that the Scottish M.P.s are a group set apart and that they are entitled to legislate for Scotland whether their proposed legislation accords well with the ideas of the majority of the House of Commons or not. Hence there are regular complaints from Scottish M.P.s, when the Labour party has a majority of the Scottish members and the Conservatives have a majority in the House of Commons as a whole, of English 'Dictatorship'. In the House of Commons as a whole there is a tendency to blame the Scottish members for forcing unpalatable measures on England, when they constitute a large part of a Labour

[1] Harry Escott, *A History of Scottish Congregationalism* (Glasgow, 1960), pp. 202–4.

majority. And on one outrageous occasion in 1928 it was the Scottish members, headed by Rosslyn Mitchell, who were largely responsible for defeating a proposed change in the Prayer Book of the Church of England, which, on the usual Scottish argument, was none of their business. Certainly, there would be a great Scottish outcry if the House of Commons as a whole decided to turn down proposals from the Church of Scotland.

III

What makes the demand for Scottish control of Scottish affairs so persuasive is that since 1918 the Scottish economy has gone through a very testing period. Before 1914 and for some years afterwards it was possible to argue that on a *per capita* basis Scotland was almost as wealthy a country as England.[1] But this calculation was largely based on the demand for the products of two industries, coal and shipbuilding, which were extremely prosperous before 1914, but have since sharply contracted.[2] There are no satisfactory figures for the Scottish national income, but there is no doubt that it is well below that of England. Wage income is significantly lower and so, therefore, is average family income (Table 2).

Table 2. INDEX OF AVERAGE WEEKLY INCOME[3]

	England	Scotland	Scotland as percentage of England
1961	135	118	87·4
1962	142	116	81·7
1963	151	125	82·8
1964	160	137	85·6
1965	171	149	87·1
1966	185	159	85·9

Unemployment, exceptionally high during the last years of Conservative rule, has been kept in check largely as a result of government support for the economy, but it has remained consistently higher

[1] See also Archie Lamont, *Scotland: the Wealthy Nation* (Glasgow, 1952).

[2] There is a useful summary of Scottish overseas trade in M. W. Flinn, 'Overseas Trade of Scottish Ports, 1900–1960', *Scottish Journal of Political Economy,* 13 (1966), 220–37.

[3] Source: 760 H.C. Deb. 5 ser., *c333*.

than the overall British rate for many years.[1] Unemployment would, however, have been much greater had it not been for emigration. The estimated emigration rate for Scotland has been over 43,000 a year since Labour took office in 1964 (Table 3).

Table 3. Net Loss by Migration[2]

Year ended 30th June	Total	To rest of U.K.	To overseas countries
1963	34,000	21,000	13,000
1964	41,000	24,000	17,000
1965	43,000	22,000	21,000
1966	47,000	22,000	25,000
1967	45,000	16,000	29,000

As nationalists do not fail to point out, this exodus shows clearly that there is a good deal of disillusionment not merely about prospects in Scotland but also about prospects in the United Kingdom as a whole. Given these figures, it is difficult at the lowest to persuade the average Scot that things would be any worse off if there were a greater degree of Scottish control over the Scottish economy than at present.

Nor is the average Scot alone in thinking thus. Many Scottish businessmen are appalled at the extent to which ordinary business decisions have come to be made in London. Though there is a separate Scottish banking system and there are many important finance companies in Scotland, there has been a steady concentration of investment decision-making in London, whether at the Board of Trade or in the financial institutions of the City of London. This is partly the result of the relatively small scale of financial operations in

[1] The percentage rate of unemployment for February of each year since 1960 was:

	England and Wales	Scotland
1960	1·7	4·3
1961	1·3	3·4
1962	1·6	3·5
1963	2·6	5·3
1964	1·7	4·3
1965	1·3	3·5
1966	1·2	2·8
1967	2·2	3·8
1968	2·4	4·1

Source: 761 H.C. Deb., 5 ser., c251.

[2] Source: 755 H.C. Deb., 5 ser., c239.

Scotland, partly of the relatively low return on Scottish investments, because of the lack of rapid-growth industries in Scotland, partly of government policy. At any rate, a considerable body of Scottish businessmen find themselves travelling to London roughly once a week if they are at all concerned with the raising of money or with investment. Moreover, the trade unions with whom businessmen negotiate are mainly United Kingdom unions, anxious to negotiate national (i.e. United Kingdom) wage agreements, and the trade associations to which businessmen belong are organized on a United Kingdom basis. There is a strong desire to make some sort of stand against the smothering embrace of London and to give a new vitality to Scottish financial and business institutions, but very little idea of how such a stand can be made. The Scottish Council (Development and Industry) has done something, notably by encouraging American and Canadian investment in Scotland as a counterweight to the London-based companies whose chief interests are in the south. There are the makings of the sort of commercial and financial structure that an independent Scotland would need, but it seems inevitable that even an independent Scotland would for a long time be financially dependent on the capital market of the City of London. Scots wish to create strong Scottish-based firms but at the moment the economic tide is flowing the other way.

The one thing that Scotland has got is a Scottish administration which works relatively well. There is a disposition in Scotland to complain about its methods, which (in common with those of all government offices) tend to be somewhat bureaucratic. But by international standards the Scottish Office does rather well. It is arguable that it would do better if the Scottish Office were almost entirely staffed by Englishmen and Irishmen, who would not be handicapped by sharing the preconceptions of the mass of Scots and would, therefore, take a more detached view of Scottish affairs, like the best administrators in the days of the British Raj in India. But any gain in efficiency which such an administration might bring would be more than counterbalanced by Scottish hostility. So far from Scotland having a less adequate administration than Northern Ireland, as has sometimes been suggested, the evidence tends to suggest that the advantages and disadvantages of the two systems tend to cancel one another out.[1]

[1] R. J. Lawrence, *The Government of Northern Ireland: Public Finance and Public Services, 1921–1964* (Oxford, 1965), pp. 174–5.

The Scottishness of Scottish Society

Of the short-term practical advantages of the link between England and Scotland in the post-war period there can be no doubt. *Per capita* incomes are lower in Scotland (and in Wales) than they are in England, yet for the most part *per capita* public expenditure is higher, because of the distinctive economic and social structure and the geographical remoteness of Scotland. It is argued by nationalist spokesmen that the available figures are incomplete, and that in any case they merely illustrate the fact that Scotland is being badly governed. If the Scottish economy were managed by a Scottish government, so the argument goes, the differences between Scotland and England would be reduced to those where the distinctive features of the Scottish scene would call for different types of public expenditure, in education, for instance, and in housing, where Scottish traditions are very unlike English.[1] Be that as it may, Scotland has in narrow budgetary terms done quite well out of the Union since the war, however badly it may have done in terms of economic development. It seems that successive United Kingdom governments have preferred to give Scotland a little more than the Scottish share of national expenditure in certain fields as compensation for their relative failure to promote dynamic policies of industrial redevelopment.

As the logic of this argument would suggest, the strongest nationalists are usually those who argue not in terms of the pounds, shillings and pence of nationalism, but in terms of national reconstruction. Indeed, it is significant that the most vehement nationalists have often been those who have a good knowledge of countries other than Scotland and who have a vision of a new future for the Scottish people. The opponents of nationalism, by contrast, are those who fear that a Scotland separated from England might be somehow cut off from the jobs and financial advantages which the Union is believed to secure.

[1] *Scotland v Whitehall No. 1: Winifred Ewing's Black Book* (Scottish National Party [1968]), p. 10.

CHAPTER TWO

The Problem of Anglicization

I

Nationalism in Scotland has never been confined to the relatively small proportion of Scots who have in the past adopted nationalist political views. There has always been a debate in Scotland about the way in which Scotland should develop, and in the course of this debate the predominant emphasis has always been on how to retain what is most distinctively Scottish about Scotland. In cultural matters, indeed, the strongest nationalists have sometimes been those who in politics were the strongest unionists. As a result, Scottish nationalism must be discussed in the light of the continuing debate over the future of Scotland which has traditionally taken the form of complaints about anglicization, as well as in terms of nationalist organizations.

Nineteenth-century nationalists for the most part stood outside the mainstream of Scottish life. Most Scots found a substitute for political nationalism in nostalgia about the Scottish past and pride in those specifically Scottish institutions that had survived the Union. This was particularly the case with those who saw in the Scottish presbyterian tradition the mainspring of Scottish life. For them nothing had been lost at the Union which really mattered, though there was widespread resentment at the restoration of lay patronage in the Church of Scotland in 1712. Indeed, so late as 1951 one finds a distinguished Scots minister still reiterating the old tradition.

The Scots had no reason to set any value on their Parliament. The Scots Parliament was a time-serving institution and echoed the voice of whoever was in power. It was to the General Assembly of the Church that the Scots looked as the guardian of their liberty. Thus, in 1707, they sold their Parliament at a very low price, but they insisted, as the primary condition of the Union of the Parliaments, that the first act of every new Sovereign would be swearing the oath of maintaining the Scottish Church as established.[1]

Scots were, none the less, acutely aware of the fact that they must fight to maintain their own characteristic institutions lest they simply be replaced by English ones. Scots, as a consequence, deservedly acquired the reputation of being almost absurdly sensitive to slights to their homeland. James Boswell may not have been altogether a typical Scot, but he reacted much as Scots were *expected* by their fellow countrymen to react when the audience at Covent Garden greeted some Highland officers with the cry of 'No Scots! No Scots! Out with them!'.

> My heart warmed to my countrymen, my Scotch blood boiled with indignation. I jumped on the benches, roared out, 'Damn you, you rascals!', hissed and was in the greatest rage. . . . I hated the English; I wished from my soul that the Union was broke and that we might give them another battle of Bannockburn.[2]

The significant thing about this sensitivity to supposed insults to Scotland was that it was as marked among those who championed the Union of 1707 as among those who regretted it. Scottish pride in the distinctive features of Scottish life was much stronger than enthusiasm for the Union. Most Scots welcomed the Union but at the same time regretted that it had been necessary and wished that they could be free of English insolence. This ambivalence emerged most clearly when the anglicization of Scottish institutions seemed to be threatening. When prominent Englishmen were so rash as to suggest that some characteristically Scottish institution was unsound—the Scottish banks, for instance, or the Scottish marriage laws—the immediate reaction was to resent the fact that an Englishman was interfering in Scottish affairs. Assessment of the merits of what he was saying came later. But for the most part the debate about anglicization was conducted by the Scots themselves. It was an internal Scottish dialogue, not a dialogue between Scotland and England.

Pressure for anglicization began to be felt in Scotland about the middle of the eighteenth century. Educated Scots became concerned about the prevalence of Scotticisms in their speech and writing, which made them uncomfortable in English company. Scots lawyers found

---

[1] Norman Maclean, *The Years of Fulfilment* (London, 1953), p. 147.
[2] F. A. Pottle, ed., *Boswell's London Journal* (London, 1950), pp. 71–2.

that they had difficulty in making themselves comprehensible to the House of Lords. And wealthy Scots began to feel that a Scottish education would put their children at a disadvantage in the struggle for life and began to send their children to English schools where they might learn to pass as Englishmen. Textbooks began to appear which enabled English to be taught to Scots almost as if it were a foreign language. Elocutionists, headed by Thomas Sheridan, visited Edinburgh to give lessons in English pronunciation.[1] About the same time there was in England a move to standardize the writing of English according to classical taste (Dr. Johnson's dictionary being the yardstick), and the new formalism quickly took hold in Scotland. Scottish writers began to write English of a classical purity and grace. So much so, indeed, that the *Edinburgh Review*, half a century later, was apt to chide English writers, including the romantic poets, for the impurity of their language and their ignorance of the rules of English expression. And even to this day, Scottish schools teach English in a much more formal way than do their English counterparts.

There is one excellent eighteenth-century account of just how this process of anglicization affected Scottish practice, that of Principal William Robertson, the historian, in his *History of Scotland*. England and Scotland in the sixteenth century, he wrote, used much the same language, but there was a great deal of variety of usage in both countries and Scotland seemed on the way to developing a distinctive version of English and a literature of her own, the yardstick of which would be Latin. But in 1603 the Scots lost one of the yardsticks of national speech, a court, and in the early eighteenth century, that other yardstick, Latin, dropped out of use.

> ... the Scots, being at once deprived of all the objects that refine or animate a people; of the presence of their prince, of the concourse of nobles, of the splendour and elegance of a court, an universal dejection of spirit seems to have seized the nation ... no domestic standard of propriety and correctness of speech remained; the few compositions that Scotland produced were tried by the English standard, and every word or phrase that varied in the least from that, was condemned as barbarous; whereas, if the two nations had continued distinct, each might have retained idioms and forms of speech peculiar to itself.[2]

[1] Thomas Somerville, *My Own Life and Times, 1741–1814* (Edinburgh, 1861), pp. 56–7.
[2] William Robertson, *History of Scotland* (12th ed., London, 1791), II, 264–5.

The Problem of Anglicization

Robertson's contemporary, Professor James Beattie of Aberdeen, who did much to discourage the use of Scotticisms, and wrote a textbook on the subject, recognized that the great problem was how to enable Scots to use English naturally.[1]

> We who live in Scotland are obliged to study English from books, like a dead language. Accordingly, when we write we write it like a dead language, which we understand, but cannot speak; avoiding, perhaps, all ungrammatical expressions, and even the barbarisms of our country, but, at the same time, without communicating that neatness, ease, and softness of phrase, which appears so conspicuously in Addison, Lord Lyttleton, and other elegant English authors. Our style is stately and unwieldy, and clogs the tongue in pronunciation. . . .

What the Scots were worried about was not that they couldn't write well—David Hume, Adam Smith and William Robertson among others demonstrated that Scots could write extraordinarily well—but that language would create a barrier between England and Scotland that would condemn Scots to provincial backwardness for all time. Scots were preoccupied with the poverty of their country and recognized that both jobs and economic progress must come from England. In the 1750s a young advocate, who later made a great career at the English bar, pointed out that

> The memory of our ancient state is not so much obliterated, but that, by comparing the past with the present, we may clearly see the superior advantages we now enjoy, and readily discern from what source they flow. . . . If countries have their ages with respect to improvement, *North Britain* may be considered as in a state of early youth, guided and supported by the more mature strength of her kindred country.[2]

The main advantage to individuals of learning to speak English in the English manner was that it opened up the opportunity of a great career in England, and was almost a necessary qualification for success in the House of Commons. Sir John Clerk of Penicuik sent his son to Eton because 'I thought it wou'd be an additional qualification to him that he understood the English language, which since the Union wou'd

[1] W. Forbes, *An Account of the Life and Writings of James Beattie, LL.D.* (2 vols., London, 1824), I, 417.
[2] Alexander Wedderburn in *Edinburgh Review* (Edinburgh, 1755–6), preface, p. ii, cited in Phillipson, op. cit., pp. 65–6.

always be necessary for a Scotsman in whatever station of life he might be in, but especially in any publick character'.[1] And there were many who shared the view so bluntly put in 1783 by R. R. Hepburn, M.P. for Kincardineshire, that the only worthwhile career for a Scot was an English one: 'It is natural for people who can afford it to get near the seat of Government; in England . . . you feel you are in a better country . . . amongst a richer and happier people. . . . We are only fit to supply England with inhabitants, and very few of those that can help it will ever return except for a visit.'[2] But there was also the problem that without an English type of schooling it was very hard for Scottish students to do justice to themselves at Oxford or Cambridge, where they were now sent in considerable numbers. The Scottish schools set a relatively low standard in the ancient classical languages, and the traditions of the Scottish universities also placed far more emphasis on a general understanding of classical texts than on textual learning or on Latin and Greek composition. A demand therefore soon arose in Scotland for a change in Scottish schooling to bring it up to English standards in classical scholarship. Inevitably this demand was strongest in Edinburgh, where the lawyers were numerous, and anxious to give their children a good start in life. One result was the creation in 1824 of an entirely new school, The Edinburgh Academy, whose founders intended it to set new standards for education for the middle and upper classes.[3] These founders—Henry Cockburn and Leonard Horner, who had the backing of Sir Walter Scott—were Scots who wanted to create in Scotland a school on English public school lines, which would set the highest standards of classical scholarship and enable Scottish boys to stay in Scotland for their education. It is indicative of the then quality of Scottish teaching that they had to go outside Scotland to get a suitable headmaster.

The creation of The Edinburgh Academy was only one step in a wider scheme of reform intended to raise the standards of all the bigger Scottish schools, beginning with the High School of Edinburgh, and extending also to the universities. The object, which was not fully achieved until near the end of the nineteenth century, was a purely patriotic one: to bring Scottish educational standards into line with those of England, so that young Scots would not have to be sent

[1] John M. Gray, ed., *Memoirs of the Life of Sir John Clerk of Penicuik* (Scottish Text Soc., Edinburgh, 1892), pp. 86–7.

[2] Sir Lewis Namier and John Brooke, *The History of Parliament: the House of Commons 1754–1790* (3 vols., London, 1964), I, 169.

[3] Henry Cockburn, *Memorials of His Time* (Edinburgh, 1910), pp. 388–9.

abroad to be educated in England to give them the same sort of start in life as their English contemporaries. Moreover, the policy was a success, in so far as the schools were concerned. Most Scots middle-class children continued to be educated in Scotland in town schools, and were not, like the sons of the English middle classes, sent away to public schools. Scottish society was, therefore, spared the social cleavage based on education which has afflicted modern English society.

With the Scottish universities the policy was less successful. The pull of Oxford, and to a lesser extent of Cambridge, was stronger than that of the English public school system. As a result, many of the ablest Scots were likely to end up in Oxford, whether they went direct from their schools or passed through a Scottish university *en route*. This meant that the pressures on the Scottish universities were rather more intense than those on the Scottish schools. The Scottish universities were expected to fulfil their traditional function of training every Scot who aspired to a University education, while at the same time preparing some students to go on to Oxford or Cambridge (though until the 1770s many Scots still went to a Dutch university), and endeavouring to compete with Oxbridge by persuading the best students that Scottish courses were good enough and intensive enough to enable any student to receive as good an education in a Scottish university as he would get in England. Furthermore, after the introduction of open competitive examinations for the Indian Civil Service and later for the Home Civil Service, the Scottish universities were in direct competition with Oxford and Cambridge for the placing of their graduates. So many Scots aspired to a career in India or the home civil service that there was an irresistible pressure for the Scottish universities to come into line with Oxbridge practice. Arts Faculty syllabuses were reorganized so that Scottish graduates would not be at a disadvantage in these public examinations, and the four Scottish universities at the beginning of the twentieth century even went so far as to appoint lecturers in Political Science because it was a compulsory subject in certain civil service examinations.

Inevitably the education question led to a clash in Scotland between two different patriotic points of view. The Whigs who founded The Edinburgh Academy, and those who then and subsequently have shared their viewpoint, argued that the only way to preserve the distinctive features of Scottish life was by raising Scottish standards high enough to make it worth while for young Scots to stay in Scotland for their education. This might mean making a substantial concession to English ideas, which was in many ways regrettable, but it did have overwhelming compensatory advantages. The social structure of Scotland was left intact, Scots would continue to be educated in a presbyterian (i.e. Scottish) environment, the traditional mixture of social classes in Scottish schools which underpinned the traditional presbyterian democracy of the country would be sustained, specifically Scottish elements in the educational curriculum would be retained (such as the distinctive method of teaching English and History), the Scottish method of evaluating school work (represented today by a distinctive system of school examinations which includes no 'A' Levels such as the English have) would survive, and, above all, Scottish standards would be improved—a big gain in itself. Furthermore, such a move had a special appeal to the sort of municipal patriotism which resented the loss to the burgh schools of children sent to England. It gave municipal worthies great pleasure to be able to say, as Treasurer Leishman of Edinburgh did in 1911, that 'it was strange that people should send their boys to England to be taught, when they could get such an excellent education here'.[1]

The contrasting argument—equally patriotic—was that by changing the Scottish educational system to bring it into line in some respects with that of England something valuable would be lost. The Scottish primary school system and the Scottish universities, it was argued, were expressions of a distinctive national point of view which put more emphasis on making education freely available to all and on a 'philosophical' approach to learning than on examination achievements. Moreover, the Scottish educational system, like the legal system, was much closer to that of the continent of Europe than that of England. If changes must be made it would be better to seek continental models than English ones. The leading exponents of this point of view, such as Professors James Lorimer and Alexander Campbell Fraser of Edinburgh University, preferred to look to Germany rather than England for inspiration, and under their leadership German jurisprudence and German philosophical techniques established a firm footing in Edinburgh. But Germany was not the only possible source of example, and Dr. George Davie, in his remarkable book *The Democratic Intellect: Scotland and her Universities in the Nineteenth Century*, rightly emphasizes the close connections between French and Scottish philosophy in the early part of the nineteenth century.

The two approaches which I have outlined here both drew their

[1] *The Thistle*, III (1911), 123.

inspiration from national sentiment—or patriotism if that is a better word. But neither of them necessarily involved any association with political nationalism. Political nationalists, then as now, were divided on educational issues. Nationalism was only an avowedly important factor in education for the small body of ultra patriots who were prepared to put emphasis on the national spirit before all else. And appropriately enough, the most fervent educational nationalist, Professor John Stuart Blackie of Edinburgh, had picked up his educational ideas in the ultra-nationalist atmosphere of the German universities. For him the national spirit was everything. He championed the Scottish pronunciation of Greek and denounced the English. He disapproved of the English public school and university system. And he was prepared to make of even his philological studies a weapon to be used against English educational encroachments. He also won a certain notoriety as a champion of Highland Celtic culture against its English and Lowland detractors, and was almost imperceptibly impelled by his championing of the Highland crofters into the forefront of Scottish politics, and in this way became the first chairman of the Scottish Home Rule Association. But most Scots regarded Blackie as a picturesque eccentric and preferred to keep overt nationalism and Home Rule politics out of the education question.

There was, however, more to be said for Blackie's point of view than was usually appreciated at the time. Blackie realized that those who started by wishing to anglicize the schools for patriotic reasons might end up by believing in anglicization for its own sake. And this, indeed, seems to have been very much what happened to those distinguished Scots who rose to high rank in science and in the English and Scottish Education Departments during the nineteenth century. For them only the management of Scottish education from Whitehall would be capable of saving the Scots from themselves. When it was proposed in 1885 to transfer responsibility for Scottish education from the Education Department (which dealt with both English and Scottish education) to the Secretary for Scotland, the members for the Scottish Universities opposed the change on simple utilitarian grounds. Sir Lyon Playfair, a distinguished educationalist, who had once been Professor of Chemistry in Edinburgh, argued in the House of Commons that the move was a retrograde one. The differences between the English and Scottish systems of education were slowly disappearing, his argument went, and it was to the advantage of all that the two systems should be entirely assimilated so that all the citizens of the

United Kingdom would start life on more or less the same footing. The Bill would create a ground for English jealousy, lead to a reduction in the education grant, and above all

> accentuate the differences between England and Scotland for the future, and . . . tend to convert Scotland into a Province, with the narrower peculiarities of Provincial existence. No country can less afford than Scotland to narrow the ambition of its educated classes or to parochialize its institutions. If it separates itself from England in administration and education it need not be surprised if in time England becomes less of an outlet for Scotch enterprize.[1]

Stated thus baldly Playfair's argument may seem to be a narrow one, but it must be placed in the wider context of his thought. Playfair was a pioneer evolutionist and he was terribly afraid that Scotland would fall behind in the struggle for the national survival of the fittest. 'Communities,' he once said, 'like animals, may remain stationary . . . they may develop into a higher existence; or they may degenerate. . . . As competition becomes keen among nations, the country which stands still while its environments are constantly changing must be content with a low place for a time, and must ultimately perish.'[2] Scotland, in other words, would lose its national being and be destroyed unless it consented to an inoculation of anglicization.

Patriotic sentiment was so strong that Playfair's views were disregarded. But his remarks serve to remind us that the case for the anglicization of education has always been stronger than has usually been recognized in Scotland. Scotland has hitherto always been a net exporter of men and women and the Scottish schools and universities have, therefore, always been geared for the production of graduates for export. Or, as Lyon Playfair put it, 'Education in Scotland is the essential source of its prosperity, for it has scarcely any natural sources of wealth.'[3] So long as this is so, any educational arrangement which tends to put young Scots at a disadvantage education-wise, such as the present Scottish Certificate of Education Higher Grade examination, which is not of a high enough standard to secure for those who have passed it admission to English universities, requires some special justification, for on strictly utilitarian grounds it must be regarded as a distinct handicap to many Scottish school leavers. The Scottish Higher

---

3 *Hansard*, CCC, 922–23.

[2] Andrew Reid, ed., *Why I am a Liberal* (London, [1885]), p. 79.

[3] Playfair to Gladstone, 8th December 1884. B.M., Add. MS. 44280, f. 205.

41

Grade examination must, therefore, be justified either on such educational grounds as that it promotes a better overall pattern of education, or on such patriotic grounds as that it keeps most Scottish school leavers in Scotland where they will imbibe a distinctive approach to life which is worth acquiring.

II

The problem of anglicization began to assume a specifically twentieth-century character in the 1890s. Sir Patrick Geddes, remembered today chiefly as a pioneer town planner, was one of the first Scots to say publicly that Scotland had lost ground in the nineteenth century by comparison with other nations. In a speech in Dundee he spoke what he called 'some unpleasant truths' about the state of Scotland in general and about the Scottish universities in particular.[1] He argued that while Scotland was 'naturally proud' of Scottish missionaries, Scottish thinkers, Scottish inventors and Scottish writers, these men were not typical of Scotland. Scotland as a whole had always lived on the fringes of civilization and 'all the great world-movements have reached us slowly'. The Romans came late to Scotland, so did Christianity, so did cathedrals and universities, so did printing, so did the renaissance, and, as for 'our Scottish Reformation, however proud we may be of it', it 'was a full generation behind that of England, as England in turn was behind Germany'. Flodden and Dunbar were battles fought over dead causes, while at Culloden men fell 'for a race of worn-out tyrants, who had run away nearly 60 years before'. 'There are indeed few more continuous tragedies than this history of ours—the noblest of our ancestors, in each century, dying manfully for a dead cause, that of the ideas of the century before.' Nor were things better in recent times:

> ... culture and prosperity alike find their way but slowly over the border. Even with the largest discount for Dr Johnson's obvious limitations and prejudices, it is hopeless to deny that that general inferiority to England did exist upon which he so tiresomely harped. Our industrial prosperity, too, in almost every great town, is one or two, or even three whole generations newer and cruder; and our justly-boasted leadership in agriculture has been gained within the memory of living men. And when we have done something we go to sleep again. Witness the Edinburgh advocate living upon the

[1] P. Geddes, *Scottish University Needs and Aims* . . . (Perth, 1890).

literary and social glories of his guild, two generations back; while from the city which not so long ago was both the Weimar and the Leipzig of the English-speaking peoples, the last writer has long vanished, and the last publisher will doubtless soon have fled.

The general fact of history, then, is that along with the strength and intensity of our individual types, of which we are so proud, we must also recognise the fact that all the great world-movements have reached us slowly. In short, our history may be summed up in this one sentence—that while the Scotsman has often led the age, Scotland has no less often lagged in it.[1]

The point of Geddes's oration was that Scotland was not spending enough money on the right things to keep abreast of world movements. He was chiefly anxious that Scotland should spend more money on universities (Edinburgh was the only university in Scotland at this time with a record of successful money-raising on a large scale). But what he said was equally applicable to science and industry. France and Germany—and particularly Strasbourg and Montpellier—seemed to him to have taken a great leap forward since 1870, whereas Scotland had done little or nothing. 'A mighty national revival in well-nigh every department of thought and action is being made by the men who were young enough to be in the terrible year of 1870.' Scotland, by contrast, seemed a European backwater. Edinburgh University might in some respects be a university of European stature, but the 'present low standing among the Universities of Europe' of the Scottish universities as a whole was justified. Indeed, the Scottish universities now ranked with the new English provincial university colleges.

Geddes's remedy was to create links with the 'new renaissance' on the continent of Europe by re-establishing Scots colleges and by introducing continental ideas to Scottish readers, notably in his journal *The Evergreen*. To look to Germany for a lead was also the policy of Principal Donaldson and Professor John Burnet of St. Andrews, who were intimately concerned with the revival of that terribly decayed ancient seat of learning. Both of these men looked to Germany for a solution of Scotland's problem, because Germany was in the forefront of European science and letters. All three men recognized that Oxford and Cambridge had far outstripped the Scottish universities,[2] and,

[1] ibid., p. 4.
[2] Burnet wrote 'The older Universities and the Public Schools do much the best educational work that is done in this country [i.e. Great Britain] to-day'. J. Burnet, *Higher Education and the War* (London, 1917), p. 32.

fearful that if Scotland merely followed in the wake of England the special characteristics of Scottish education might be lost, they wished to catch up by jumping a stage in educational development. As Scottish patriots they wanted what Germany had already, a 'Scots Renascence'.[1]

Yet at every step there were difficulties. If the Scottish universities were to put themselves on the map, they must develop the study of History. But History was not taught effectively in any of the Scottish universities and there had not since Robertson been any Scottish tradition of historical writing. Professors of History must therefore be recruited either from England or from Germany. Since suitable Germans were not forthcoming, this meant a choice between Scottish men of letters and Oxford or Cambridge dons. And when it came to the choice, Englishmen usually proved to be better qualified than Scots. Historical teaching in the Scottish universities, therefore, came to reflect the pattern of teaching at Oxford and Cambridge. Patriotic Scots had only two ways of fostering a distinctively Scottish approach to History. They might foster the creation of chairs of Scottish history —even though this meant the isolation of Scottish from European history—or they might insist on the writing of history simply as a branch of national patriotism, which was the object of old-style nationalists like T. D. Wanliss, who thought of the nation as very much like an individual, and, therefore, to be treated with a certain reticence.

> For the history of a living nation, which ought to be suitable for being placed on the table of any family, or on the bookshelves of any library, should treat the domestic doings of that nation or people, with a certain amount of decent reserve, in the same way as a respectable biographer would treat the private life of the subject of his biography. For a nation, like that of Scotland, England, or Ireland, which are still living entities, have national or corporate feelings, which even now, vibrate with emotion, when their cherished traditions are treated.[2]

The call for a national renaissance on German lines naturally received a check with the outbreak of war in 1914, and in 1917 John Burnet of St. Andrews published a book, *Higher Education and the War*, which pointed out just what was wrong with the German system,

[1] P. Geddes, 'The Scots Renascence', *Evergreen*, Spring 1895, pp. 131–9.

[2] T. D. Wanliss, *The Muckrake in Scottish History* . . . (Edinburgh, 1906), pp. 36–7.

although it still shows a nostalgia for the possibility of adapting the best of the German educational system to Scottish needs. It was left to an Irish M.P., Arthur Lynch, to remind the Scots during the war that they should not forget the need for a revival of the Scottish universities. In a debate in the House of Commons in 1915 he commented that 'The intellectual product of Scotland in these latter days is not a credit to Scotland', and added that both Scottish mathematics and philosophy, once great, were in a bad way.[1] He concluded by offering the Scottish universities a piece of advice:

> Instead of following their routine derived in great part from England, they should become exemplars, marching in the foremost ranks of thought, capable of vying with the great universities—I will dare say it—of Berlin and Paris. This is due to Scottish genius, Scottish thought, Scottish courage, to those qualities which throughout the ages have illuminated and honoured the Scottish race.[2]

When the war was over literary men returned to the theme of the contrast between Scotland and France and Germany. They were dismayed to find that Frenchmen thought even the best Scottish writing provincial and were determined to put Scotland on the intellectual map.[3] Francis George Scott, in particular, is remembered for the emphasis he put on 'standards' in the arts and on the need to make regular comparisons with artistic developments in France, Belgium and Holland. This emphasis on international comparisons explains much of the preoccupation of Hugh MacDiarmid with the 'Scottish idea', which was to be one element in a great international interaction of national ideas—a parallelogram of ideas—from which some sort of neo-Hegelian synthesis was to emerge. It also explains the pride with which Scots writers greeted the news that a Frenchman, Denis Saurat, had discovered the 'Scottish renaissance' of the 1920s and reported his discovery to his fellow countrymen.

The result was to create in the Scottish literary world a sort of permanent confrontation between those writers who looked habitually to the continent (including Scandinavia and Russia) and those whose horizons were set by Britain and the United States. For Hugh MacDiarmid and many of the younger poets between the wars, England

[1] *5 Hansard* (*Commons*), LXXIII, 2227–8.
[2] ibid., 2229.
[3] I owe the theme of this paragraph and the one that follows to Dr. George Davie, who knew all the people involved.

was an evil thing, not merely because it represented a form of imperialism, but because English domination of Scotland meant the imposition of second-rate standards on Scotland. Like Patrick Geddes, they thought of culture and ideas as having their origin on the continent of Europe and wished to get them direct from the fountainhead, not filtered and a generation late via England. For such people Gaelic culture was important because it gave Scottish writers a stock of distinctive ideas, attitudes and memories to draw on which were not part of the common currency of Europe. The Lowland Scots tongue, too, had a special merit as something distinctively Scottish, while for a time a revived older Scots, 'Lallans', looked as though it could be made into a suitable vehicle for the expression of Scottish ideas that could not be suitably expressed in English.

Given such a background of ideas, it was inevitable that MacDiarmid and writers who shared his preconceptions should regard Scots who habitually wrote for the English market as choosing to be second-rate Englishmen, churning out works that would sell on the English market rather than ones that would develop the Scottish idea. From this it was but a small step to regarding papers like *The Scotsman* and the *Glasgow Herald* as traitors to Scotland and hirelings of the English ascendancy. The whole question of anglicization acquired, as a result, an explosive significance during the 1930s. Hence the great stir made by Edwin Muir's *Scott and Scotland* in 1936, because it seemed to champion the anglicization of Scottish letters.

But anglicization was not merely a matter of concern to writers. Anglicization of the universities continued, and they became each year more and more like English provincial universities. When Sir Henry Craik claimed in 1915 that the distinctive feature of the Scottish universities was that they were 'popular institutions . . . in the sense of being framed to meet the needs of the country. . . . The students . . . are drawn from every corner of the country, the remotest glens and the humblest purlieus of the city',[1] he was behind the times. For the English provincial universities were by then doing exactly the same sort of job as the Scottish universities, and in some fields they were doing it rather better. In the educational hierarchy of the United Kingdom the position of the Scottish universities was already by 1915 inferior to what it had been a generation before, not in absolute but in relative terms.

Anglicization became also an important factor in industry and

---

[1] 5 *Hansard* (*Commons*), LXXIII, 2225–6.

commerce. The English chain stores moved in on the High Streets. More and more Scottish factories were taken over by branches of big international firms. And even control of whisky distilling seemed about to pass into English hands. For a time in the late thirties the growing provincialization of Scottish industry and commerce provoked a passionate outburst among patriots of all sorts, which was by no means confined to nationalist meetings and journals. Lists began to be compiled of Scottish-made goods[1] (they were revised again after the war, and stalwart patriots like Wendy Wood will still not use English electric light bulbs), and there was a great deal of pressure to resist the southern invasion.

The battle none the less was lost. For what Patrick Geddes had been gloomily talking about in the 1890s was repeated once again. Scotland was following England after a time lag. English firms moved into Scotland only after they had been established in the English provinces. In business, as in education, the Scots had not bestirred themselves to create equally efficient counterparts, so that the English giants had an easy passage. The S.N.P. might write into its programme proposals for the halting of the march of the English multiple store, as it did in 1946. But in the short term they were of no more avail than the protests of English pharmaceutical chemists against the multiplication of the shops of Boots the Chemists.

What most troubled thinking Scots was that the ordinary Scottish man-in-the-street, so far from supporting the campaign against anglicization, seemed to welcome the fact that he could now get in Scotland the advantages his southern counterparts enjoyed in England. For this made for a marked psychological dependence on England. The ordinary Scot since the 1930s has simply sat back and waited until the good things from the south have at last reached Scotland—new shops, new social security benefits, new industries, new towns. There has been a clamour when they have not come soon enough to please him. But there has been little disposition to do anything positive to help, or appreciation of the invaluable work done in Scotland by the Scottish Council (Development and Industry) or other bodies devoted to the fostering of Scottish industry. The ordinary Scot has been prepared to accept that his more enterprising fellows will emigrate as a matter of course and that Scotland will become a pensioner dependent on England. In recent years there has been some evidence that the atmosphere

---

[1] A typical list is given in Archie Lamont, *Buy Scottish Goods; How to Reduce Unemployment and Emigration* (Glasgow, [1954]).

has begun to change and that the importance of balanced economic growth has begun to be recognized by the electorate. But it would be a bold man who would say that many people in Scotland, other than members of the Scottish National Party, have been willing to do anything positive to put Scotland back on the map of Europe as a nation with a distinctive culture and a distinctive economy that are worth France or Germany taking into account.

III

There are two yardsticks that show the extent of economic anglicization. One is the growing number of people born in England and Wales attracted to Scotland by United Kingdom based industries, the civil service and the armed forces (Table 4). The atomic energy establishment at Dounreay, the naval bases on the Forth and on the Clyde, the universities, the electronics industry, and the motor industry among others, have been forced to seek trained staff outside Scotland. Some of those attracted are the sons of Scots living in the South. Many are English or Welsh by birth and origin. The result is that at a time when the Irish in Scotland are becoming more and more Scottish in their loyalties, and the number of Irish-born people living in Scotland is steadily falling, anglicizing influences are greatly strengthened by an influx of people with an English education and English ideas. This is a process that has occurred before, but never in recent times on so large a scale.

The second yardstick of anglicization is the extent of non-Scottish ownership of Scottish industry and commerce. This is notoriously a difficult subject on which to arrive at satisfactory figures. But various more or less satisfactory estimates have been made. One good yardstick is the ownership of manufacturing firms employing over 200 persons. For these *The Scotsman* gives the following breakdown:[1]

Headquarters in Scotland	292
Headquarters in England	253
State owned	30
Headquarters in Europe or North America	73
	648
Others	52
	700

[1] *The Scotsman*, 4th July 1968.

The Problem of Anglicization

These figures suggest that in terms of economic development the Union with England is the source of much of the dynamism that there is in modern Scottish industry. This has been the view of the business-oriented *Glasgow Herald* for many years. And it is of course very much in line with the experience of the Scottish universities which recruit a large proportion of their staffs from England in order to keep abreast with modern developments and have become geared to the standards of the London-based University Grants Commission.

For the most part Scottish opinion accepts this growing anglicization. There is no sense of popular resentment that mobile Scots are leaving Scotland and being replaced by better-qualified Englishmen. English control of Scottish businesses is shrugged off as of subsidiary importance: 'they bring jobs, don't they?' Even Scottish lawyers now find that their more lucrative business comes from firms outside Scotland. The ordinary Scot may sympathize with the desire of the nationalists to put Scotland once more on the map and may cherish a fierce pride in the past of his country. But he is for the most part not prepared to bestir himself. Things are better than they were in the past and that is enough. As for emigration, that can be attributed to the age-old wanderlust of the Scots. Small wonder that nationalists feel that they are swimming against the tide and are liable to become a little shrill.

Table 4. ENGLISH AND WELSH-BORN AND IRISH-BORN PERSONS IN SCOTLAND, 1861–1961[1]

	English and Welsh-born	Irish-born
1861	56,032	204,683
1871	70,482	207,770
1881	91,823	218,745
1891	111,045	194,807
1901	134,023	205,064
1911	165,102	174,715
1921	194,276	159,020
1931	168,640	124,296
1951	231,794	89,007
1961	246,917	80,533

[1] Source: *Census 1961: Scotland* (H.M.S.O., 1966), 5, xvii–xviii.

CHAPTER THREE

The Scottish System of Government

I

It might be supposed, from the persistence of Scottish complaints about the way in which Scotland is governed, that it is entirely governed from Whitehall. Such, however, has never been the case. Ever since the Union the emphasis has been on the preservation of Scottish institutions, although there have been occasional cases of English 'interference'. And in the last hundred years a new Scottish system of government has come into being which with little modification would be capable of providing the basis for an independent Scottish administration. Home Rule may not have succeeded in the sense that there is not yet a parliament in Edinburgh, but in every other respect devolution has gone remarkably far.

The Acts of Union passed by the parliaments of England and Scotland in 1707 in constitutional theory put an end to the existence of both the kingdoms of England and Scotland. Henceforth only the new kingdom of Great Britain was to have any existence in law. But because England was so much bigger and wealthier than Scotland, and because the capital of the new state was the English capital, both parties to the union recognized that in most everyday affairs English traditions would prevail over Scottish ones. That is why the Union settlement included safeguards for Scottish institutions such as the church, the legal system and the local government system with which the parliament of Great Britain might be tempted to interfere. The great difficulty about the Union, however, was that English constitutional traditions did not give constitutional legislation any special status. Whatever the Treaty of Union and the Acts which incorporated it might say, the parliament of Great Britain could at any time alter its terms or ignore them because there was no authority recognized as unquestionably superior to that of an Act of the parliament of Great Britain.

50

The Scottish System of Government

In the years immediately after the Union it did, indeed, look for a time as though the ministers and parliament of Great Britain were determined to behave as though the Union Treaty and the Acts which incorporated it were worthless scraps of paper.[1] The Scottish treason law was assimilated to that of England in 1709. In 1712 the law relating to patronage in the Church of Scotland was altered to make it fit in better with English ideas, in spite of the express provision in the Act of Security of 1707, which became part of the Union settlement, that the affairs of the Church of Scotland were to be left undisturbed. There were also lesser changes, as when the law relating to the Scottish peerage was changed to suit the exigencies of party politics, and the Scottish privy council was abolished. For most of the eighteenth century, however, English ministers and English parliamentarians were content to leave the Scots to manage their own affairs. They grumbled about the way the Scots did things, and about Scottish legal appeals to the House of Lords, but they did not interfere. Scotland was regarded very much as a state within a state, as the Treaty of Union had suggested that it would become. Nor did the English show themselves very much more interested in Scottish affairs in the first half of the nineteenth century. English ministers, instead, complained bitterly that they were expected to deal with Scottish problems which they did not understand, and to intervene in disputes where they had nothing to gain but hard knocks. Moreover, even after a Secretary for Scotland had been created in 1885, we find the same attitudes persisting among English ministers. Thus Sir George Trevelyan, an Englishman who was Secretary for Scotland on two occasions because he sat for Scottish constituencies in the House of Commons, replied in 1892 to Gladstone's invitation to resume the office, with a seat in the cabinet: 'I am much honoured by the offer of the Scotch Office, and shall do my best to assist your general policy by trying to conduct that department to the satisfaction of the Scotch members. . . .'[2]

The great problem left unresolved by the Acts of Union was how changes were to be made in Scotland in institutions which were exclusively Scottish in character, now that there was no Scottish parliament or privy council. The Treaty of Union was on this point of little

[1] For this period see James Mackinnon, *The Union of England and Scotland . . .* (London, 1896), Ch. XII, 'Unconstitutional Legislation'. There is a more up-to-date account in W. Ferguson, *Scotland: 1689 to the Present* (Edinburgh, 1968).

[2] Trevelyan to Gladstone, 15th August 1892. British Museum Add. MS. 44,335, ff. 230–1. It was very unusual for a minister to regard himself as the servant of any particular group of M.P.s.

help. Article XVIII of the Treaty provided that 'Laws which concern Public Right, Policy, and Civil Government, may be made the same throughout the whole United Kingdom'. But Scottish institutions were so very different from those of England that the English ministers, after their experiment with the law of treason, preferred to leave most Scottish public institutions untouched, so that this provision of the Treaty was of little immediate utility. In any case there were restrictions in the Treaty on how far the United Kingdom parliament could legislate for Scotland in the public law field, such as the provision in Article XIX that the Court of Session must 'remain in all time coming within Scotland, as it is now constituted'. The most important of these restrictions was contained in part of Article XVIII which ruled that 'no alteration be made in Laws which concern private Right, except for evident utility of the Subjects within Scotland'. What 'private right' included was not defined, but the implication was clear enough. The parliament of Great Britain was only to pass legislation of which the people of Scotland approved.

Eighteenth-century English ministers made no pretence of knowing anything about the affairs of Scotland. So far from being determined anglicizers, they preferred to let Scottish dogs lie sleeping as long as possible. When confronted with a Scottish problem they expected the Scottish members of the government—which usually meant the Scottish law officers, the Lord Advocate and the Solicitor General—to sort things out. Because in the first three-quarters of the eighteenth century Scottish legislation was on a small scale, it was, therefore, easy enough to work out a procedure for dealing with it. Measures involving changes in the law were sponsored by the Scottish law officers, vetted by the judges, referred for comment to the Faculty of Advocates and the Society of Writers to the Signet (the two societies of Edinburgh lawyers), and discussed by the county freeholders and other interested parties before being introduced into parliament.[1] Other measures, such as the act creating the Board of Trustees for Improving Fisheries and Manufactures, which was sponsored by the Convention of Royal Burghs and the Society of Improvers in the Knowledge of Agriculture in Scotland, got through because they were popular with the landed interest and, therefore, commanded support among the Scottish landowners in parliament once the landed interest had been given the

[1] On this whole question see N. T. Phillipson, *The Scottish Whigs and the Reform of the Court of Session, 1785–1830* (Unpublished Ph.D. thesis, Cambridge, 1967).

chance to express its views. The result of experience with a series of quite small Bills was that a 'normal procedure' was developed, in which the management of Scottish legislation was placed in the hands of the Scottish law officers, subject to widespread preliminary consultation in Scotland, centring in the Scottish legal profession. Scotland, therefore, found itself launched on a system of government by public debate, in which the lead was taken by the Edinburgh lawyers, with the English ministers in London acting as ultimate arbiters.

The process of government by public debate, coupled with the practice of giving judicial appointments to political partisans—a practice which survives down to the present day—led to the creation among Scottish lawyers of a party system very much on English lines. From this it was but a short step to the bitter party animosities of the time of the French Revolution, of which Lord Cockburn makes so much in his *Memorials*, and the subsequent journalistic pugilism of the *Edinburgh Review* and *Blackwood's Magazine*, the noise of whose combat echoed round the world. Sir Walter Scott, who tried to keep out of the fighting, wrote caustically in 1826 of this in-fighting among lawyers:

> We, the Whigs and Tories of Scotland, have played in our domestic quarrels the respectable part of two bull-dogs, who think it necessary to go by the ears under the table, because their blue-sleeved beef-eating masters have turned up for a set-to. The quadrupeds worry each other inveterately, while not a soul notices them till the strife of the bipeds is appeased or decided, and then the bleeding and foaming curs are kicked separate by their respective owners.[1]

The result of this constant strife was that towards the end of the eighteenth century the process of consultation which had been a prelude to previous Scottish legislation was supplemented by a party disputation and a continuous trial of strength in Edinburgh. Measures were still initiated by the law officers, the judges and the societies of lawyers were still consulted officially, and until 1832 the county freeholders also had their say, but measures were now, in addition, fought over by party warriors drawn from the legal profession. Scotland, in other words, had evolved a specifically Scottish method of dealing with Scottish legislation, so that it could clearly be shown that a discussion had been held as to whether a measure was for the 'evident utility of the Subjects within Scotland'.

---

[1] [W. Scott], *A Second Letter . . . from Malachai Malagrowther . . .* (Edinburgh, 1826), p. 13, quoted by Phillipson, op. cit., p. 54.

Many features of this legislative system continued virtually unchanged down to 1885. The county freeholders dropped out of the picture in 1832, but the Convention of Royal Burghs continued to play an active part in public affairs and so did the Edinburgh lawyers. The Convention of Royal Burghs, indeed, after the reform of the burghs in 1833, often posed as the legitimate spokesman of the people of Scotland, and occasionally sponsored public meetings, like that in 1884 which demanded the creation of a Scottish minister. The Faculty of Advocates met regularly to consider the application and implications of changes in the law, as Lord Rosebery's papers, among others, show. The advocates also campaigned hard to retain the old system of government by lawyers unchanged. And even the judges were regularly consulted on political matters. Lord Justice-Clerk Hope was the recipient of one of Sir Robert Peel's most persuasive self-justifications in 1846, and had encouraged the government to take the line it did with the Church of Scotland before the disruption of 1843. And prominent judges, like Lord President Inglis, were active in public life throughout the nineteenth century, even though they did not take an avowedly party-political stand. Nor was there much change in the twentieth century. There was, indeed, a complaint from the Lord Advocate in July 1968 when one of the judges, Lord Avonside, agreed to serve on the Conservative party's constitutional committee for Scotland,[1] but the fact that the complaint was resented shows how strong the tradition of judicial participation in public life still is.

One major change was brought about by the Reform Act of 1832. The introduction of a system of free elections gave a new lease of life to the Scottish members of parliament. Hitherto largely the nominees of ministers and landed notables, and usually passive supporters of government in the House of Commons, the Scottish M.P.s after 1832 became much more active. Because until 1886 they were overwhelmingly Liberal in their politics, they came to form a recognizable group in the House of Commons. They held occasional meetings to discuss Scottish business, they expected the Lord Advocate to explain to them in advance any measures that he was proposing to introduce, and they expected a certain amount of parliamentary time to be regularly reserved for Scottish business and complained bitterly when they did not get it.[2] Indeed, though they produced few leaders of any note, the

---

[1] Later he resigned. See *The Scotsman*, 26th July–6th August 1968.
[2] Charles Cowan, *Reminiscences* (privately printed, Edinburgh, 1878), pp. 260–3.

Scottish M.P.s by the 1860s had begun to claim that they alone were the rightful spokesmen of the people of Scotland.

In fact, the history of the Scottish members during the nineteenth century is largely the history of their attempt to create a specifically political leadership for Scotland and to oust the Parliament House (i.e. the Faculty of Advocates, who practise before the Court of Session, which sits in Parliament House) from its political monopoly. There were regular complaints down to 1885 that the only Scottish minister of standing was a lawyer, the Lord Advocate, and a variety of gibes at government by lawyers. Sir George Campbell was only expressing the common view when he commented that 'he was inclined to think that Lawyer Government was not altogether good for any country'.[1] Yet even after a new Scottish minister had been created in 1885 Scottish politics long continued to be lawyers' politics, and one of the classical descriptions of Scottish lawyer politics was given by John Buchan so late as 1913:

Few will be found to defend the system under which legal office in Scotland is determined mainly by politics, so that a party when it comes into office is faced with rows of hungry and expectant claimants, and if it remains long in office may have to go into the highways and hedgerows of faction to hunt for nominees. One advantage it has, however, along with its many drawbacks. It keeps the combative forces of party in fine fighting trim. Apathy is made difficult by stern professional needs, for politics to a Scots advocate are a matter of bread and butter. The country may be bored to tears by their name, but not so the Parliament House. From its portals champions go forth daily to do battle for or against some Government measure. A body of energetic and highly intelligent men cannot exercise their brains constantly on a subject without something happening, and accordingly we find in the Scots Bar a rare level of political knowledge and capacity. . . .

One result of the system is that the Scots Bar rarely shows a conversion. When a man has selected his side he must stick to it; otherwise his earlier service will have been so much waste of time—not ranking, so to speak, for promotion. Hence we see Tories by instinct miserably doing lip-service to Radical propaganda, and natural revolutionaries chafing under the fate which has made them defenders of the *status quo*. Only once in a century comes a dis-

[1] *3 Hansard* CCXXXII, 932.

ruption so tremendous that all the old boundaries are obliterated and men start afresh on a basis of conviction.[1]

Because Scottish issues were first discussed by Scots, the intention of Article XVIII of the Treaty of Union was clearly fulfilled. English intervention in Scottish affairs occurred only when the Scots were unable to settle their differences. There was no English design, such as some Scottish lawyers have been inclined to imagine, to intervene in Scottish affairs and to force English solutions down Scottish throats. The real problem was that there was insufficient vitality in many Scottish institutions to enable them to produce specifically Scottish solutions to Scottish problems. Anglicization was not forced on the Scots by the English: it was a deliberate policy pursued by Scots who did not have any alternative ready to hand. Only in the middle of the twentieth century have Scots begun to think seriously of Scandinavia as an alternative source of ideas and institutions. French and Dutch influence, so important before the Union, has counted for little since 1745.

II

The debate in 1884 and 1885 about the ministerial arrangements for Scottish education also illustrates very well just how English ministers regarded Scottish legislation. Pressure for the creation of a Scottish minister had slowly built up among the Scottish M.P.s before 1880, when the cause received a notable adherent in the person of Lord Rosebery, Gladstone's host during the Midlothian campaign. Rosebery chose to stake his political future on pressing for a Scottish minister, and after much travail got his way because he could always argue that the people of Scotland were behind him. Gladstone conceded that Rosebery had a case, but, like a number of other members of the cabinet, he found it hard at first to believe that there was any urgency about the matter. In parliamentary terms, the Scots appeared to be at the end of a queue for new ministers—a queue headed by Agriculture and Education. It was Rosebery's achievement to get Scotland to the top of the queue by persistent lobbying.

When it came to the question of whether Scottish education should be allocated to the new Scottish minister the issue became much more complicated. The existing Education Department was dead against

[1] John Buchan, *Andrew Jameson, Lord Ardwall* (Edinburgh and London, 1913), pp. 78–81.

the change. The Vice President of the Committee of Council for Education, A. J. Mundella, an Englishman, felt that his dignity was being attacked: the Lord President of the Council, Lord Carlingford, an Irishman, wanted to defend the integrity of his department: the senior officials in the department, all Scots (Sandford, Cumin and Craik), felt that Scottish education would do better under a United Kingdom minister than under a Scottish one and preferred a centralized educational bureaucracy to a fragmented one. The big Scottish school boards agreed with the Education Department, as they made clear by passing appropriate resolutions. The Scottish Catholics deprecated any change because they were afraid that a Scottish department would be less sympathetic to denominational education than a United Kingdom department accustomed to dealing with English and Irish denominational schools. The educational experts of the other Scottish churches were pretty evenly divided. The spokesmen of the Scottish universities in the House of Commons were, as we have seen, strongly opposed to any change. And the Faculty of Advocates objected to the proposal that a Secretary for Scotland should be appointed, whatever his powers, on the ground that the Lord Advocate managed Scottish affairs perfectly well as things were. By contrast, there was strong public feeling in Scotland that the change was desirable on patriotic grounds, and the change was also supported by *The Scotsman* and other opponents of centralization. The Scottish Liberal peers almost to a man favoured the change and so, rather unexpectedly, did Lord Salisbury (partly on the ground that it is better not to do things by halves, partly because he was opposed to administrative centralization on principle). The Scottish M.P.s, as a result of cross pressures, were confused and divided, though the majority favoured the change, and required a strong lead to bring them into line. The result was that initiative in the matter was thrust squarely into the hands of an English minister, Sir William Harcourt, who, as Home Secretary, had charge of the Secretary for Scotland Bill.

Harcourt took the traditional ministerial line that he should try to do what the Scots wanted, provided that he himself agreed with them. He therefore took soundings to find out what Scottish public opinion really wanted, and at the end of 1884 came to the conclusion that Education should be transferred to the Scottish Secretary.

When I first framed the Scotch Minister Bill I left Education where it was and did not propose to transfer it to the new depart-

57

ment. At that time I was not aware of the strength of feeling on this subject amongst all sections of Scotch opinion. Since that time that opinion has been so distinctly and almost unanimously pronounced that I have no hesitation in saying it is perfectly hopeless to propose a Scotch Minister without transferring Scotch Education to his control.[1]

Harcourt at this point was overstating his case, as he well knew, and it was some months before he was able to bring most of his colleagues round to his point of view. In April 1885 he contemplated calling a meeting of the Scottish M.P.s to demonstrate to his colleagues that the Scots were really behind him. But Lord Rosebery warned him to do no such thing.

As regards Education I am against a meeting of Scottish members, and for this reason: they are so equally divided that you could get no result from it. I do not believe that it is denied that Scottish feeling on the whole is in one direction and those who are specially interested in education in the other. But meetings of the Scottish members are never harmonious and never successful, and a gathering where they are so equally divided could only distract the Government and would probably end in personal violence.

I have come to the conclusion (whatever that may be worth) that the Govt. should include the charge of education in the bill, because the mass of Scottish opinion demands it: and if that be the case you will never have done with this Scottish Secretary business until education is put under the Minister. I have always been strongly of opinion that this should be so, but my personal opinion and the opinion of Scotland are two different things, and I have been watching the latter carefully ever since the first cabinet meeting which I attended, when my opinion was asked.[2]

We therefore have the curious spectacle, for those who are not familiar with the intricacies of Scottish politics, of an English minister pushing a measure through the House of Commons against determined *Scottish* opposition, because he is backed by the leading Scottish Liberals in the House of Lords, most of the Liberals in the House of Commons, the Leader of the Opposition in the Lords (Lord Salis-

[1] Harcourt to Gladstone, 11th December 1884. B.M. Add. MS. 44, 199, ff. 121–2, quoted in H. J. Hanham, 'The Creation of the Scottish Office, 1881–87', *Juridical Review*, 1965, p. 217.
[2] Rosebery to Harcourt, 19th April 1885. B.M. Add. MS. 44, 199, f. 201.

bury) and by Scottish public opinion. Such a spectacle was, however, entirely characteristic of the management of Scottish affairs and continues to be so, with the Secretary of State for Scotland now in the position of the Home Secretary in 1884–5. In such cases the problem was not English intervention in Scottish affairs, but simply the fact that the Scottish system of government by public debate tended to lead to a stalemate unless there was a *deus ex machina* to force a decision.

III

The creation of the office of Secretary for Scotland in 1885 was the first stage in the development of a separate modern administration for Scotland. This was required not merely to replace the lawyer-government of the Lord Advocate, but also to give a sense of purpose to the curious collection of little offices in Edinburgh, which dealt with much of the day-to-day business of Scottish administration. These offices were nearly all run by boards, some of whose members gave their services part-time, but there were also some outposts of the Whitehall departments, such as the Queen's and Lord Treasurer's Remembrancer who represented the Treasury.

The case for the creation of a Scottish minister had been clear enough since the early years of the nineteenth century, and when the second Viscount Melville ceased to be Scottish 'manager' it became urgent. Lord Melville himself wrote to Peel in 1829:

> There is one topic . . . on which I have for several years felt very desirous that the Govern^t. should adopt some remedial measure—I mean the inconvenience frequently complained of by the natives of Scotland, particularly the Members of Parliament, that there is no special officer or office in London for the transaction of the Parliamentary or other business connected with that part of the Kingdom, though from the dissimilarity of our laws and institutions it is even more necessary than a similar office for Ireland. It has hitherto devolved chiefly on the Lord Advocate, most improperly and inconveniently for the public service. There are various modes of effecting the object. . . . It should be a House of Commons office held during pleasure under either the Treasury or the Secretary of State. . . .[1]

The Scottish Whigs were thinking along the same lines. In a letter to

[1] Melville to Peel, 15th November, 1829. Copy by courtesy of Dr. N. T. Phillipson.

T. F. Kennedy, James Abercromby, later Speaker and Lord Dunfermline, agreed that the best move would be to create a junior minister for Scotland

> Scotland is too small for a Secretary. Without the patronage the Sec. would be nobody, & the little that there is could not well be taken from the Home Office & the Treasury. But then there is certain business to be done, in which both the Home Office & Treasury require aid.[1]

The Whigs accordingly appointed T. F. Kennedy to be a Lord of the Treasury, and thereafter there was normally a Scottish Lord of the Treasury to act as Scottish Whip in the Commons and to deal with the day-to-day requests of individual M.P.s.

The new system never worked well. The Home Secretary was still the minister responsible for Scottish affairs and the Lord Advocate was still regarded by members of parliament and Scottish public opinion as the sole Scottish minister. The Scottish Lord of the Treasury and his counterpart on the Opposition benches became, therefore, simply his party's election manager for Scotland and Whip in the Commons. The Conservatives in 1878 introduced a Bill to provide for an additional Under-Secretary at the Home Office to deal with Scottish affairs, but the Bill was not proceeded with. For a short time in the early 1880s Lord Rosebery was appointed to the existing under-secretaryship at the Home Office, but the arrangement did not work because of misunderstandings, and in 1883 the Gladstone government decided to create a Scottish minister, though the necessary legislation was actually carried by the Conservatives in 1885 as an agreed non-partisan measure.

At the time of its creation the Scottish Office, headed by a Secretary for Scotland who was not a Secretary of State, had little work to do. The general tone of public opinion still strongly favoured *laissez faire*, and the troubles in the Highlands which were to be one of the major concerns of the new Office were seemingly little more than a passing phase. The first Secretary for Scotland, the Duke of Richmond, was told by the Prime Minister, Lord Salisbury, when he was asked to take the post that 'The work is not very heavy' and Richmond himself, in his letter of acceptance, commented 'You know my opinion of the office, and that it is quite unnecessary'.[2] But the Scottish Office got off

---

[1] Abercromby to Kennedy, 16th July 1832. Kennedy Papers.
[2] Hanham, 'The Creation of the Scottish Office, 1881–87', op. cit., p. 229.

to a good start—with a levee in Edinburgh—and in a short time had become very busy. In addition to the problem of maintaining law and order in the Highlands and running the Scotch Education Department, there was a great deal of legislative and administrative work to be done in the 1880s and 1890s. The powers of the Scottish Office itself were extended in 1887, there were big new measures relating to Scottish education, the Scottish universities, emigration, and Highland development, and there was a big backlog of minor matters to be dealt with. As a result, the Secretary for Scotland and the Lord Advocate were both very busy, and it was usual for the Secretary for Scotland down to 1905 to sit in the Lords and the Lord Advocate to represent the Scottish Office in the Commons. After 1892 the Secretary for Scotland was always in the cabinet, and very gradually he came to be accepted by his colleagues as the spokesman for every aspect of Scottish affairs. And after 1905 the demand for special legislation for Scotland was so great that the Scottish Secretary was nearly always in the Commons.

The Scottish Office was given Dover House in London as its headquarters. Routine administration had, therefore, to be managed either by quasi-independent boards in Scotland or direct from Whitehall.[1] Administrative theory had long disapproved of such a divided administration, and of the uncertain constitutional relationship which it created in terms of the answerability of boards to parliament. Moreover, for the most part Scottish opinion disliked the Scottish boards, because they seemed to be remote from the day-to-day problems of the country. Yet there was seemingly no easy way out of the difficulty so long as the Scottish Office was London-based. By the end of the First World War, however, the pressures to bring all Scottish administration into line with the Scotch (from 1918, Scottish) Education Department, which was directly answerable to the Secretary for Scotland, had become overwhelming. In 1919 a new Scottish Board of Health was created to take over the work of the Local Government Board for Scotland and other Scottish health authorities. This was in all but name a branch of the Scottish Office, since the Secretary for Scotland was President and a new junior minister, the parliamentary Under

---

[1] The Boards in existence in 1914 were Fisheries Board, Trustees for the National Galleries of Scotland, Scottish Insurance Commissioners, Highlands and Islands (Medical Service) Board, Local Government Board for Scotland, General Board of Commissioners in Lunacy in Scotland, Prisons Commission for Scotland, Board of Agriculture for Scotland. There had formerly been other Boards as well.

61

Secretary for Health, was Vice President. In 1926 the process was carried a stage further when the Secretary for Scotland became a Secretary of State and the Under Secretary became an Under-Secretary of State. In 1928 the two major Scottish boards, the Board of Health and the Board of Agriculture, became departments, and in 1939 the 'general department' of the Scottish Office became the Scottish Home Department. Furthermore, in 1939 the Scottish departments were brought together in a new building in Edinburgh, St. Andrew's House, which became in effect the Scottish seat of government. These administrative developments had the effect of creating in Scotland something very like four separate Scottish government departments (Home, Health, Education, Agriculture) which could easily, if required, be removed from the control of the Secretary of State and become the basis of a Home Rule Scottish government. As it is, the ministerial arrangements for Scotland are such that there is normally a junior minister attached to each of the Scottish departments, since there have since 1952 been a Minister of State and three Under-Secretaries of State for Scotland under the Secretary of State.

This is not the place to describe the work of the Scottish Office, which has been ably done elsewhere.[1] What is important to recognize is that the Scottish administration, after a slow start, has now become a comparatively big one employing a large number of civil servants.[2] Complaints in Scotland about the growing bureaucratization of the country are wide of the mark, but there is no doubt that the Scottish civil service, in the fields where it operates, is very nearly large enough to become the civil service of an independent Scottish state. It must be added, however, that its range is still limited. United Kingdom departments like the Post Office, the Inland Revenue, the Ministry of Social Security and what used to be called the Ministry of Labour[3] still employ larger staffs than the Scottish departments.

The unglamorous work of the Scottish Office is frequently overlooked in Scotland, where it is not realized just how far devolution has gone. Yet Scottish opinion takes for granted a number of other forms of devolution which are no less remarkable as a recognition of Scottish distinctness from the rest of the country. Edinburgh has the trappings

---

[1] Sir David Milne, *The Scottish Office and other Scottish Government Departments* (London, 1957) and *Scottish Administration: a Handbook prepared by the Scottish Office* (rev. edn., Edinburgh, 1967).

[2] The staff of the Scottish Office increased by 1,036 between October 1964 and April 1967: 744 H.C. Deb. 5 ser., *c. 263*.

[3] Now the Department of Employment and Productivity.

of a national capital as much because national museums and galleries, a national library and a national botanic garden exist in the city as for any other reason. Yet all these are relatively new. The National Museum of Antiquities of Scotland became a national museum in 1851, the Royal Scottish Museum dates from 1854, the National Gallery from 1859, the Scottish National Portrait Gallery from 1889, the National Library of Scotland from 1925, while the National Gallery of Modern Art is even more recent. The national museums are, indeed, one of the few practical legacies of the national agitations of the 1850s, and their maintenance and development, along with the development of Scottish science, has always been a matter of concern to serious-minded nationalists.[1]

[1] Cp. H. C. MacNeacail, 'The Starving of Scottish Science', *Scottish Review*, 40 (1917), 118–24.

CHAPTER FOUR

The Beginnings of Modern Nationalism

Scottish nationalism is as old as the Scottish nation. Scots throughout the ages have been fearful of English domination, and Scottish verse and story have always abounded in anti-English asides. But there is also a respectable Scottish patriotic literature, devoted chiefly to the careers of the great Scots patriots, Wallace and Bruce. The earliest of the great Scots poets, John Barbour (*c.* 1320–95) is remembered for one big poem *The Bruce*, whose most famous passage is printed in the anthologies under the simple heading, 'Freedom':

> Ah! Freedom is a noble thing!
> Freedom makes man to have liking;
> Freedom all solace to man gives;
> He lives at ease that freely lives!

A later work, Blind Harry's *Wallace*, became one of the foundations of folk-legend. Generations of humble Scots learned to be patriots from Barbour and Blind Harry in the way which Hugh Miller describes in the autobiography of his childhood in Cromarty:

> I first became thoroughly a Scot some time in my tenth year [i.e. 1812 or 1813]; and the consciousness of country has remained tolerably strong within me ever since. My uncle James had procured for me from a neighbour the loan of a common stall-edition of Blind Harry's 'Wallace', as modernized by Hamilton; but after reading the first chapter . . . I tossed the volume aside . . . and only resumed it at the request of my uncle. . . . But I now . . . read on with increasing astonishment and delight. I was intoxicated with the fiery narratives of the blind ministrel,—with his fierce breathings of hot, intolerant patriotism, and his stories of astonishing prowess; and, glorying in being a Scot, and the countryman of Wallace and the Graham, I longed for a war with the Southron, that the wrongs and sufferings of these noble heroes might yet be avenged. . . . it was not until some

years after, when I was fortunate enough to pick up one of the later editions of Barbour's 'Bruce', that the Hero-King of Scotland assumed his right place in my mind beside its Hero-Guardian. . . . the recollections of this early time enable me, in some measure, to understand how it was that, for hundreds of years, Blind Harry's 'Wallace', with its rude and naked narrative, and its exaggerated incident, should have been, according to Lord Hailes, the Bible of the Scotch people.[1]

There was, however, much more to the Scottish patriotic tradition than Barbour and Blind Harry, and modern nationalists have agreed that the most important single literary contribution to the nationalist tradition was the Declaration of Arbroath of 6th April 1320, now available in a variety of translations.[2] Drawn up in Latin by a churchman at the great abbey of Arbroath during the War of Independence, it took the form of an appeal by the Scottish barons to the Pope, who had refused to recognize Robert Bruce as king of Scotland and Scottish independence of England. The Declaration sets out a skeleton history of Scotland which might well have come from Blind Harry,

. . . we learn from the deeds and records of the men of old, that among peoples of renown our Scottish people have been distinguished by many tributes to their fame. Passing from Greater Scythia over the Tyrrhenian Sea and by the pillars of Hercules, abiding for long courses of time in Spain among the fiercest of warriors, by none how barbaric soever could they be anywhere brought under the yoke. And thence coming, twelve hundred years after the setting forth of the people of Israel, they won for themselves by victory after victory and travail upon travail the abodes in the west which now they hold, the Britons expelled, the Picts utterly destroyed, assailed again and again by Norseman, Dane and Angle; and this their home, as the histories of the ancients bear witness, they have kept evermore free from any servitude. Within their realm have reigned one hundred and thirteen kings of native royal stock, never an alien upon the throne.

[1] Hugh Miller, *My Schools and Schoolmasters*, ch. III.
[2] For the pre-1707 patriotic tradition see M. P. Ramsay, *The Freedom of the Scots from Early Times till its Eclipse in 1707: Displayed in Statements of our Forefathers who Loved and Served Scotland* (Edinburgh, 1945). For a nationalist appraisal of the Declaration see Agnes Muir Mackenzie, *On the Declaration of Arbroath* (Saltire Society, Edinburgh, 1951).

But the Declaration's most celebrated passage was an eloquent declaration of loyalty to Robert the Bruce and a plea for liberty.

Unto him, as the man through whom salvation has been wrought in our people, we are bound both of right and by his service rendered, and are resolved in whatever fortune to cleave, for the preservation of our liberty. Were he to abandon the enterprise begun, choosing to subject us or our kingdom to the king of the English or to the English people, we would strive to thrust him out forthwith as our enemy and the subverter of right, his own and ours, and take for our king another who would suffice for our defence; for so long as an hundred remain alive we are minded never a whit to bow beneath the yoke of English dominion. It is not for glory, riches or honours that we fight: it is for liberty alone, the liberty which no good man relinquishes but with his life.[1]

The Union with England of 1707 created a new patriotic literature. Andrew Fletcher of Saltoun, the leading opponent of the Union, was a fluent pamphleteer, and there was much about the Union to which a pamphleteer could object. So far from being the consequence of 'a free and an honest decision', to quote the words of an English commentator,[2] the Union had been forced through without any effective attempt at popular consultation and long remained unpopular on both sides of the border. As a result, anti-union pamphlets have been part of the stock-in-trade of Scottish nationalists from 1707 to the present day.[3] The fundamental point made by the anti-unionists was that if there must be a union it should have been a federal not an incorporating union—that the Scots should have retained their own government and parliament in any deal which might be made with the English. And there has always been a good deal to be said for their case. It is at least arguable that Texas got better terms when it joined the United States than Scotland got when it joined Great Britain.

One immediate consequence of the Union was the sending of Scot-

---

[1] The text of the Declaration of Arbroath given here is that in W. C. Dickinson, Gordon Donaldson and Isabel A. Milne, *A Source Book of Scottish History*, Volume I (London and Edinburgh, 1952), pp. 131–5.

[2] Sir Reginald Coupland, *Welsh and Scottish Nationalism: a Study* (London, 1954), p. 111 and Ferguson, *Scotland: 1689 to the Present*, Ch. II.

[3] Among modern ones Charles Waddie, *How Scotland Lost her Parliament and What Came of It* (Edinburgh, 1891, 3rd edn. 1902), Oliver Brown, *The Anglo-Scottish Union of 1707: Then and Now* (Stirling, n.d.) and *The Treaty of Union between Scotland and England 1707* . . . (Scottish Secretariat No. 62, Glasgow, 1955).

tish peers and Scottish members in quite small numbers (sixteen peers and forty-five M.P.s) to the English parliament of Westminster. The move had important social consequences in Scotland, because it soon created among the Scottish landed aristocracy a group which was as much at home in England as in Scotland and which tended to send its sons to English schools to be educated. And this anglicization which began at the top of Scottish society, was soon to affect the whole of Scottish life. But for most of the eighteenth century the social mores of England and Scotland were so different that both the English and the Scots were preoccupied with national differences. English parliamentarians were at first scornful of their new Scottish colleagues and rumour made their reaction sound stronger than it was. But the predominant English reaction, as in the time of James VI and I, seems to have been one of jealousy that so many prizes were in future to go to Scots. The post-Union influx of Scots looking for better jobs than they could get at home, inevitably led to much hostile comment. And such comment was much less playful than Dr. Johnson's comments on the Scots that were so much resented in Scotland. (Especially his remark that 'the noblest prospect a Scotchman ever sees, is the high road that leads him to England!'.) John Wilkes's satirical paper the *North Briton* drew on a good deal of anti-Scottish venom as well as on prejudice against the unpopular Scottish Prime Minister, the Earl of Bute. Scots who wished to be liked, like David Hume the philosopher, found it much easier to be accepted in France than in England, and became covertly or openly anti-English. Indeed, Hume even went to the length of praising the institutions of France as better than those of England. Nor was Hume alone in this. Eighteenth-century Scotland found in the legend of the 'auld alliance' with France an escape from the realities of the smothering embrace of England and dreamed that the auld alliance might be re-created in literature.

But the great watershed in eighteenth-century Scotland was the 1745 rebellion. By raising the bogy of Celtic domination over Anglo-Saxon Scotland it drove the Lowlands unequivocally into support for the Union. It made the crushing of the Highland clans inevitable. And it tainted opposition to the Union of 1707 with Jacobitism. The harrying of the clans had solid backing in the Lowlands, and it was only when the real danger was over that romantic Jacobitism took root there. Even then it was strongest among those who had suffered from their association with the Jacobite cause, notably the episcopalians who had become a persecuted sect driven to holding their services in barns and out-of-the-way places. What is surprising in retrospect is that after the Forty Five the number of the proscribed in the Lowlands was so few, and that so much of the Jacobite intellectual tradition became absorbed into Scottish thought.

The truth of the matter seems to be that all intelligent Scots in the eighteenth century were preoccupied with the problem of national development. They were aware that Scotland was an extremely poor country which, when it came to the crunch, had not been able to hold out against its economically much more powerful neighbour, England. But they felt within themselves that Scotland stood for spiritual values superior to those of England. How were they to reconcile the two? Perhaps the most successful attempt was that made by the Presbyterian Jacobite, Sir James Steuart.[1] He argued that national differences depended on the relationship of two factors, the economic and the spiritual. In countries where a backward agriculture predominated over industry, the values of the agricultural community permeated all aspects of the national life: or, as Steuart put it, 'Pipers, blue bonnets, and oat meal, are known in Swabia, Auvergne, Limousin, and Catalonia, as well as in Lochaber.'[2] In industrial places like Geneva, by contrast, the tone was set by industry. Yet the economy was not necessarily the determining factor. Each nation has a spiritual character which need not necessarily be related directly to the economy. A combination of official doctrine, history and 'established habits' might combine to give countries with a very similar economic structure a very different spiritual character or ethos. Steuart, like Hume, saw in Scotland a country with a distinct ethos of its own, which helped to add to the range and colour of European culture and must be preserved if civilization were not to be impoverished.

The great writers of the Scottish enlightenment had no need to exaggerate the contribution of Scottish culture to European civilization because from the 1750s to 1820 they were in the forefront of European literature. David Hume, Adam Smith and Walter Scott were all writers in the first rank and there were many in the second. Moreover, they witnessed in the beginnings of the New Town of Edinburgh (1767) a deliberate attempt to create in Scotland a capital worthy of one of the leading nations of Europe. That it proved to be primarily a

[1] On this see G. E. Davie, 'Anglophobe and Anglophil', *Scottish Journal of Political Economy*, XIV (1967), 291–302, a review article on an edition of Steuart's *An Inquiry into the Principles of Political Oeconomy*, edited by Andrew Skinner (2 vols., Edinburgh, 1966).

[2] Steuart, *Political Oeconomy*, I, 108.

literary capital did nothing to lessen the satisfaction of writers who believed in the dignity of literature. Scottish writers still suffered from a deeply rooted sense of inferiority and subordination because Scotland was no longer a nation state, but they were determined to make the best of it, and to outdo the English in the eyes of the most cultured nation in Europe, the French. Indeed, the Scots might rightly claim that the Edinburgh of Adam Smith, Dugald Stewart, Sir Walter Scott, Robert Burns and the *Edinburgh Review* set the tone not merely for Scotland, but for England and for much of Europe.

From the position of literary confidence which they had now reached, the leading Scots writers could afford to be generous about the English, though Burns could never resist making pleasant quips against them, much in the spirit of those present-day nationalists who published a booklet of *Nationalist Variants of Auld Scots Sangs*. Acceptance of the economic advantages of the Union was now general. And Scots basked in the reflected glory of Scots generals, admirals and proconsuls who won such renown during the Napoleonic wars and the years that followed. Thomas Campbell became a patriotic *British* poet, and won a certain notoriety among subsequent generations of Scottish patriots by writing those stirring lines about:

> Ye Mariners of England!
> That guard our native seas;
> Whose flag has braved, a thousand years,
> The battle and the breeze!

And

> The meteor flag of England
> Shall yet terrific burn;
> Till danger's troubled night depart,
> And the star of peace return.

But this growing association by Scots of Scotland with England was linked with an intense patriotic fervour for things Scottish. There has never been a stauncher Scottish patriot than Sir Walter Scott or Robert Burns and both did their best to foster what they considered the characteristic ethos of the Scottish nation. Scott, by reviving ballads and by writing verse about the Highlands, notably 'The Lady of the Lake', created a new awareness of the beauties of Scotland and of the picturesque aspects of Scotland's past. Burns, by writing 'Scots Wha Hae', identified himself with Barbour and Blind Harry.

> Scots, wha hae wi' Wallace bled,
> Scots, wham Bruce has aften led,
> Welcome to your gory bed,
>   Or to victorie.
> Now's the day, and now's the hour:
> See the front o' battle lour!
> See approach proud Edward's power—
>   Chains and slaverie!

But though Burns went on to remark:

> Liberty's in every blow!
> Let us do, or die!

he was quite prepared to recognize that the Scotland of Wallace and Bruce was no longer in being, and to take a job as an excise officer. So too with Scott. The Waverley novels are full of Scottish propaganda but they are not directed against the *status quo*. For Scott the Union was a timely settlement of an ancient rivalry, which must not be disturbed unless there were the strongest reasons for a change.

Scott's main achievement was the creation of a new vision of Scotland, the Scotland of the modern tourist industry. Scottish story, Scottish dress, Scottish castles, Scottish scenery, blended together in a romantic vision of a Scotland inhabited by chiefs and clansmen, over which Scott himself, the wizard of the north, in some way presided. This was the vision which Scott himself encouraged Edinburgh to live up to in 1822, when King George IV visited Scotland, the first monarch to do so for more than a century. The gentry dressed themselves up in fancy tartans and glengarry bonnets, their costumes specially tailored for the occasion, the Lord Mayor of London wore a splendid tartan concoction, and even the King appeared in Highland dress. The visit was an immense success, established the kilt as one of the dresses of the gentry, and gave a boost to the woollen manufacturers who from now onwards produced ever more elaborate books of tartans. Indeed, a tartan cult was established which spread across Europe and the world and came to symbolize one aspect of Scottish culture.

The Royal visit of 1822 proved to be the last great landmark of the literary predominance of Scotland over England. Already the Scottish universities had lost much of their attractiveness for Englishmen and Americans, though three future Prime Ministers, Melbourne, Russell and Palmerston had been partly educated in them. The predominance

70

of the great Scottish reviews—the *Edinburgh Review* and *Blackwood's Magazine*—was being challenged in the south by the *Quarterly* and the *Westminster* reviews, although the writers for the latter were often Scots, and Lockhart, Scott's son-in-law, for a time edited the *Quarterly*. More important, the almost exclusively Scottish character of Scottish administration was breaking down. From 1745 down to 1828 there was nearly always a Scottish manager in the government, who was a Scot himself and was given a pretty free hand to run things in Scotland. The effect of this was to encapsulate Scotland in the United Kingdom. While Scots had the advantage of being able to seek a career in England or the Empire they were left very much alone in Scotland. The longest-serving of the Scottish managers, Henry Dundas, first Viscount Melville, saw Scotland through the tense period which followed the outbreak of the French Revolution, and, when he lost his parliamentary position at Westminster as a result of party hostility which led to his impeachment, he was able to hand over his Scottish duties to his son Robert, the second Viscount Melville. By the 1820s, however, it was becoming increasingly difficult to manage Scotland simply by a judicious attention to patronage and the management of elections. Because most of the talent at the Scots bar was on the Whig side Tory ministers found that they could no longer with a clear conscience appoint only Tories to the judicial bench. Rising administrative standards at Whitehall made Home Secretaries, who were nominally responsible for Scottish affairs, uneasy that they were not themselves doing in Scotland the job that they were paid to do. Periodic outbreaks of disorder in the industrial districts suggested that there was need to keep a closer eye on Scotland than hitherto. And there was in any case no Scottish politician on the Tory side who looked as though he had the makings of a future Home Secretary. When the second Lord Melville refused to serve under Canning in 1828, no Scottish 'manager' was appointed to succeed him, and the old system quietly came to an end. Scotland was at last placed directly under English ministers at Whitehall. For a time this did not seem to matter, because Scotland was about to enjoy the revivifying effect of parliamentary and local government reform. But 1828 was eventually to prove one of the decisive dates in the history of Scottish nationalism, because it marked the beginning of the move to create a Scottish Office to handle Scottish business.

The Reform Act of 1832 for a time channelled Scottish political energies almost exclusively into Whig and Liberal political channels.

For Scotland reform was more important than for England because the great magnates and the Scottish manager had between them established a stranglehold over the small Scottish parliamentary constituencies. Reform meant for Scotland the creation for the first time of a system of free elections. And because the bad old system was associated in Scots minds with Toryism, and because the Whigs undoubtedly enjoyed an intellectual ascendancy in Scotland, the Scottish M.P.s for over fifty years after 1832 were almost entirely Whig or Liberal in politics. Indeed, at the height of Liberal enthusiasm in 1880 it was said that all the Scottish Conservative M.P.s could have travelled to Westminster together in one first-class railway compartment (built to hold six).

The Liberal supremacy in Scottish elections coincided with a bout of enthusiasm for the Union, which even the disruption of the Church of Scotland in 1843 did little to modify. Indeed, even the Chartists were strong Unionists. Though all was not well with Scottish society, Scotland was now more prosperous than ever before, and people attributed this prosperity in part to the Union. Free churchmen, in particular, riding on the crest of a wave of religious fervour, felt that the Union gave them the opportunity to share in the management of a world-wide empire and to carry Free Church principles to the far corners of the earth. The Free Church journal, the *North British Review*, gave in 1854 the classic summary of the Unionist case, written by David Masson:

> Increased quiet, increased commerce and wealth, increased liberty, increased civilisation—these have been the consequences to Scotland of the once detested Union. That Scotland, if left to pursue her separate career, would still have made progress in these respects, need not be doubted; but that the degree and the kind of the progress she *has* made are traceable to the fact of the Union, admits of historical proof . . . since the Union, Scottish talent and Scottish energy have had a wider and richer field to expatiate in than they would otherwise have possessed. There can be no doubt that, in the general field of British activity, in all its departments, Scotchmen have, during the last century and a half, done a disproportionate share of the work, and earned a disproportionate share of the recompense. There have been Scottish Prime Ministers of Britain; Scottish Chief Justices of England; Scottish Lord Chancellors; Scottish Generals of British armies, and Admirals of British fleets;

Scottish Governors of India, and other colonial dependencies of Britain. England is full of Scottish merchants and manufacturers. London is full of Scottish literary men, and Scottish editors of newspapers.[1]

Dissent from the Unionist consensus was left to small, but not unimportant minorities, who first began to make themselves heard at the end of the forties.

Modern nationalist ideas were first formulated by three distinct groups of people with very different points of view. First there were the practical reformers and the businessmen in Glasgow, who found that the abolition of the Scottish manager in 1828 seemed to make it impossible to get things done quickly, except by extending English laws to Scotland, and who found that there never seemed to be enough parliamentary time for Scottish business. Hence their characteristic cry that the needs of Scotland were neglected. Secondly, there was the Scottish Tory literary establishment in Edinburgh, which was geared to the production of stories and verse about the Scottish past, plus the few Scottish counterparts of the Radical writers of the Young Ireland movement. For them the main theme was English insults to Scotland and the need to restore Scotland to her former glories. Thirdly, there were the few Radical thinkers who saw in the political arrangements made for Scotland a yardstick for Scottish inadequacies and wanted so to arrange the affairs of Scotland that Scots were forced to stand on their own two feet. Their motto was 'Scotland arise'. In addition there lay behind all this a strong sense of frustration at the extent of the anglicization discussed in an earlier chapter, and a profound irritation at the way in which the English seemed to misunderstand the Scots and at the pinpricks that appeared in English newspapers.

The early nationalists also had powerful allies in the Scottish newspaper press, which was periodically convulsed by irritation at English newspaper stereotypes of Scottish life. Scots could afford to laugh at such *Punch* jokes as the one about the Scotsman visiting London for whom 'Bang went saxpence'. But they found the relish with which English journalists printed what they regarded as anti-Scottish propaganda quite repulsive. Partly this arose from the traditional Scottish habit of turning a joke into an affront. But it was also the product of a long history of derogatory English remarks about the Scots going back to the Union of the Crowns in 1603 and even beyond. The English had

---

[1] *North British Review*, XXI (1854), 82.

long made much of Scottish poverty, the lack of Scottish skill at handicrafts, the smallness and dirtiness of Scottish houses, the lack of personal cleanliness of the people ('many of their women', noted Whitelocke in 1650, 'are so sluttish, that they do not wash their linen above once a month, nor their hands and faces above once a year'),[1] and the badness of Scottish inns. Now that things were rapidly getting better Scots took it amiss that relics of the bad old days were still harped on, and that a quite disproportionate emphasis was given to the bad conditions which existed in decaying Scottish villages and in the Highlands. Like many Africans today they wanted visitors and journalists to concentrate their attention on the modern side of the Scottish economy, not its backward side. But they had no means of enforcing such a ban as that which one government imposes today on photography—'It is forbidden to photograph derogatory objects'—and could only respond by way of a press campaign. A whole book could be made out of English jokes and cartoons about Scotland and about the Scottish reaction to them. Scots detested being treated as if they were a backward people and bitterly resented English comments which (rightly) suggested that the Scots were more drunken than the English and that Scottish standards of sexual morality were lower than those of England. Indeed, looking back to the origins of the first Scottish nationalist movement one of its leaders attributed its formation to the 'revival of the old scurrilous spirit towards Scotland that prevailed in the South more than a century ago. . . . Scotland—her institutions, her manners, and customs—were railed at in every imaginable shape and form, until the Thistle could stand it no longer'.[2]

The first Scottish nationalist agitation began early in January 1850 with an outburst by one of the leaders of the Free Church, the Reverend James Begg of Edinburgh. Begg was foremost among those who wanted to promote a regeneration of Scottish life in all its aspects. He carried on the Chalmers tradition of social work in the poor districts of the towns, he was a champion of popular education and of the extension of the franchise, and he was a fundamentalist in religion, who placed much emphasis on the purity of Free Church doctrine. In 1850 his object was to start a national revival by recalling the nation to its senses:

---

[1] Quoted among other derogatory remarks in Buckle's *History of Civilization in England* (new ed., London, 1902), III, 25n.

[2] Speech by William Burns quoted in Hanham, 'Mid-Century Scottish Nationalism, op. cit., p. 153.

The Beginnings of Modern Nationalism

We are sinking in our national position every year, and simply living on the credit of the past. . . . A people that might match the world for energy, and who have heretofore stood in the first rank of nations, sinking under a combination of increasing evils—the efforts of ministers paralysed—our universities locked up, dwarfed, and comparatively inefficient—crime increasing—drunkenness and Sabbath-breaking making progress—Christianity languishing—pauperism threatening to swallow up the whole property of the country —hundreds of our best people flying from our shores under the pressure of want, or at the command of tyranny—the great natural resources of our whole country locked up in the iron embrace of feudal despotism—little intelligence amongst the people to understand this, far less to battle with it—the very passes of our mountains interdicted—the fishings of our rivers monopolized—our public grounds and gardens shut up—the Parliament of England despising us, our natural guardians joining in the oppression.[1]

Begg did not spell out all his points in 1850, but when he returned to the subject in 1871, in a pamphlet appropriately entitled *A Violation of the Treaty of Union the Main Origin of our Ecclesiastical Divisions and Other Evils*, he argued that the reason why the Scots were in such a plight was that Scotland was rent by ecclesiastical divisions, that these divisions were 'mainly caused by a deliberate violation of the Treaty of Union on the part of England' and that there was a well-thought-out plot to subordinate Scotland to England. Hence it was urgently necessary to act in order to preserve Scotland's status 'not as a conquered province of England, but a distinct independent kingdom, which has united with England on equal terms, and under a clear and solemn treaty'.

Begg's solution in 1850 was the reconstitution of a Scottish government headed by a Secretary of State and the strengthening of the Scottish representation at Westminster. But he was willing to contemplate the creation of a subordinate Scottish parliament

. . . if no attention were to be paid to their affairs,—if a Secretary of State were not appointed for Scotland, with a Council of Scotchmen,—if some effectual plan were not fallen upon, he was not sure but they must endeavour to get such a change in the existing system

[1] James Begg, *National Education for Scotland practically considered* (Edinburgh, 1850), pp. 35–6.

as would secure them some legislative body in their own country to dispose of purely Scottish questions.[1]

For a time Begg's remarks made little impact outside his own immediate circle. *The Witness*, under the editorship of Hugh Miller the most powerful Free Church newspaper in Scotland, was vaguely sympathetic. The other newspapers merely groused about the neglect of Scottish business by the government and the House of Commons, which had delayed a long string of Scottish bills.

Support for Begg's position first came from a very unlikely source in 1852, when James Grant, a historical novelist and Edinburgh antiquarian, published a series of letters and articles on the theme of 'Justice to Scotland' in two minor Edinburgh newspapers. The core of his argument was that England had broken the terms of the Union, both in the letter and in the spirit and that England was getting very much more out of the Union than was Scotland. To support his argument he went through a list of Scottish grievances since the Union, and then attempted to show that during the last few years public expenditure had been largely for the benefit of England. Administrative economies had meant a reduction in the number and size of government offices in Edinburgh and the concentration of civil service expenditure in London. Naval expenditure was almost exclusively allocated to English dockyards, shipyards and arsenals. And every day Scottish talent was being drawn off to London to the impoverishment of Scotland.

> vast numbers of respectable and well-educated young men pining for lack of employment, are forced to emigrate to become private soldiers in India, while their unmarried sisters (as Belhaven prophesied of old) must resort to the most humble means for subsistence— to labour with their hands, or become poor dependents, teachers and governesses amongst that very English people, into whose pockets and Exchequer *nine millions* of our Scottish money are annually poured.[2]

Grant's solution to the problem, as befitted one the heroes of whose novels were often Cavaliers or Jacobites, was to put the clock back, to restore the various government offices and courts that had been abolished in the nineteenth century, to restore the Scottish Secretary of

[1] Thomas Smith, *Memoirs of James Begg, D.D.* (Edinburgh, 1888), Vol. II, pp. 149–50.
[2] Quoted in Hanham, 'Mid-Century Scottish Nationalism', op. cit., p. 158.

State and Privy Council which had been abolished in the eighteenth century, and to strengthen Scottish representation in the United Kingdom parliament.

Probably nothing further would have been heard of Grant's ideas had he not stumbled across a means of conducting a public agitation to give them publicity. Late in 1852 he and his brother John, along with a trio of sympathizers, hit the headlines by a bizarre gesture. They appealed to the Lord Lyon King of Arms, the official heraldic authority in Scotland, through his depute, asking him to suppress various irregularly quartered royal arms, and improperly made flags used by public offices, and also the new florin coins, on the ground that they were in contravention of the laws of heraldry and the Acts of Union and were further an insult to Scotland. Lyon Depute hastily disclaimed responsibility, but for some reason the subject caught the public fancy. Ever since there has been a steady procession of little booklets about English infractions of the Acts of Union by the use of the wrong flags. The Acts clearly prescribed the use of the Union flag in all circumstances, but the English went on using the flag of St. George, notably in the Royal Navy.[1] Since 1852 there has been a revival of Scottish interest in heraldry which in the twentieth century has become one of the main interests of the right wing of the nationalist movement. In 1852 the 'heraldic grievance' immediately became a popular issue. All the major town councils and the Convention of Royal Burghs petitioned the Queen to ask for a redress, and the newspapers had a field day. The English newspapers and *The Scotsman* denounced the agitation as a puerile exhibition of wounded feelings (one English paper asked why the Welsh rabbit did not appear in the arms of Great Britain), but the Grant brothers had made their point. They had shown that it was possible to get up a nationalist agitation in Scotland, even on a trivial point.

During 1853 and 1854 the first effective nationalist movement, the National Association for the Vindication of Scottish Rights, or Scottish Rights Society, was formed to follow up the Grants' agitation. Supported by both Dr. Begg and the Radical Duncan McLaren on one wing and by the Tory romantics on the other, it had for a time the makings of a great national crusade. The politicians held aloof, but the town councils supported it, so did the Convention of Royal Burghs, so did a considerable number of men who felt that they had a grievance

---

[1] There is a temperate and brief account of the matter in William McMillan and John A. Stewart, *The Story of the Scottish Flag* (Glasgow, 1925).

against the way the existing system worked, and so did most of the old-fashioned Tories once they had been given a lead by *Blackwoods*. There were great meetings in Edinburgh and Glasgow, long lists of supporters, a series of pamphlets, and then—nothing. The bubble burst with the outbreak of the Crimean War and the Indian Mutiny and nothing was left except memories.

But Scottish nationalists were not left long without a cause. They were soon enlisted in the campaign to create a national monument at Abbey Craig near Stirling to that greatest of Scottish fighters against English oppression, Sir William Wallace. The Wallace monument, in the form of a giant stone tower on a great rocky hill, proved to be a much more important landmark in the history of the nationalist movement than the Scottish Rights Society had been. For it symbolized the aspirations of Scottish patriots much better than the long list of miscellaneous grievances, which James Grant had drawn up for the Society. As *The Witness* put it:

> Either Scotland has no history at all, or that history finds its centre in Wallace. Either it is not desirable that the nation should understand its history at all, or it is desirable that it should understand the historical place and significance of Wallace. Either Scotland contributes nothing distinctive to the philosophy of history, offers nothing remarkable to the student of man or of nation, or her contribution is all summed up in the name and in the work of Wallace.[1]

Moreover, the Wallace monument project attracted attention because it appealed to extremists of all sorts. John Steill, an isolated supporter of Young Ireland, came forward to speak for the lunatic fringe. For him England was an imperialist power which would stoop to anything, and had not changed since Wallace's day. As for Wallace:

> England took care not to let the people of Scotland have amongst them the sacred ashes of Wallace to kneel over; for when she could not subdue, she got the patriot by treachery into her hands, and hewed his body to pieces.[2]

For him the Wallace monument was to be a symbol of Scotland, 'the last object that the emigrant may set his eyes on when he leaves Scotia's

[1] *The Witness*, 13th March 1858.
[2] *Daily Bulletin*, 9th April 1856.

shore, and the first that he welcomes when it is his lot again to return to his native land'.

Nor was enthusiasm for the Wallace monument project confined to Scotland. Wallace monuments became a symbol of Scottish patriotism all over the world, and many Scottish communities did their best to erect one. Perhaps the most famous was at Ballarat in Victoria, Australia, which was unveiled with some panache in 1889 and cost £1,000. For not only was it a fine statue, but it is associated with lines by Francis Lauderdale Adams that soon sprung to fame and are now included in the *Oxford Book of Scottish Verse*.

> This is Scotch William Wallace. It was he
> Who in dark hours first raised his face to see:
> Who watched the English tyrant nobles spurn,
> Steel-clad, with iron hoofs the Scottish free:
>
> Who armed and drilled the simple footman Kern,
> Yea, bade in blood and rout the proud Knight learn
> His Feudalism was dead, and Scotland stand
> Dauntless to wait the day of Bannockburn!
>
> O Wallace, peerless lover of thy land
> We need thee still, thy moulding brain and hand!
> For us, thy poor, again proud tyrants spurn,
> The robber rich, a yet more hateful band!

Furthermore, from the Ballarat statue movement was to stem much other Scottish nationalism in Australia, including the Scottish National Association of Victoria.

Perhaps the Wallace monument would have mattered less if the English had not shown every sign of being upset by it. *The Times*, which maintained that 'the Wallace himself . . . is the merest myth', regarded the monument project as simply another example of the Scottish fondness for grousing. But in a famous article beginning, 'Scotland is manifestly a country in want of a grievance' it launched what is probably the most effective attack ever made on modern Scottish nationalism:

There is a widespread feeling that Scotland has not within the present generation quite upheld her own past reputation. Edinburgh, indeed, continues to affect literary airs, and a coterie of writers live together on terms of mutual admiration. Numbers of young Scotchmen, as of yore, come south, and reap the reward of energy and ability, but on the whole, Scotland has lost way. She remains motionless, relying on past achievements, boasting of great men that are dead and gone, repeating maxims which were discoveries once, but are mere platitudes now, and showing few signs of intellectual or moral vigour. Past generations gave the country good primary schools, and the present has added nothing. The Universities are inferior, the schools for the middle and higher classes are inferior, professional education and professional spirit are not what they are in England. The clergy are comparatively an unlettered class of men. Hardly a single idea on political or social subjects comes in the present day from Scotland. Literature is merely a faint and worthless imitation of old models. Poems in the style of Burns, which can be written by any human being who can write at all, are actually still produced in incredible quantities. The old metaphysics, the old divinity, are quite worn out with the discussions of cliques, who cannot get beyond them. Scotchmen, in fact, seem to do nothing but masquerade in the garments of their grandfathers.

Now, it seems to us that this general poverty of thought is the cause why Scotch Lords and professors and men of letters are continually harping on their nationality and their historical renown. When there really was a national mind the world heard nothing about the Abbey Craig, the Royal arms, and the rights of the Scottish heralds. Now, by their exclusiveness, and what we will make bold to call their provincialism, the Scotch have not only kept out English influences which might have done them good, but they have driven the best of their own countrymen to England. There can be no doubt that we get nearly all the talents that the northern kingdom produces, and the cause is not difficult to ascertain. It is not merely because Parliament sits in London that England draws away the best brains from the other two kingdoms, but because Englishmen have thrown away those confined notions of nationality which still prevail in Scotland and Ireland. We south of the Tweed have risen to the conception of a United Kingdom; nay, more, of a British Empire, and every subject of the Queen finds here a career in which he may advance without fear of jealousy or prejudice. But in Edinburgh the cry, or at least the feeling still is, Scotland for the Scotch. Yet the more Scotland has striven to be a nation, the more she has sunk to be a province.[1]

[1] *The Times*, 4th December 1856.

This attack was, alas, never effectively met by any Scots contro-versialist. The Scots nationalists, for the most part, chose easier targets. The most persistent of them was William Burns, a Glasgow solicitor who acted as adviser to the West of Scotland coal owners and ironmasters. As a nationalist Burns has three claims to fame. He was the first man to bring home to Scots the enormity of allowing Great Britain to be referred to as 'England' and of the use of 'Scotch' instead of 'Scottish'. He was one of the first to recognize that no nationalist movement can thrive without a nationalist historiography to back it, and for this reason himself composed a substantial book, *The Scottish War of Independence: its Antecedents and Effects* (2 vols., Glasgow, 1874). And, finally, he was the first of those patrons of nationalist endeavours in journalism and other fields, who have played such an important part in modern nationalism. In particular he supported Patrick Edward Dove, a man of astonishingly wide interests, who tried his hand at all sorts of literary ventures, and served as one of the few links between the middle-class nationalists and working-class nationalism.

William Burns's lasting claim to fame is that he and his disciples virtually killed the use of the word 'England' and 'English' as applied to Scotland, and that they made it hard for conscientious people to use the adjective 'Scotch'. There were those who thought that this pre-occupation with the 'national names' was unimportant, but it was in fact a matter of some significance. Those who were brought up during the revolutionary wars had been prone to accept, as Thomas Campbell the poet did, that Scotland was in process of being swallowed up by her bigger neighbour and might be included in 'England'. Further there were already Scots who identified themselves with the English past rather than with that of Scotland. Men like Sir Archibald Alison, the historian, who was long Sheriff of Lanarkshire, and Lord Palmerston habitually used the word England when they meant Great Britain and English when they meant British, much as Americans do today. They spoke of the greatness of England, of England's power, English victories, and English civilization. And they were followed by many ordinary Scots. The perpetuation of such a usage was bound to make for national assimilation, and must therefore be resisted by any conscientious nationalist. Hence Burns's pamphlets such as *'England' versus 'Great Britain'* and *Scottish Rights and Honour Vindicated*. It was too late to change the habits of the older generation, but Burns had the satisfaction of seeing that the younger generation were gradually adopting his precepts. As for the word 'Scotch', Burns's attack produced an immediate change. The *North British Daily Mail* attacked the word as 'modern' and 'vulgar' in 1858, and abandoned it at once, and the *Glasgow Herald* promptly followed suit. It agreed with Burns that 'Scotch' was 'a horrid vulgarism, and as barbarous as vulgar', and that 'No correct writer ever uses it'.

Meanwhile the campaign for a Scottish minister and for the redress of Scottish grievances quietly simmered on. A little more time was found for Scottish legislation. The abolition of Scottish offices was almost entirely halted. And governments began to show themselves willing to contemplate the creation of a special minister for Scotland, even if the present moment should not be an opportune one for action. The initiative, however, remained almost entirely in the hands of staunch supporters of the Union who regarded themselves as Scottish patriots rather than as nationalists. James Begg's fulmination against the Union in 1871 was but little noted, whereas the steady manœuvring by his old ally of 1853, Duncan McLaren, by 1868 the leading Scottish Liberal in the Commons, was pretty effective.[1] The Conservatives in 1878 introduced a Bill to create an Under Secretary for Scotland, though it was not proceeded with, and after 1880 the Liberals were committed to more ambitious legislation, though what form it might take was still uncertain. As a result when the office of Secretary for Scotland was created in 1885, the move was more a result of steady political pressure from within the establishment than of nationalist agitation from outside. A great demonstration in Edinburgh in January 1884, under the auspices of the Convention of Royal Burghs, at which all parties were strongly represented, showed that it was still possible, given appropriate circumstances, to re-create some of the atmosphere of 1853–4.[2] But now such demonstrations were managed by sober politicians rather than by nationalist writers and agitators.

Nationalism needed the impetus of the rise of the Parnell movement in Ireland to get it going again as a political force. However, the status of Scottish nationalism was now different. After 1886 Gladstone's conversion to Home Rule for Ireland made the idea of Home Rule for Scotland seem much less revolutionary than hitherto. In a later chapter, just what this meant in practical politics will be examined

[1] J. B. Mackie, *The Life and Work of Duncan McLaren*, 2 vols. (Edinburgh, 1888).
[2] *The Scotsman*, 17th January 1884.

in more detail. Here it is only necessary to look briefly at the literary side of the Scottish Home Rule movement that came into being after 1885.

The main achievement of the ten years after 1885 was the creation of a substantial pamphlet literature, much of it published under the auspices of the Scottish Home Rule Association. In one sense it added little to what early pamphleteers had said. But it did make clear the range of nationalist opinion and it did link up the agitation of the 1880s with earlier movements. One of the earliest of the Scottish Home Rule Association pamphlets was *Home Rule for Scotland, as advocated by Andrew Fletcher of Saltoun, our first Home Rule Statesman, nearly 200 years ago*. Another pamphlet gave *Burns's Opinion of the Union of 1707*. A leaflet linked the S.H.R.A. with William Burns's campaign against the misuse of the national names—*Protest by the Scottish Home Rule Association against the misuse of the terms 'England' and 'English' for 'Britain', the 'British Empire', its Peoples and Institutions*. There was revived talk of national monuments. There was a deliberate move to cultivate Scottish opinion abroad, indicated by the S.H.R.A.'s publication of *Home Rule in America: a Political Address by Andrew Carnegie, Esq*. Dr. Begg's views were resurrected in a pamphlet entitled *What the Rev. Dr. Begg said in 1871 about Home Rule for Scotland*. Above all there was a new confidence about the pamphleteers. All sorts of backwoods nationalists began to emerge and to make themselves heard, and for a time after 1890 the Scottish Home Rule Association virtually took over the *Scots Magazine*.

The most interesting feature of this pamphleteering was that it covered the whole of the modern nationalist spectrum. On the right there were now two distinct groups. There were the aristocrats who were convinced that all was not well with Scotland and that something must be done about it. Of these the most interesting was the third Marquess of Bute—the Lothair of Disraeli's novel—who as a Roman Catholic Tory philanthropist and antiquarian was outside the realm of ordinary party politics. He was one of the first to evolve something like a distinctive Catholic nationalist point of view. But he was chiefly notable as a convert to the idea of creating a national legislature for Scotland, even before the Home Rule question became popular. In a letter to Lord Rosebery in 1881 he argued his case, both by reference to Scottish grievances, much in the manner of the nationalists of 1853–4, and by bringing forward views characteristically his own about the Scots peers:

It is commonly said that the Government contemplate some measures for relieving the House of Commons of the plethora of business which chokes it, and that this will be done either by restrictions upon the freedom of debate or by withdrawing matters non-Imperial from its ordinary cognizance.

What I am writing for now is to urge upon you that, if the latter of the two above courses be adopted, the internal legislation of Scotland ought to be committed to some nationally representative body, to meet, not in London, but in Edinburgh, if necessary, at a different time to the Imperial Parliament; and which, if the title of Parliament were not given it, might at least deserve the scarcely less historic and honoured one, of National Convention.

I have never pretended to be an admirer of the Union of 1707, nor do my historical and especially, ethnological, studies, make me like it any the better. Putting, however, everything else aside, and granting for the sake of argument that there may have been reasons (probably dynastic) in its favour in the time of Queen Anne, it seems to me to do nothing now but prevent any public Scotch business of a Parliamentary kind being done at all, to place what is done or left undone in the hands of English authorities, whereby *inter alia*, public money is unfairly spent (look at the fact that there is not in Scotland a single arsenal or harbour of refuge, and that the lives of the Shetlanders were sacrificed only a short time ago to the absence of a telegraph,) to subject litigants and others to enormous expense in taking their business to London to be managed by lawyers who do not understand their law, and to drain a lot of the best people and a lot of money out of the country.

Allow me to say that I think there are many Tories like myself who would hail a more autonomous arrangement with deep pleasure. We would prefer the rule of our own countrymen, even if it were rather Radical, to the existing state of things.

It seems to me that Peers ought, were such a Body as I suppose, to exist, to be eligible to be members of it by election, like other citizens. It is true that I should see with a certain regret (more antiquarian, perhaps, than anything else) some families ousted, in that way, from an hereditary legislative power which they have enjoyed (more or less, for the Union was not generous in that way) some of them, for 600 or even 700 years, but I cannot help thinking that peerages are the production of a medieval and normalized, rather than of an aboriginal and national epoch, and that whatever claim they may at one time have possessed to represent a very important stratum of society, they are now little more than an arbitrary distinction. I think it might be concluded that, in Scotland at any rate, they are little more than an obsolete relique of a not inglorious past, whose claim to practical veneration at the present day could not justly go much farther than the legal recognition of their titles.

I do not think much expense would be entailed by such an arrangement, and there would certainly be more money to meet it with, by money being kept in the country which is now expended elsewhere through litigation and otherwise. Some adjustment might ultimately be effected, by which we should get more result for the taxes we pay. (You will perceive from the above that I am not scared by the words 'Home Rule' and that even the terrific phrase 'dismemberment of the Empire' fails to deter me from thinking of practical convenience. (If the Irish could manage their own affairs too, I don't see why they shouldn't, any more than Canada or the Isle of Man—but my impression is that they are incapable. No one would say the same thing of us.)[1]

The other main body of thought on the right was that associated with the few remaining Tory romantics of the school of James Grant. But they found a new, and not altogether welcome recruit from an unexpected source in the person of Theodore Napier. Napier was of Scottish parentage and was educated at the High School and University of Edinburgh, but he had been born in Australia and owned land there. Introduced to Scottish national politics by T. D. Wanliss, a politician of some note in Victoria, who when in Scotland published nationalist pamphlets in Dundee, Napier gradually went the whole hog as a nationalist. He became a Jacobite and secretary of the Legitimist Jacobite League of Great Britain and Ireland. He organized the Scottish 1897 jubilee petition to Queen Victoria against the misuse of the national names, he became secretary of the Wallace Robroyston memorial, he started a nationalist-cum-Jacobite journal, the *Fiery Cross*, and he took to wearing the costume of a Highland chieftain of the Cavalier period and paying annual visits to Culloden on the anniversary of the battle, and to Fotheringay Castle, where Mary, Queen of Scots was beheaded. Though embarrassing for his nationalist

[1] Marquess of Bute to the Earl of Rosebery, 3rd November 1881. Rosebery Papers, National Library of Scotland, RB57.

allies, he was a remarkable man, whose career would repay more attention than it can be given here.[1]

Still to the right, but nearer the centre, there was a group of nationalist lawyers and businessmen of very diverse views. Charles Waddie, who became secretary of the Scottish Home Rule Association, was perhaps the most characteristic figure among them. Moved by a sort of romantic nostalgia he published a number of 'patriotic' poems even before he became a Home Ruler. He then graduated from publishing poems with such titles as *Dunbar: the King's Advocate: a Tragic Episode in the Reformation in Scotland*, and *Wallace: or, the Battle of Stirling* to more ambitious political verse under the improbable title *Scotia's Darling Seat: a Home Rule Sermon, and other Poems*. But Waddie was also a good businessman and churchman—he was a printer in Edinburgh—who attempted much more ambitious exercises in the theory of political economy and of local government. And in one of his pamphlets he gives one of the few accounts we have of how this generation of nationalists came to their nationalism.[2]

In the early part of 1882 our attention was drawn to the subject of which this little work treats. The attempts of the English Courts to found jurisdiction over domiciled Scotsmen was creating some considerable stir in the country, and every now and then reference was made to the Treaty of Union. As they were all of a very vague and sometimes contradictory character we looked carefully into the question, and in the early months of 1883, we gave the result of our studies in the shape of a little pamphlet entitled 'The Treaty of Union between Scotland and England', with an Historical Introduction. Up to this time we had only a suspicion of the fraud perpetrated upon the Scots, and accepted the general verdict that the Union, however corruptly brought about, had been of signal service to the Scottish people. We felt many a pang of regret at the loss of our Parliament, with all the pomp and circumstance of the Court and the offices of state which surrounded our ancient seat of Government; yet as our people were prosperous and contented we accepted without question this oft-repeated assertion that the Treaty of Union

---

[1] There are brief lives in *The Jacobite*, May 1921, pp. 27–8, and in W. T. Pike and A. Eddington, *Edinburgh and the Lothians* . . . (Pike's New Century Series No. 12, Brighton and Edinburgh, 1904), p. 128.

[2] Charles Waddie, *How Scotland Lost her Parliament and What Came of It* (Edinburgh, 1891), pp. v–vii.

was the cause of all our happiness. This was the common opinion of Scotsmen; it was taught to them at school, shouted on the platform, dinned into their ears in newspaper articles, and constantly admitted and gloried in by our public men. The English looked upon themselves as the benefactors of Scotland, and no one from Scotland ever entered their country without being made aware of the interesting fact. This was a little galling to our pride, but what everybody admitted to be true could not be questioned. The little pamphlet above referred to, and which forms the opening chapter of this book, had created some suspicion in our mind that all was not as it should be; our studies had pointed to a very different conclusion from the generally received opinion, but the tumult of the political world over Home Rule for Ireland left us little leisure to prosecute our studies further, so for a time the question had to stand aside. The constant reference by both parties engaged in the political war of our times to the Union of Scotland and England as an example which pointed a moral in the case of the Union between Great Britain and Ireland, compelled us to look a little closer into the subject, and the result of our studies is now set before our readers in the following pages.

On the left the Home Rule debate introduced a much more Radical pamphleteer, whose nationalism was quite as fervent as that of Napier or Waddie. This was John Morrison Davidson, a journalist in London, whose name is still a by-word among older nationalists of left-wing views. His rather frantic denunciations of kings, bishops and lords, his emotional nationalism, and his sympathy for socialism, made him a symbol for the left. And he also had the advantage for them of claiming to act as a spiritual link with the Radical nationalists of former generations, from whom he traced his intellectual line of dissent through Patrick Edward Dove.[1] Morrison Davidson never had a paper of his own to edit, probably for the reason suggested in the somewhat wry comment by Guy Aldred:

In [W. Stewart Ross's] office I met that strange person Morrison Davison [*sic*], who exuded rare and disconnected scholarship. He was a crony of Ross, a defender of Christian Socialism, an authority on Winstanley the Digger, and had a manner replete with engaging

[1] This is what Davidson said himself in conversation and is borne out by his articles on Dove.

Radical memories. He was a splendid man if you permitted him to do all the conversation and later applied wisdom to all that he had said. I liked him but his love of John Barleycorn made close association impossible.[1]

In his rather incoherent way, however, Davidson became a very effective pamphleteer. Davidson's works *Scotia Rediviva: Home Rule for Scotland with the Lives of Sir William Wallace, George Buchanan, Fletcher of Saltoun and Thomas Spence, Scotland for the Scots: Scotland Revisited*, and *Leaves from the Book of Scots*, were well received at the time,[2] but they are so disorderly in their presentation that they make rather sad reading today.

On the left, however, the main importance of the Home Rule debate was that it brought to the fore a new type of working-class nationalism which will be discussed more fully in a later chapter.

Here it need only be said that by the 1880s the main patterns of modern nationalism had emerged. On the right nationalism was represented by individual Tory peers like Lord Bute, by romantic Tories in the tradition of James Grant, and by a small band of Jacobites. Nearer the centre were businessmen like William Burns and Charles Waddie, for whom nationalism was a discovery to be propagated in a businesslike way. And on the left there were Radical writers like Morrison Davidson, and working-class nationalists like some of the early Labour leaders. Nationalists could now work through the Scottish Home Rule Association in a climate more favourable to nationalist ideas than at any time in the past, conscious that there lay behind them a tradition both of nationalist ideas and nationalist agitation.

Nationalist ideas were still, however, largely held by fairly unsophisticated people. One suspects that the doggerel verse, that has always been a feature of Scottish life, meant more to them than controversial pamphlets. The Scottish Home Rule movement had no Barbour among its versifiers, but it had at least a substitute for Blind Harry in Charles Waddie, who produced for it the masterpiece with which this chapter must close.[3]

[1] Guy A. Aldred, *Dogmas Discarded, Part II* . . . (Glasgow, 1940), p. 31.
[2] See for instance the *Fiery Cross*, October 1902, p. 6, and *The Thistle*, VII (1915), 106–9.
[3] Charles Waddie, *Scotia's Darling Seat: a Home Rule Sermon, and other Poems* (Edinburgh, 1890), pp. 16–18.

The Beginnings of Modern Nationalism

Is Scotland to get Home Rule?

Wake! Scotland, wake! from thy long sleep.
Thy foes with stealthy footsteps creep,
And try to rob thee of thy name,
The dowry of a deathless fame,
Which Wallace, Bruce and Douglas too,
Left as a heritage to you.
With sneering lip and scornful glance,
They look upon thy broken lance,
And fettered limbs—thy treaty torn,—
A nation of its freedom shorn.

Rouse! Scotland, rouse! from sloth and fear,
Again the cry of freemen here,
Tell Gladstone, Morley, and their crew,
That Scotland to herself is true;
Nor will consent her lion's paw
Shall chestnuts from the furnace draw;
Nor slave to party; but shall fight,
And strike a blow for her own right;
No more to England will we bow,
But hold aloft our manly brow.

Shame! Scotland, shame! to be the slave
Of every canting English knave.
Shall London lawyers loudly brag
They've but to come with carpet bag
And stroke thee down with flattering speech,
And tell thee how they'll wisely teach,
Along the English road to trudge,
A patient, loyal, obedient drudge?
What need there then her chains to sever,
'Tis Ireland now, but Scotland never!

Rise! Scotland, rise! in all thy might,
With vision clear and aspect bright;
From distant isles, from hill and dale,
From mountain hoar, and lowly vale,

The Beginnings of Modern Nationalism

From barren glen and fertile strath,
By metalled road or mountain path,
From teeming workshop, mart, or street,
Let all the sons of Scotland meet,
A true, a loyal, a patriot band,
And sweep all traitors from the land.

CHAPTER FIVE

Home Rule All Round

I

Support for Scottish Home Rule within the United Kingdom was confined to a tiny minority before 1886. The overwhelming majority of Scots thought that they could get what they wanted through the ordinary mechanism of the United Kingdom parliament and that a Scottish parliament would be superfluous. There was a certain amount of interest in administrative devolution, of the sort which Joseph Chamberlain favoured for Ireland, and in building up a Scottish Office on the same lines as the Irish Office. But that was all. Gladstone's conversion to Home Rule for Ireland, however, entirely transformed the situation. The majority of Scottish Liberals accepted the new policy (though there were numerous dissenters who created a strong Liberal Unionist organization in Scotland) and as a result found themselves committed to a reassessment of the whole structure of the United Kingdom. After the 1886 general election Gladstone—who sat for a Scottish seat—chose, indeed, to go out of his way to force his followers to think what they were doing by publishing a pamphlet on *The Irish Question* in which he invited Wales and Scotland to rethink their position in the United Kingdom, and to contemplate replacing the Union by a federal structure:

The recent contest has been fought upon the question of nationality.... this very fact ... of itself gives a new place to nationality as an element of our political thought. Secondly, these nationalities will be inclined to help one another. Ireland has received signal assistance from Scotland and from Wales on the great and capital subject of her nationality. Should there be, and will there not be?—questions coming forward, in which Scotland or Wales have a special national interest or feeling, it is probable that Ireland, so long at least as she continues to have a voice through her members in

91

British affairs, will reciprocate the boon. What is not less likely, and even more important, is that the sense of nationality, both in Scotland and in Wales, set astir by this controversy, may take a wider range than heretofore. Wales, and even Scotland, may ask herself, whether the present system of intrusting all their affairs to the handling of a body, English in such overwhelming proportion as the present Parliament is, and must probably always be, is an adjustment which does the fullest justice to what is separate and specific in their several populations. Scotland, which for a century and a quarter after her Union was refused all taste of a real representative system, may begin to ask herself whether, if at the first she felt something of an unreasoning antipathy, she may not latterly have drifted into a superstitious worship, or at least an irreflective acquiescence. Of two things I feel assured. First, whatever practical claims either of these countries may make on their own behalf will be entertained and disposed of without stirring up the cruel animosities, the unworthy appeals to selfishness, the systematic misrepresentations, which have told so fearfully against Ireland. And, secondly, that the desire for Federation, floating in the minds of many, has had an unexpected ally in the Irish policy of 1886; and that, if the thing, which that term implies, contains within itself possibilities of practical good, the chance of bringing such possibilities to bear fruit has thus been unexpectedly and largely improved.[1]

A Scottish Home Rule Association was founded in Edinburgh in 1886 and Home Rule feeling steadily mounted in the Scottish Liberal associations. Some prominent Liberals, including John Morley, James Bryce and Lord Rosebery, regarded this development with some alarm, and the leaders of the Scottish Liberal Association did their best to damp down enthusiasm. After a good deal of discussion in 1888, the conference of the Scottish Liberal Association in the following year was accordingly advised to pass a holding resolution which read:

> That this National Conference is of opinion that Home Rule should be granted to Scotland, so that the Scottish people could have the sole control and management of their own National Affairs, and suggests that the true solution of the question may be found in

[1] W. E. Gladstone, *The Irish Question: I. The History of an Idea. II. Lessons of the Election* (London, 1886), pp. 36–7.

granting Home Rule legislatures on a Federal basis to Scotland, England, Ireland, and Wales; but in respect to the urgency of the claim of Ireland, declares that that country must have first consideration.[1]

Local conferences of Scottish Liberals for a time toyed with alternative formulations of the proposition that Scotland should wait its turn, and one at Hawick invented the curious title of 'the United Empire of Great Britain'. But action was clearly left to the leaders of the Liberal party who alone could carry Irish Home Rule. As a result, though a number of Home Rule resolutions were carried in the House of Commons when the Liberals were in power, beginning in 1894, they meant very little in terms of practical politics.

There was not even much discussion as to what form Scottish Home Rule should eventually take. The Scottish Home Rule Association favoured such discussion, but it was suspected of desiring to embarrass the Liberal leaders and of backing those Liberal Unionists who were willing to try a measure of devolution in Scotland, where it would be safe to make the experiment, but were opposed to what they considered Gladstone's foolhardy Irish policy.[2] Such Liberal Unionists could, moreover, claim that they had thought out their position fairly carefully, for it was logically an extension of Joseph Chamberlain's Irish devolution proposals which Gladstone had rejected before the Liberal party broke up.

The main long-term achievement of the Scottish Home Rule Association was to confirm in their Home Rule sympathies many of the Radical leaders in the Highlands and many of the leaders of the Labour movement. The list of Vice Presidents in 1892 included the names of such Highland leaders as G. B. Clark, Myles McInnes, Charles Fraser-Mackintosh, Alexander Mackenzie, Surgeon General Maclean, John Macleod and J. McGilchrist Ross and such Labour leaders as R. B. Cunninghame Graham, J. Keir Hardie and Robert Smillie. Moreover the local branches of the Association fell quite soon into ultra-Radical hands: for instance, Ramsay MacDonald was for some years secretary of the London branch. The result was that although the Scottish Home Rule Association had right-wing Liberal officers in Edinburgh, its branches were associated with Radicalism

---

[1] From the Minutes of the Scottish Liberal Association in Edinburgh University Library.

[2] Cp. the speech by Charles Fraser-Mackintosh in *The Scotsman*, 19th April 1892.

and Labour. In the House of Commons motions for Scottish Home Rule were introduced by two prominent Radicals who were officers of the Association, Dr. G. B. Clark in 1889 and 1892 and Dr. W. A. Hunter in 1892. And Home Rule ideas were very much to the fore in Scottish labour politics.

Keir Hardie was particularly active as a Scottish Home Ruler. His Scottish Parliamentary Labour Party was committed to 'Home Rule for each separate nationality or country in the British Empire, with an Imperial Parliament for Imperial affairs'.[1] He himself advocated it in his election address at Mid Lanark in 1888,[2] and, as has already been seen, early became a Vice President of the Scottish Home Rule Association. Inevitably, Keir Hardie drifted out of Scottish Home Rule politics when he moved south to further his political career. But he never abandoned his Home Rule ideas, although they were never fully elaborated. The best statement of the Home Rule case that he ever made was probably that with which nationalists made great play in the 1920s:

> I am of those old-fashioned people who place considerable value on National life, customs, and language. These are all the growths of the ages, and as such are a part of our very being, and not to be lightly regarded or set aside. No better means for retaining all that is best in the life of a nation has yet been devised than that of a National Parliament, through which National sentiment finds expression and embodiment in the laws of the land.[3]

II

Although the Scottish Liberal Association was in favour of Scottish Home Rule after 1888 the Liberal party leaders took very little notice until 1912. They argued that the Irish question was of such paramount importance that Scotland, like Wales, must wait until Irish Home Rule was out of the way. Those, like John Morley, who disliked the whole

---

[1] David Lowe, *Souvenirs of Scottish Labour* (Glasgow, 1919), p. 2.

[2] Hardie wrote 'I am also strongly in favour of Home Rule for Scotland, being convinced that until we have a Parliament of our own, we cannot obtain the many and great reforms on which I believe the people of Scotland have set their hearts'. Both the Edinburgh headquarters and the London branch of the Scottish Home Rule Association endorsed Hardie's candidature. William Stewart, *J. Keir Hardie: a Biography* (London, 1921), pp. 38–9.

[3] *Scots Independent*, II (1927–8), 134.

idea of Scottish Home Rule, hoped that this would in fact mean the indefinite postponement of Home Rule All Round. And the famous Newcastle Programme of 1891 did not include any reference to it. But Home Rule for Scotland never ceased to be Liberal policy in Scotland. In October 1911, with the Parliament Bill through the House of Lords, the General Council of the Scottish Liberal Association passed a resolution reminding the government that a Scottish Home Rule Bill should follow the Irish one. And in November 1912, with the Irish Bill more or less safe, the same body put on record 'its belief in the urgent need for a federal system of Home Rule', and stated that 'the time has now come when a measure granting Home Rule to Scotland should be introduced by the Government and passed through all its stages without delay'.[1]

There were those who found the snail's pace of the advance towards Home Rule dispiriting and were anxious to ginger up the Liberal party on the subject. After 1900 they were represented by the Young Scots Society, which for a time published a journal, *The Young Scot*, and issued Home Rule pamphlets. But the activities of the Young Scots, headed by J. M. Hogge, were not much approved of by the party leaders, and even some of the Young Scots themselves were pretty cool on the subject. J. W. Gulland, afterwards Chief Liberal Whip, reminded them in 1903 that their programme should be 'Scotland for Liberalism' and not any form of separatism: 'the formation of a separate Scottish National Party . . . is unnecessary, and would be unwise'.[2] The Young Scots, however, went on their way vigorously enough, pleased like all party youth groups to be able to cock a snook at their elders. But the leading Young Scots nearly all found seats in parliament after 1906, and by 1910 the Young Scots were not the force they had been before 1906.

One result of the decline of the Young Scots was that a substantial body of Scottish Liberal M.P.s became alarmed lest the Home Rule cause should not receive adequate backing in Scotland once Irish Home Rule was out of the way. As a result a body of twenty-one M.P.s, instigated by Captain Duncan Vernon Pirie, M.P. for North Aberdeen, constituted themselves a Scottish National Committee to press for Home Rule. Their chairman was R. C. Munro Ferguson, not hitherto a keen supporter of Home Rule, but a keen Imperial Federationist and a useful man to have in the chair because he had been a

[1] Entry in the minutes of the Association.
[2] *The Young Scot*, I (1903–4), 16.

former Scottish Liberal Whip. Their manifesto issued in August 1910[1] was well received by nationalists as well as by orthodox Liberals. And for a time while the new organization was coming into being, unwary nationalists talked of Pirie with considerable enthusiasm as the man who had organized a 'Scottish National Party' in parliament.[2] Indeed, T. D. Wanliss of *The Thistle* became at once a convert to the official Liberal cause, and began to encourage his contributors to write of 'The Revival of Scottish Nationality' and of a 'National Renaissance',[3] while a perfectly straightforward Liberal meeting was reported under the heading 'The Nationalist Meeting at Aberdeen'.[4]

A Scottish National Committee of M.P.s was not by itself enough to secure widespread support for Home Rule, so the Liberal party managers arranged to supplement it with a pair of political organizations, the Scottish Home Rule Council, which was simply an *ad hoc* committee of the existing Liberal organizations in Scotland, and a publicity machine, the International Scots Home Rule Association— called International to attract North American financial support. This Association, with Principal Sir James Donaldson of St. Andrews as Honorary President, and Councillor F. J. Robertson, an Edinburgh insurance man, as secretary, was founded in May 1913 and started its own journal *The Scottish Nation* in the following November. Most of its money was spent on the distribution of leaflets, but its secretary was also employed on all sorts of odd jobs. He acted as election agent for the Lord Advocate, as fund raiser in the United States and Canada, and as lobbyist in the Edinburgh Town Council. With his aid a substantial municipal Home Rule campaign was got under way which secured the support in general terms not only of Edinburgh Town Council, but of a string of smaller burghs, and the Convention of Royal Burghs itself.[5] With the outbreak of the war in 1914, however, the International Scots Home Rule Association immediately went over to war work, and though *The Scottish Nation* continued to appear for several more years, the Association itself quickly died.

---

[1] *The Scotsman*, 5th August 1910.
[2] *Fiery Cross*, July 1910, p. 8.
[3] *The Thistle*, II (1910), 46; VII (1915), 70.
[4] ibid., IV (1912), 25.
[5] Convention of the Royal Burghs of Scotland, *Local Self-Government for Scotland: Report, 11th March 1914.*

III

The Asquith government found the concept of 'Home Rule All Round' a difficult one to turn into concrete terms. As early as February 1911, before the Irish Home Rule Bill had gone through the Commons, Winston Churchill as Home Secretary was at work on the matter. But he found his terms of reference extraordinarily difficult. There was no great problem about the creation of new parliaments for Ireland, Wales and Scotland, but what was to be done about England?

> It seems to me absolutely impossible [he wrote in a Cabinet paper] that an English Parliament, and still more an English Executive, could exist side by side with an Imperial Parliament and an Imperial Executive. . . . Imperial affairs could not in practice be separated from English party politics, which consist principally of domestic questions. . . . The external sphere touches the internal at almost every point. The fortunes of the country abroad and at home are interdependent and idissoluble.[1]

Churchill therefore suggested in the following month a policy of devolution which would lead to the creation of regional legislatures in England to counterbalance those in Ireland, Scotland and Wales:

1. The Imperial Parliament to remain unaltered, except by a strict numerical redistribution between countries.

2. The United Kingdom to be divided into ten areas, having regard to geographical, racial, and historical considerations.

3. A legislative and administrative body, separately elected, to be created for each area.

4. In Ireland, Scotland, and Wales these bodies to be clothed with Parliamentary form so far as may be desirable in each case.[2]

Churchill, at this time M.P. for Dundee, ceased to be the minister responsible for devolution when he became First Lord of the Admiralty in October 1911, but he continued to take an active interest in the subject for a number of years. In a speech at Dundee in September 1912 he made public the main outlines of the scheme he had put to the cabinet in the previous year, and discussed the case for devolution in what was to have been a sober and persuasive speech, until it was

---

[1] Public Record Office Cab. 37/105/16.
[2] Cab. 37/105/18. Printed in full in H. J. Hanham, *The Nineteenth-Century Constitution* (Cambridge, 1969), pp. 131–3.

disrupted by suffragette demonstrators.[1] Other ministers said very little about the subject, presumably on the principle that it would be wise to let the members of the House of Commons have their say before the government showed its hand.

In the House of Commons the virtual unanimity of the Scottish Liberal members for Scottish Home Rule kept the question alive, and a series of Home Rule resolutions was carried between 1894 and 1914. It was 1912, however, before the government was willing to concede that Scottish and Welsh Home Rule had any likelihood of finding a place in the government's legislative timetable. Asquith, as prime minister, committed the government to a general Home Rule programme when on 11th April 1912 he introduced the Government of Ireland Bill, with the remark that it was 'only the first step in a larger and more comprehensive policy' and the confession that a further measure of administrative devolution was 'admittedly overdue'.[2] With the Irish bill safely through the House of Commons the Scottish Liberal members determined to get their own equivalent. They, therefore, agreed upon a measure which was introduced on their behalf by William Henry Cowan, M.P. for East Aberdeenshire, in a speech which gave a very good summary of the position as it stood on 30th May 1913. Though this speech was a long one, I make no apology for printing a large part of it here:

> The principle of the Bill has already been endorsed by the House. It is not a new thing. In 1894 my right hon. Friend the Member for Kirkcaldy (Sir H. Dalziel) proposed a Resolution in these terms:—
>
> > That it is desirable, while retaining intact the power and supremacy of the Imperial Parliament, to establish a Legislature in Scotland for dealing with purely Scottish affairs.
>
> In the following year again, on the Motion of my right hon. Friend, this House resolved:—
>
> > That it is desirable to devolve upon Legislatures in Ireland, Scotland, Wales, and England, respectively, the management and control of their domestic affairs.
>
> And so recently as last year my hon. Friend the Member for Stirlingshire (Dr. Chapple) moved and the House adopted the following Resolution:—

[1] *The Scotsman*, 13th September 1912.
[2] *5 Hansard (Commons)* XXXVI, 1403.

That in the opinion of this House, the measure providing for the delegation of Parliamentary powers to Ireland should be followed in this Parliament by the granting of similar powers of self-government to Scotland as part of a general scheme of devolution.

But that is not all, for in the year 1908 my hon. Friend the Member for Aberdeen (Mr. Pirie) introduced a Bill granting self-government to Scotland. That Bill was passed on the First Reading in this House by a large majority. Again, in 1911, my right hon. Friend the Member for Kirkcaldy, who has done so much for the cause of Scottish Home Rule introduced a Bill to grant self-government to Scotland, which again was passed on First Reading by a large majority. . . . But that is not all, for much has happened since the 28th February, 1912, when my hon. Friend the Member for Stirling-shire introduced his Resolution. An epoch-making event has occurred; the Irish Home Rule Bill has been passed in this House through all its stages under circumstances such as never existed before and which I am profoundly thankful to find exist now and which ensure for the Bill a safe passage to the Throne. . . . Therefore I say with absolute confidence that Ireland is safe, and Scotland has a right to come next. Mr. Gladstone, at the very beginning of his Home Rule campaign, used these words:—

> I will consent to give to Ireland no principle, nothing that is not upon equal terms offered to Scotland, and to the different parts of the United Kingdom;

while the present Prime Minister, on the 6th May, 1912, in reply to a deputation of Scottish Liberal Members, declared that

> Home Rule for Ireland only would leave the Constitution 'lop-sided', incoherent, and logically inconsequent.

We do not desire that the Constitution should be left in that position. . . .

The Scottish Liberal Members to a man are declared and convinced Home Rulers. . . . The mere fact of their associating themselves with the measure that we are discussing to-day, is evidence that Scotland is behind them. . . . A Scottish Office in London can never be other than a geographical absurdity. It is admittedly the centre of an efficient bureaucracy. . . . It governs Scotland more or less autocratically—largely by methods of administrative decree. I do not blame the members of that bureaucracy. They are courteous and considerate, especially to Scottish Members. But they can do very little to mitigate evils for which they are not responsible. Scottish legislation—what there is of it—is initiated mainly by the permanent heads of the various Departments. If these Departments are situated in Edinburgh they are out of touch with the Scottish Members here. If they are situated in London they are out of touch with the Scottish people.

Let me call attention to one or two Scottish grievances—briefly. The Scottish People have been clamouring for a simple measure of temperance reform for more years than most of us care to remember. . . . To my knowledge there has been a Scottish majority in this House in favour of Scottish temperance reform since 1885—a majority which, being a minority of the House, has been always voted down by the English Members. So the Scottish Members have found it impossible to make effective the mandate that they have been given. . . . In the second place, let me call attention to an urgent and pressing question, second only to that of self-government—land reform. Hon. Members are well aware that Scotland is being depopulated. . . . They must know that emigration from Scotland, according to the last Government Return, is double that from Ireland. What is the explanation? Surely that feudalism, unchecked by legislation, survives in Scotland. . . . Scotland has become a reservoir for the filling up of Canada. We recently had the Crofters Act extended to the non-crofting counties of Scotland. You gave it too late. We had to wait twenty-five years for it. . . . If we had had a Parliament in Scotland this would have been given to us, and given to us in time, and thus saved to Scotland thousands of her worthiest sons who have been driven into exile by the callous indifference of this House. Scotland has seventy-two representatives in a House of 670 Members. Surely this is a predominantly English institution. In the future perhaps we may have to deal with the question of Disestablishment, and Scotland may decide by a majority of her Members to Disestablish her own Church. If that demand is made by Scotland and the matter comes before this House we shall have to refer this definite mandate from Scotland to a jury of 598 persons who know little or nothing of Scotland or her ecclesiastical system, and it is to those people we have to submit that question. . . .

Let me return to administration. The present Lord Advocate [Alexander Ure], speaking in October, 1911, used these words:—

A single permanent official rules Scottish education with almost despotic sway.

A most admirable official. . . . I am not here to make any attack on any official, but on the system, and it is a scandalous thing that it can be said by a Member of the Government that a single Scottish official rules Scottish education with almost despotic sway. And why? Because in the early seventies this Scottish Department was transferred to London. That was a gratuitous insult to the nation, which had its own national and democratic system of education before England ever dreamt of educating her people at all, and if Scotland has not fully maintained her lead during the forty years since that transfer we must attribute it to this attempt to Anglicise Scotland, and that that attempt has largely failed, as it has, is one of the strongest evidences of the vitality of Scottish nationality.

Then take the case of the Scottish Estimates. This House grudgingly allows to Scotland one day of seven hours in each Parliamentary year for the discussion of Scottish Estimates, on which alone any question regarding Scottish administration can be effectively raised. . . . Is it any wonder Scotland is tired and demands a Parliament of her own? That she demands her own legislation for land, for the liquor trade, for education, for housing, for fisheries, for ecclesiastical affairs, for one-hundred-and-one matters of purely local concern?

We have tried other palliatives. This House has tried all-night sittings; it has tried autumn sittings; Guillotine and Kangaroo Closure; it has tried setting up Grand Committees, and has set up even a Scottish Grand Committee, encumbered by the presence of fifteen 'undesirable aliens'. Yet 75 per cent. of the moneys voted by this House is voted under Closure and without a word of discussion, and half the Bills the Government introduce each year are jettisoned because they have not the time to carry them through. We are attempting an impossible task; the machine is breaking down, the men working [it] are giving way under the strain. Devolution is the only cure. . . .

. . . the Government of Scotland Bill revives three ancient institutions—the Scottish Parliament, the Scottish Privy Council, and the Lord High Commissioner in his political capacity. The Scottish Parliament will consist of His Majesty the King and a Single Chamber, which, again, will consist of 140 Members, practically two for each of the existing constituencies and four for Dundee, and we propose to omit the representation of the universities. . . . The supremacy of the English Parliament is safeguarded in precisely the same manner as in the Irish Parliament, and we have lifted from the Home Rule Bill Sub-section (2) of Clause 1, which provides that:—

> (2) Notwithstanding the establishment of the Scottish Parliament or anything contained in this Act, the supreme power and authority of the Parliament of the United Kingdom shall remain unaffected and undiminished over all persons, matters, and things in Scotland and every part thereof.

We desire nothing but the power of local legislation and administration. The Lord High Commissioner, as the King's representative, will be the head of the Administration, and he will be advised by a Cabinet, which will be an Executive Committee of the revived Scottish Privy Council. The powers of the Scottish Parliament will closely resemble those of the Irish Parliament, with the exception that we do not desire to control the Post Office, and there will be no reserved services. We shall take over the administration of old age pensions, national insurance, and Labour Exchanges—in fact, the Bill will give Scotland control of purely Scottish affairs. . . .

As regards the judiciary the Bill simply recognises existing conditions, but provides that the judges of Court of Session, sheriffs, and other judges shall be appointed by the Lord High Commissioner. The Judicial Committee of the Privy Council is substituted for the House of Lords as the final Court of Appeal, and will determine all constitutional questions.[1]

The scheme propounded by the Scottish Liberal members, with its proposals for reviving the ancient Scottish Privy Council and for giving a new status to the Lord High Commissioner, whose functions up to date had been primarily ecclesiastical, was much more nationalist in tone than any bill that the ministry was likely to have sponsored. By contrast the Government of Ireland Bill was a down-to-earth document which eschewed nationalist overtones. But there was in fact no opportunity for the government to bring forward a measure of its own. Indeed, at the end of the war the position was rather worse than it had been in 1913, because Irish Home Rule seemed as far off as ever. When Cowan (now Sir Henry) in 1919 reintroduced a measure

---

[1] *5 Hansard (Commons)* LIII, 471–81.

very similar to that of 1913 he found that the Lloyd George government was much less sympathetic than its predecessor had been. The
coalition government took it for granted that any proposal for devolution would have to secure the consent of the Conservatives as well as
the Liberals. A move by a Coalition Conservative and a Coalition
Liberal led to the creation of the Speakers' Conference on Devolution,
which reported in 1920, but when the report of the Speakers' Conference was ignored nothing further happened. Initiative passed as a
matter of course to the Labour party.

IV

One consequence of Home Rule for Scotland being associated
before 1914 with Home Rule for Ireland and with the political left, was
that Conservative and Unionist opposition to it was inevitable. There
were always a few Scottish home rulers in the Conservative party, just
as there were a few Conservatives who were sympathetic to the grievances of Ireland. But the mass of the party before 1914 was strongly
opposed to any tampering with the existing structure of the United
Kingdom. As a result, Scottish Home Rule was always opposed
in the House of Commons by the Conservative members.

This was not just a matter of opposition by English Conservatives to
Scottish claims, as Liberal propaganda sometimes suggested. Scottish
Conservatives seem to have been much more hostile to Home Rule
than their English counterparts, and the chance that the Conservative
party leaders in the Commons from 1891 to 1920 were Scots (or semi-
Scots)—A. J. Balfour and Andrew Bonar Law—gave the Conservative
opposition to Scottish Home Rule something of the flavour of a
domestic dispute between Scots about the future of their country.
Conservative spokesmen, indeed, were sometimes inclined to argue
that Home Rule was being forced on Scotland by outside pressure.
Thus on the Liberal motion that was carried through the House of
Commons in 1894 the *Campaign Guide* commented:

> The motion was made by Englishmen sitting for Scottish seats, and
> men whose interests in life lay in England. The opposition to it was
> led by men of Scottish birth, of local Scottish interests, and of
> Scottish residence.[1]

[1] *The Campaign Guide, 1900: a Handbook for Unionist Speakers* (8th edn.,
Edinburgh, 1900), p. 335.

But the main emphasis of Conservative comment was on the damage which Home Rule would do to Scottish career prospects:

> Scotsmen are not prepared, as are Irish Nationalists, to renounce their share in the Government of the Empire. This would certainly follow the establishment of separate Parliaments in the three kingdoms, for as England has four times the population and wealth of Scotland and Ireland combined, and her Capital is the seat of Imperial Government, if there are to be separate Parliaments the advisers of the Crown must enjoy the confidence of the English Parliament. Taxes could not be levied in England to carry out an Imperial policy of which the majority in the English Parliament disapproved. Under a Scottish Home Rule Scheme, public life in England would cease to be a career open to Scotsmen. The late Prime Minister, the leader of the House of Commons, and the leader of the Opposition, are Scotsmen; so are the President and the ex-President of the Board of Trade, the Attorney-General and the ex-Attorney-General, and the Governors-General of Canada and Australia. Multitudes of Scotsmen, too, have made for themselves successful business careers in England. But separate the Parliaments of the two countries, and Scotsmen will be *quasi* foreigners in London and Liverpool, will be regarded with the utmost jealousy, and will no longer be able to compete on equal terms with Englishmen.[1]

The strongest Scottish opponent of Home Rule was Sir Henry Craik, who had been head of the Scotch Education Department for many years before he entered the House of Commons as member for Glasgow and Aberdeen Universities in 1906. Like Lyon Playfair, Craik feared on patriotic grounds that if the Scots were left to manage their own affairs they would soon sink into a provincial backwater. Or worse, that England and Scotland would drift apart. In an eloquent speech on the 1924 Government of Scotland Bill he used all the by now classical arguments against Home Rule.

> I would ask hon. Members who press this Bill to remember that they have not a monopoly of love for their country, of patriotic feelings, or of heartfelt, innate attachment to every association of romance or of characteristic quality that we have had handed down from our ancestors in Scotland. I do not feel that these things,

[1] ibid., p. 590.

sacred as they are, can be bolstered up by, or require the fictitious aid of, any of your Parliamentary machinery. They are planted too deeply, they have too strong a root, their growth is too sure, to require to be supported by any scaffolding of petty regulations about this or that legislative assembly.

Of all the ills the human race endure,
How small the part that laws can cause or cure.

Do not think that our national characteristics, our national history, our national romance, our national courage of the best sort, are due to your legislative arrangements from one generation to another. You got, by the Act of Union, a great step in advance, and that man is a maniac who, after a study of history, will stand up and deny that that Act of Union was an advantage. . . .

I want the House to consider what is this national entity which you are going to cut off from the whole of Southern Britain and constitute a national item by itself. Is there that intimate sympathy of race and feeling between the remote fishermen of the Hebrides and the Orkneys and Shetland, or even Inverness-shire, and the Lanarkshire population, or that thick population in Glasgow constituted very largely by an influx during recent years of 1,500,000 from Ireland? Is that exactly a homogeneous population? Where do you think the strong sympathy exists which is to bind together the Hebrides with the coal mining districts of Lanarkshire? Do you think the Northern parts of Scotland will be so very pleased to be ruled, as they inevitably would be, by the packed population in the slums of Glasgow and the mining districts of Lanark? . . .

Then have the hon. Members ever considered whether there is not a very close connection between certain parts of England and Scotland? Are they aware that there are many businesses carried on in Glasgow and Manchester the partners of which live half of each week in Glasgow and half in Manchester? Manchester and Glasgow are far more closely connected in sympathy and in daily intercourse than Glasgow and Edinburgh, certainly than Glasgow and Inverness. Do hon. Members know that the pilots of Aberdeen and Newcastle know each other by name, meet each other constantly and feel like brothers to one another? Aberdeen and Newcastle are far more closely connected together than Glasgow and Aberdeen. You cannot draw these distinctions exactly. It would not be true in race, in religion, in feeling, or in business relations.

Do you think we have not drawn enormous advantage from our brothers South of the Tweed, to their advantage too? We have sent them Prime Ministers, Lord Chancellors and Archbishops of Canterbury and of York. Do you think that will go on when you have built a high wall of division between the two countries? Do you think you will be accepted readily and easily as the rulers of your brothers South of the Tweed when you have told them 'No, you shall have nothing to say in the least to any concern of ours. We shall do you the pleasure of coming and voting upon your water Bills and anything else, but we will not allow you to intervene in anything whatever except the Post Office and Foreign Affairs.' Do you think you will get great advantage for your own country in the long run by this? Hon. Members on this side may say, 'We will have a compromise. We will go so far with you.' I am against the whole thing. It is mischievous from beginning to end. I will not temporise with it. Is it not perfectly certain that if you establish two separate Parliaments the line of political complexion of those two Parliaments will be violently opposed, that the Government of one will be absolutely different in spirit and in tone from the other? That must extend not merely to domestic affairs but to foreign affairs, and you may have two Governments ruling within this island absolutely opposed to one another, not only in private and domestic matters, but on the large issues of peace and war and of foreign policy. Will that add to the strength and respect in which we are held?[1]

Even within the Conservative party there was, however, a move towards a federal concept of the United Kingdom in the years just before the First World War, which originated with Lord Milner and the Round Table movement. Whether the idea came first from Liberals in the Milner kindergarten or not is uncertain. What is clear is that between 1909 and 1919 a good many influential Conservatives were ready to flirt with the idea of Home Rule All Round, so long as it was associated with the idea of imperial federation.[2] During the 1918 election most of the Coalition candidates in Scotland, both Liberal and Conservative, gave a cautious endorsement to the idea of Home Rule, which was associated with support for Lloyd George.[3] And in 1919 the

[1] 173 H.C. Deb., 5 ser., c. 838–9, 841–3.
[2] For an over-narrow account of the origins of this Conservative flirtation see J. E. Kendle, 'The Round Table Movement and "Home Rule all Round"', *Historical Journal*, XI (1968), 332–53.
[3] *Scottish Review*, 42 (1919), 160–1.

curious combination of one of Milner's English disciples, Edward Wood (afterwards Viscount Halifax, Viceroy of India, Foreign Secretary, and Ambassador in Washington) acting in harmony with a prominent Scottish Liberal supporter of the Lloyd George Coalition, the Rt. Hon. John Archibald Murray Macdonald, M.P. for Stirling and Falkirk, carried a motion in the House of Commons which called for the appointment of a committee to investigate just how it would be possible to introduce a federal system in the United Kingdom.[1] The government accordingly appointed the Speaker's Conference on Devolution, which was presided over by Speaker Lowther and went into the whole matter in considerable detail, and came up with two rival schemes of Home Rule.[2]

The report of the Speaker's Conference was one of the many schemes for post-war reforms which came to nothing. Like the Bryce Conference on the Reform of the Second Chamber and the Haldane Committee on the Machinery of Government, it attracted little public attention and its report soon disappeared into limbo. Unlike the Machinery of Government Committee it failed even to produce the sort of intellectually satisfying scheme on which academics might fasten. The two schemes which it discussed were both essentially tentative, and one sometimes has the impression that the Conference did not believe very much in its own work.

The failure of the report of the Speaker's Conference demonstrated clearly enough the new power of the Conservative party after 1918. Except in the short-lived parliaments of 1922, 1923 and 1929, the Conservatives did pretty well in Scotland by the standards of the nineteenth century and of the 1906 and 1910 elections. In terms of seats in parliament they did not have a convincing majority in 1918 and 1935 but they and their Liberal allies taken together did have a clear majority, while in both 1924 and 1931 the Conservatives alone had a clear majority in Scotland without counting their Liberal allies. Home Rule was no longer the danger which it had seemed to Conservatives before 1914.

V

Home Rule sentiment before 1914 had something artificial about it, because it was so closely associated with Home Rule for Ireland. Few

[1] 116 H.C. Deb., 5 ser., c. 1873.
[2] *Conference on Devolution: Letter from Mr. Speaker to the Prime Minister* [Cmd. 692] H.C. (1920), XIII, 1151–88.

Scots were forced to ask themselves what it would mean, and ministers who were in principle committed to Home Rule never put forward positive proposals for a Scottish 'parliament'. As a result, Home Rulers after 1918 found themselves in much the same position as they had been before the war, except that there was no longer a united Liberal party to champion their cause. The few active propagandists left over from the old Scottish Home Rule Association who had been Liberals before the war now inclined to support the Independent Labour Party. And the I.L.P. in turn threw up a number of eloquent supporters of Home Rule. When the Scottish Home Rule Association was revived in 1918 the key men in it were Roland Eugene Muirhead, once a Young Scot and a council member of the pre-war Scottish Home Rule Association, and Thomas Johnston, the editor of *Forward* (which Muirhead had helped to finance) and a prominent member of the I.L.P.

Muirhead (1868–1964) was a tanner by trade and became one of the best known of all Scottish nationalists by providing them with a 'literature service' which all might use, which, under the name of the Scottish Secretariat, continued in being until his death.[1] Muirhead at the end of the war was a Home Ruler rather than a nationalist. That is, he wanted a measure of devolution along the lines proposed by Cowan in 1913, and preferably the immediate creation of provisional governments for Wales and Scotland.[2] But he was not the sort of man of whom platform orators are made, so that in his rather grim way he was prepared to welcome all sorts and manner of men to help him. As a result, his monthly news-sheet, *Scottish Home Rule*, was open to contributors, including Hugh MacDiarmid, who disagreed with him fundamentally on issues of policy.[3]

Muirhead's ally, Johnston, was by temperament much more of a romantic than Muirhead was,[4] and in 1924 gave the House of Commons a fine account of what he considered the main reasons for Home Rule:

> Our land problem is vastly different to the land problem of England. Here you have no deer forest or crofter problem such as we

[1] There are biographical articles on him in *The Scots Review*, November 1948, p. 108, and *Glasgow Herald*, 9th July 1964, and an autobiographical one in *Scots Independent*, II (1927–8), 81–3.
[2] *The Thistle*, X (1918), 95–6.
[3] C. M. Grieve, *Contemporary Scottish Studies, First Series* (London, 1926), pp. 260–7.
[4] Thomas Johnston, *Memories* (London, 1952), *passim*.

have, and our ecclesiastical problems are different. I notice that you are going to settle the Scottish Church question here this month. You are going to deal with the question of teinds, and you do not know the meaning of the word. Our local problems are different and our local phrases are different. For example, what Englishman knows the meaning of the word 'hamesucken'? Our local adminis-trative problems are entirely different from those in England and our education problems are quite different. Every Secretary for Scot-land, at any rate under the last six Governments, of every party has been a declared Scottish Home Ruler. . . .

Our historical and cultured traditions are different; our racial characteristics are different. The Celt has long memories, the Eng-lishman forgets quickly. There are Members on these Benches and on those Benches too who fight their electoral battles upon, say, the battle of the Boyne. We have Members on these Benches who fight them on the battle of Bannockburn. But the Englishman forgets quickly. We can never obliterate these national characteristics, and a jolly good job too! There is always, for each one of us, some place that he calls 'home,' some memories that he has of his childhood days, and, thank God, they cannot be obliterated. I think it was Robert Louis Stevenson who once wrote about a vision that he had of a Scots army in the service of the Dutch Government marching beneath the polders in the Low country, and he pictured an officer stopping suddenly and taking off his bonnet because he felt on his brow the soft wet rain of the Hebrides, and a private stepping out of the ranks because he recognised the old aroma of the peat reek. As Kipling puts it [sic]:

> God gave all earth to men to love;
> But, because our hearts are small,
> Ordained for each, one spot should prove
> Beloved over all.

And the greatest Scotsman who ever lived, Robert Burns, declared that

> The story of Wallace poured a tide of Scottish prejudice into my veins which will boil along there till the floodgates of life shut in eternal rest.

We may believe very earnestly in internationalism, but you cannot have internationalism without nations. The word 'international' means 'between nations,' and any political party in this House that seeks to destroy these national characteristics and diversities is doing something that is for the ill-being, and not for the well-being, of the British Empire.[1]

The attitude of the I.L.P. in Scotland after the war was for the most part similar to that of Tom Johnston. James Maxton, for instance, who was not an enthusiastic Home Ruler before the war, seems to have been convinced by his wartime experiences that something must be done about the existing system of government. Indeed, complaints about the dead hand of the Whitehall bureaucracy were an important element in Clydeside discontent. The Scottish Trades Union Congress and the Scottish Council of the Labour Party were also clearly ranged in the Home Rule camp.

The very fact that a Scottish Trades Union Congress existed alongside the English T.U.C. was a guarantee that it would be sympathetic to Home Rule. But the S.T.U.C. was never very enthusiastic about it before 1914. During the war, however, the S.T.U.C. became more and more militant on the subject. In 1916 a motion was carried 'That this Congress affirms its belief in the principle of Scottish Home Rule'.[2] In 1917 it was strengthened to read:

> This Congress reaffirms its demand that the control of Scottish affairs should be placed in the hands of the Scottish people by the reinstitution of a Scots' Parliament, and regrets that at this juncture the Scottish people should not be represented directly on the Imperial War Council.

The leaders of the revived Scottish Home Rule Association in 1918 began to lobby the trade unions which constituted the S.T.U.C. (the Scottish miners, among other unions, became affiliated to the S.H.R.A.),[3] and their efforts were reinforced by those of the Hon. Ruaraidh Erskine of Marr who was conducting a campaign to secure separate Scottish representation at the Paris Peace Conference. As a result of this pressure the S.T.U.C. in 1918 agreed to a surprisingly strong, though badly worded, policy resolution.

That this Congress demands the establishment of a Scottish Par-

[1] 173 H.C. Deb., 5 ser., c. 799–800.
[2] I owe these and other extracts from the reports of the S.T.U.C. to the kindness of Mr. Colin Lindsay.
[3] The miners voted to affiliate in June 1920; R. Page Arnot, *A History of the Scottish Miners from the Earliest Times* (London, 1955), p. 150.

liament to deal with Scottish national affairs; the neglect of Scottish interests and the growing congestion of public business in the Imperial Parliament render it imperative that Scottish Home Rule should be inaugurated at the earliest possible moment; the problems of reconstruction peculiar to Scotland can best be dealt with by a Scottish Parliament; further, we demand that Scotland as a nation be directly represented at the Peace Conference.[1]

The Labour party in Scotland adopted a similar stance to that of the S.T.U.C. As was to be expected of a Radical organization which had grown away from the Liberal party, the Labour party, however, tried to outdo the Liberal party in the fervour of its protestations. The Scottish Council of the Labour party regularly passed Home Rule resolutions in the years immediately after its formation in 1915 and Scottish Home Rule formed one of the main planks of its 1918 election programme. Moreover, the annual report of the Executive of the Scottish Council of the Labour Party for 1918–19 made it clear that the Labour party in Scotland was prepared to go a very long way beyond mere administrative devolution towards outright Scottish nationalism:

HOME RULE FOR SCOTLAND

Now that the War is ended and an era of reconstruction begun, Scottish problems require the concentration of Scottish brains and machinery upon their solution. Your Committee is of opinion that a determined effort should be made to secure Home Rule for Scotland in the first Session of Parliament, and that the question should be taken out of the hands of place-hunting lawyers and vote-catching politicians by the political and industrial efforts of the Labour Party in Scotland which should co-ordinate all its forces to this end, using any legitimate means, political and industrial, to secure the establishment of a Scottish Parliament upon a completely democratic basis, as briefly outlined below:—

WHEREAS,

Scotland, though temporarily deprived, without the consent of her people, and by corrupt means, in 1707, of the exercise of her right to self-determination, is presently, as anciently, entitled to legislate for the governance of her National affairs in a Parliament of her own, the full exercise of that right is hereby restored.

[1] *Scottish Review*, 41 (1918), 149.

Be it enacted by, etc.,

(1) The Secretary for Scotland, for the time being, is charged with the responsibility of making the necessary arrangements to summon a Parliament forthwith to meet in Edinburgh.

(2) Which Parliament shall be elected, on the basis of Adult Suffrage accruing at the age of 21, without distinction of sex, by the Divisions within the Borders of Scotland, which, under the Representation of the People Act, 1918, elect members to the Imperial Parliament.

(3) Men or women of the age of 21 years and upwards shall have for electoral purposes one vote each in relation alike to the Scottish Parliament and each of the local governing bodies appertaining to the area in which they are resident.

(4) All other qualifications or disqualifications for the vote as contained in the Representation of the People Act, 1918, are not to be applied so far as Scottish National and Local Government are concerned, with the exception that (a) a person shall not be disqualified from being registered as a Parliamentary or Local Government elector by reason that he or some person for whose maintenance he is responsible had received poor relief or alms; (b) that he or she has been, on proper medical certification, declared to be presently insane.

(5) All electors resident at a greater distance than one mile from the polling place or medically certified as unfit to take the journey on foot shall have the option of exercising the right of voting in the manner presently prescribed for those upon the list of 'absent voters.'

(6) The Elections shall be taken on the system of Proportional Representation, as applied at the elections to the Education Authorities of Scotland.

(7) Any person entitled to the Parliamentary vote shall be entitled to be nominated for any public election to any representative governing body, whether resident in its area or not; provided that he or she shall on nomination sign an undertaking to attend, if elected, at not less than 90% of the sittings, including sittings of any Committee to which he or she may have been appointed. Failing such attendance, unless through illness or other sufficient cause certified to and accepted by the House, the seat shall at the end of the administrative year be declared vacant and a nominee of the same public connections shall be co-opted instead.

(8) Public representatives shall be paid any necessary allowances to meet all reasonable expenditure upon travelling and maintenance, because of their attendance upon public duty, the rate of such remuneration to be fixed by statute.

(9) A candidate for the Scottish Parliament shall be required to deposit with the Returning Officer a sum of £20 along with the nomination papers, which money shall be returned to him at the declaration of the poll in the event of his having polled 500 or more preference votes.

(10) Subject to the Constitutional veto, the Scottish House of Parliament shall have powers to deal with any Scottish matters, including the levying of taxes, hitherto within the jurisdiction of the Imperial Parliament at Westminster, except such as determine the control and equipment of the Army, Navy, Civil, Diplomatic, Dominion, Colonial, and other Imperial Services.[1]

The annual conference of the Scottish Council of the Labour party endorsed this policy on 20th September 1919. But members of the conference showed that they were prepared to go even further than the Executive. Hugh Lyon of the Scottish Horse and Motor-men:

said the new Executive should send a deputation to convert the members of the Parliamentary Labour Party, many of whom did not realise the urgent need for Scots Home Rule. They could not have real social reconstruction in Scotland while they were held back by England. Freedom of government was necessary for Scotland in order that progress would be made in harmony with the aspirations and wants of the people.[2]

The Scottish Council also carried a motion proposed from the floor that:

This Conference . . . demands the Government to frame and introduce a Bill for the establishment of a Scottish Parliament to deal with Scottish national affairs, thereby applying the principle of self-determination to the Scottish people.[3]

[1] Labour Party (Scottish Council), *Report of Fifth Annual Conference . . .* (Glasgow, 1919), pp. 20–1.
[2] ibid., p. 37.
[3] ibid., p. 42.

H 113

On one point, however, the Labour party created difficulties. The Scottish executive did its best to prevent its members from becoming active in the Scottish Home Rule Association on the ground that it was established party policy to discountenance the formation or support of overlapping organizations. The executive therefore resolved that 'whilst strongly in favour of Home Rule for Scotland' it was 'of opinion that the people of Scotland can secure this measure by a fuller support of Labour at the polls, and therefore considers it inadvisable for members of the Labour Party to associate with members of other political parties in special organisations for the purpose of securing Home Rule'.[1] The resolution failed to deter a number of Labour party members from playing an active part in the Scottish Home Rule Association. But it was a timely warning to Labour supporters that some day they might have to choose between the Labour party and Home Rule—a choice that had increasingly to be made after 1929.

Labour Home Rule feeling was probably at its strongest between 1918 and 1920. Both the Scottish Council of the Labour party and the Scottish Trades Union Congress had passed resolutions in favour of separate Scottish representation at the Paris peace conference, and Labour speakers for a time vied with one another in the expression of Home Rule sentiments. But the mood soon changed. The Clydesiders were willing enough to be associated with bold nationalist gestures but they were primarily interested in the material well-being of the people of the Clyde Valley. And immediate relief could come only from England. With many of the leading Clydesiders in the House of Commons after 1922 the Home Rule enthusiasm of the Scots M.P.s began to wane. Moreover, the Labour party in England needed all the help it could get from Scotland and Wales, and was clearly reluctant to contemplate any weakening of the Labour camp which might result from even a small measure of devolution. It was also a curious feature of Labour politics that those Labour candidates who seem in retrospect to have been most closely associated with support for Home Rule were least successful in finding Scottish seats. Keir Hardie, Robert Smillie and Ramsay MacDonald were all M.P.s for constituencies south of the border, during the active part of their careers (Ramsay MacDonald was found a seat for the Scottish Universities after his retirement and sat from 1936 until his death in 1937).

Ramsay MacDonald and most of the Scottish Labour members

[1] ibid., p. 8.

114

were still quite keen Home Rulers in 1924 and so long as the Labour party was led by Ramsay MacDonald there was a chance that something would eventually be done about Home Rule for Scotland. But it was difficult to see just what the Labour party could do. In a minority in the House of Commons until 1945, the Labour party would have found it impossible to force a Home Rule Bill through both the House of Commons and the House of Lords. The best a Labour government could hope to do was to keep the issue alive by allowing a regular series of Home Rule debates, and by making another attempt at a Speaker's conference on devolution. Thus the various Home Rule debates in the 1920s launched first by George Buchanan and subsequently by the Reverend James Barr had an atmosphere of unreality about them.[1] Ramsay MacDonald studiously avoided committing himself in public to introducing a Home Rule Bill as an official party measure, and left his back benchers to make the running. The back benchers in turn recognized that there was little point in trying to get up a public agitation and left the Scottish Home Rule Association to conduct a holding operation, which it did until it was merged with the National Party of Scotland in 1928.

Home Rule sentiments continued to be expressed in the Labour party and the S.T.U.C. throughout the interwar years, but Labour interest in Home Rule steadily declined. Clement Attlee's book, *The Labour Party in Perspective*, published in 1937, puts its emphasis exclusively on London-organized measures for building a new Britain. And the new generation of trade union leaders were not nearly as friendly to Home Rule as their predecessors, and were, indeed, not altogether convinced of the value of the S.T.U.C. itself. At the time when the National Party of Scotland was being formed in 1927 and 1928 motions were each year proposed at the S.T.U.C. that it should merge with the English T.U.C. and abolish itself. As a result the S.T.U.C. was driven to debate Home Rule in a domestic context against a background of the steady centralization of the trade union movement on London. As early as 1917 there had been complaints in Scotland about the bureaucratization of the trade unions and their centralization in London. William Diack pointed out in the *Scottish Review* that:

[1] Unfortunately Barr's book *Lang Syne: Memoirs of the Rev. James Barr, B.D.* (Glasgow, 1949) is simply a scissors-and-paste affair of no value whatever on this subject.

The arguments in favour of 'Home Rule', or autonomy, for Scottish trade unionists are just as strong . . . as the arguments in favour of self-government in the great affairs of the state. Centralisation in London is equally as objectionable in connection with Trade Unions as in connection with administrative and parliamentary matters.[1]

Yet as time went on there were fewer and fewer independent Scottish Unions. The National Seamen's and Firemen's Union and the National Union of Railwaymen were denounced by Diack in 1917, as strongly 'Unionist'. But they had the future on their side. In 1923 the separate Scottish railway companies disappeared, and with them all prospect of a Scottish railwaymen's union. And in the years that followed more and more Scottish unions were absorbed into the English giants, notably Ernest Bevin's Transport and General Workers' Union. By the 1930s there was little left of the old Clydeside independence in the trade union movement, and the commitment of the S.T.U.C. to Home Rule became largely a matter of lip service.

There was also a marked shift in left-wing thinking away from the nationalism of the war years towards stressing the solidarity of the international working-class movement. This began to affect the S.T.U.C. from 1920 onwards. In that year T. Phillips of the Shop Assistants' Union, a Union which had formerly been one of the sponsors of Home Rule resolutions, deplored the emphasis placed by the S.T.U.C. on Home Rule.[2] 'The national geographical area', he argued, 'was not to be the area of the future. To pass [a Home Rule] resolution would be to support the narrow spirit of nationalism when they were all out for a broad internationalism.' In the following year other delegates argued in Marxist terms that 'Home Rule was no use to the workers under Capitalism. . . . It was not Home Rule they should be seeking, but the dictatorship of the proletariat', that 'it was disgraceful they should be wasting time over a question like Home Rule. It was of no consequence to the working class', and that 'While Capitalism continued the workers would not be any better off even when Home Rule was in operation'. This Marxist opposition was easily defeated in 1920, 1921 and 1922, but after that the Home Rule question was allowed to drop until 1931, when, after a hot debate, the S.T.U.C. abandoned its support for Home Rule.[3] Home Rule All

---

[1] *Scottish Review*, 40 (1917), 320.
[2] The speeches quoted here are from the relevant S.T.U.C. reports.
[3] See below, p. 199.

Round on pre-war lines was no longer a practical policy for the Scottish Labour movement, however much individual members might cherish it as an ideal.

VI

The declining strength of Home Rule in the House of Commons meant that the leadership of the Home Rule movement slipped imperceptibly out of the hands of the politicians and into those of the Scottish Home Rule Association. The Scottish Home Rule Association was, however, by no means a large or popular body. And it did not endear itself to the politicians by announcing in 1920 that it found neither of the schemes discussed by the Speaker's Conference on Devolution at all adequate. Founded on 9th September 1918, its first officers were a mixed bunch.[1] William Gallacher of the Scottish Co-operative Wholesale Society was the first president, Mrs. Crosthwaite, chairman of Eastwood School Board, and Peter Fyfe, chief sanitary inspector for Glasgow, were vice presidents, and Roland Muirhead was secretary. The Association set out to attract corporate members rather than individual ones and made a great feature of questionnaires to candidates at local elections. It also set about discussing a possible future constitution for a Scottish state within a federal United Kingdom. After the first few months the most prominent member was the Reverend James Barr, later M.P. for Motherwell and for Coatbridge, but most of the work was done by Muirhead.

The main hope of the Scottish Home Rule Association was that by holding conferences with M.P.s a common basis for action would be evolved. To this end it brought together a representative body of M.P.s in Glasgow on 9th September 1922 and again on 2nd February 1923, though on the second occasion the Unionists were less prominent than before. By the beginning of 1924 the Association had agreed on a draft Home Rule Bill, and it clearly hoped that the first Labour government would back it. But the failure of the 1924 Home Rule debate to achieve anything positive and the failure of the three major parties to include Scottish Home Rule in their 1924 general election programme led to speedy disillusionment.

Roland Muirhead was now convinced that nothing could be hoped

---

[1] For details of its work see *Scottish Home Rule Association News-sheet*, 1920–9, renamed *Scottish Home Rule* in October 1922. The Association also published one issue of a leaflet called *Liberty* in 1919.

for from any of the existing political parties.[1] But the majority of the Scottish Home Rule Association still hoped to win over the Scottish M.P.s and decided to sponsor a Scottish National Convention to talk the matter over after the 1924 election. The majority of Scottish M.P.s said they were in favour of such a convention being held, but only a few of them attended when it met in the City Hall, Glasgow, on 15th November 1924. The Convention set up a committee to draft yet further proposals, which were reported back to the Convention nearly two years later, on 30th October 1926. Already the Bill drafted by the Committee had been given a formal first reading on 28 July 1926, and so was available for public discussion. The new Bill went much further than its predecessors. It provided for the withdrawal of the Scottish members from Westminster and for Dominion status for Scotland 'on the basis of Scotland being a sovereign state'.[2] However, both the Reverend James Barr and the other Scottish Labour M.P.s who sponsored the Bill were prepared to accept something less than Dominion status. Unfortunately for the S.H.R.A., the 1926 Bill did not get beyond a formal first reading, its successor was talked out in 1927, and in 1928 there was simply a formal reintroduction of the Bill by Barr. Clearly Home Rule could make no progress in the House of Commons.

At this point the S.H.R.A. began to separate out into two distinct wings, the majority still in favour of lobbying M.P.s, and the minority, by now a substantial one, in favour of running independent Scottish candidates. And at this point Muirhead decided to force a decision. He availed himself of a clause in the S.H.R.A constitution which permitted the S.H.R.A. to run its own candidates and announced that he was standing as prospective independent Scottish Nationalist candidate for West Renfrewshire. And at the same time he began negotiations with the Scots National League, the Scottish National Movement, and the Glasgow University Scottish Nationalist Association with a view to starting a Scots National Party. Home Rule All Round as a policy was now moribund. A few diehards tried to keep the Scottish Home Rule Association going, but Muirhead resigned as secretary and brought its life to an abrupt end early in 1929.

[1] *Scots Independent*, II (1927–8), 81–3.
[2] 206 H.C. Deb., 5 ser., c. 866.

CHAPTER SIX

The Fundamentalists

I

The conversion of the Liberal party to Home Rule for Ireland in 1886 led to an immediate upsurge of nationalist sentiment among Scottish Liberals. The leaders of the Scottish Home Rule Association soon recognized that they were stronger nationalists than they were Liberals and resented the fact that the Scottish Liberal Association was determined to keep the leadership of the Home Rule movement in its own hands. Professor Blackie, who was the Association's first chairman, thought that Scotland was fit for immediate self-government but that Ireland was not.[1] John Romans, his successor, a gas engineer who had supported the Free Church in 1843 and had been a member of the Scottish Rights Society in 1853, resigned his office as Liberal convener in Newbattle, Midlothian, in 1893 in protest at the half-heartedness of the Liberals towards Scottish Home Rule.[2] Charles Waddie, the Association's secretary, and William Mitchell, the treasurer, also resigned office in their local Liberal associations when they saw that there was no chance of the Liberals putting Scottish Home Rule before Irish, in order entirely to devote themselves to nationalist and other patriotic causes.[3] Not surprisingly they gave a markedly nationalist twist to the list of objects of the Scottish Home Rule Association.

[1] Anna M. Stoddart, *John Stuart Blackie: A Biography* (2 vols., Edinburgh, 1895), II, 273, and J. S. Blackie, *The Union of 1707 and its Results: a Plea for Scottish Home Rule*, Glasgow, 1892.

[2] Romans' views are set out in his *Home Rule for Scotland* (Edinburgh, 1893). There are obituaries in *The Thistle*, II (1910), 29–31 (by Waddie) and the *Fiery Cross*, April 1910, p. 7.

[3] Waddie published many pamphlets and an autobiography, *The Religion of a Layman* . . . (Edinburgh, 1907). There are good accounts of him in the *Scottish Patriot*, II (1904–5), 187, *The Thistle*, IV (1912), 40–4, and the *Fiery Cross*, April 1912, p. 8. Mitchell was a prolific writer, Secretary of the Cockburn Association, and a keen supporter of the project for a national monument. See *The Thistle*, V (1913), 142.

1. To foster the National sentiment of Scotland, and to maintain her national rights and honour.

2. To promote the establishment of a Legislature, sitting in Scotland, with full control over all purely Scottish questions, and with an Executive Government responsible to it and the Crown.

3. To secure to the Government of Scotland, in the same degree as is at present possessed by the Imperial Parliament, the control of her Civil Servants, Judges, and other Officials, with the exception of those engaged in the Naval, Military, and Diplomatic Services, and in collecting the Imperial Revenue.

4. To maintain the integrity of the Empire, and secure that the voice of Scotland shall be heard in the Imperial Parliament as fully as at present when discussing Imperial affairs.[1]

By the beginning of the twentieth century the Scottish Home Rule Association was practically defunct because the Scottish Liberal Association chose to ignore it. Or as Waddie put it in 1908: 'The Scottish Home Rule Association . . . has been allowed to become a derelict because the Liberal Association had taken the matter up, and it was said there was no longer a reason for its existence.'[2] Romans and Waddie, as chairman and secretary, continued to issue occasional public statements in the name of the association, of which one of the last was a re-issue of the 'Protest of the Scottish Home Rule Association against the Denial or Delay of Home Rule for Scotland'.[3] But both men had virtually given up hope. Waddie experimented with a journal, the *Scottish Nationalist*, for a short time in 1903, but he soon had to give it up. In a sad letter published in 1908, Waddie claimed that both the major political parties had betrayed Scotland, and that he himself found it 'a source of trouble and shame to a Liberal like myself that a few crumbs have been awarded Scotland by the Tories, and nothing but fair words by the Liberals'. In a message to the people of Scotland he added:

[1] This is the form in which Charles Waddie seems to have preferred to arrange the Objects, but items 1 and 4 were interchangeable, cp. *Prospectus of the Scottish Home Rule Association* (Edinburgh, 1892). The basic document apart from this list of objects is the *Protest of the Scottish Home Rule Association against the Present Policy of Official Liberals towards Scotland* [1890].

[2] *Fiery Cross*, April 1908, p. 8. Waddie refused to support the Liberal party at the January 1910 election because it was not strong enough for Home Rule. See *The Thistle*, II (1910), 13–15.

[3] *Fiery Cross*, April 1910, p. 7, and *The Thistle*, II (1910), 31–2.

The Fundamentalists

I feel a sinking of the heart when I consider that I have spent some of
the best years of a long life trying to rouse you from your present
apathy. I have seen nearly all my old friends sink into their graves
with their hopes unfulfilled, and but a few years more and I must
follow—will it be with my hopes unfulfilled?[1]

Romans died in 1910, Waddie in 1912 and Mitchell in 1913, and the
old Scottish Home Rule Association died with them. The name of the
Association was now available to any Home Rulers who wished to
make use of it, although nobody in fact took it up again until Roland
Muirhead reformed the Scottish Home Rule Association in 1918.

Long before Waddie's death nationalism had become almost entirely a matter for a few hundred individual enthusiasts, of whom those
with sufficient money to sponsor a journal were the most important. Of
these there were four, Theodore Napier, Thomas Drummond Wanliss,
John Wilson and the Hon. Stuart Erskine. But to their number should
be added the St. Andrew Society of Edinburgh. Theodore Napier has
already been mentioned as a picturesque Jacobite. He was also
an enthusiastic propagandist and almost single-handed obtained
over 104,000 signatures to a diamond jubilee petition to Queen Victoria protesting against the misuse of the national names. Napier went
through a difficult period during the Boer War, because he supported
the Boers, but he gradually became a popular figure in Edinburgh, and
when he left the country in 1912 there was a good deal of regret.[2]
Napier's Jacobitism seemed to assort ill with his Liberal politics, his
support for Boer and Irish nationalists, and his Protestant faith,
while his gift for publicity and annual visits to national shrines were a
source of irritation to other nationalists. Charles Waddie once reacted
to a favourable article about Napier with a stern denunciation on the
theme that 'Mr. Napier's eccentricities have done incalculable harm to
the cause of Scottish Home Rule'.[3] Napier's paper, the *Fiery Cross*
(Edinburgh, 1901–12), though full of idiosyncratic articles about the
virtues of monarchy and the evils of tobacco, included a useful record
of nationalist activities and a number of articles by competent contributors, and had a freshness about it which the other nationalist papers

---

[1] *Fiery Cross*, April 1908, p. 8.
[2] There are friendly notices about him in *Scottish Patriot*, II (1904–5), 42, 45,
The Thistle, IV (1912), 178–80, and *Scots Pictorial*, 5th October 1912. The *Scottish
Patriot* emphasized that Napier was 'a patriot and a gentleman' and there was
general agreement that he was courteous and friendly to all.
[3] *Scottish Patriot*, II (1904–5), 60.

lacked. Moreover, Napier's approach was very like Waddie's. He wanted a federal system, under which, according to the *Fiery Cross,* 'all the nationalities should have their parliaments restored to them synchronously, and a *Federal United Parliament* created for the whole of the United Kingdom and its Dependencies'. This alone, it was argued, would put an end to the system whereby Scotland was 'a tributary province of England, having all its laws made for it by Englishmen'.[1]

Another Australian settler, Thomas Drummond Wanliss, published a more ambitious monthly nationalist journal, *The Thistle*, in Edinburgh from 1909 to 1918. Wanliss, a native of Perth, had lived for many years in Ballarat, which he represented for five years in the Victoria Legislative Council, and where he was proprietor of the *Ballarat Star*.[2] His book, *Bars to British Unity: or, a Plea for National Sentiment* (Edinburgh, 1885), was one of the earliest and best of the nationalist pleas of the 1880s, and is in many ways one of the classics of Scottish nationalism. The man himself, however, was rancorous and rather bitter, particularly when he wrote about the English. *The Thistle*, as a result, became a repository of anti-English propaganda not altogether dissimilar in tone to that of much German propaganda during the First World War.[3] In addition, Wanliss was a passionate champion of Presbyterianism as the essence of the Scottish national way of life, alike in speeches in Victoria, in pamphlets and in *The Thistle*.[4] Wanliss's rather grim approach would, no doubt, have killed his journal had it not been for the fact that he enjoyed the services of a competent writer on literary themes, William Keith Leask, who gave *The Thistle* at times a decidedly literary flavour. In retrospect, the chief merit of *The Thistle* was simply that it survived for ten years and appeared throughout that time regularly every month with news of Scottish organizations.

John Wilson of the *Scottish Patriot* (Glasgow, 1903–6) was much more interested in distinctively Scottish cultural activities than either Napier or Wanliss. By profession an advertising agent, he was a great

[1] *Fiery Cross*, April 1902, p. 5.

[2] See obituary notices in *The Scotsman*, 19th April 1923, and *Glasgow Herald*, 20th April 1923.

[3] The strongest anti-English propaganda appeared in a series of papers entitled 'The Matter with the Englishman . . .' by Thomas Falkland in *The Thistle* in 1915 and 1916 and in an article on 'The Anglo-Saxon Character: its Weakness', *The Thistle*, VII (1915), 121–4.

[4] Notably in *Scotland and Presbyterianism Vindicated* . . . (Edinburgh, 1905).

promoter of choirs for singing Scottish songs, and of Scottish games, notably 'The National Game of Shinty'.[1] By the standards of other nationalists he was much too prone to give prominence to the activities of the Scottish aristocracy, the monarchy, and Scottish worthies at home and abroad (partly no doubt because the *Scottish Patriot* carried numerous illustrations) but the *Scottish Patriot* made a generally favourable impact on contemporaries. Its successor was the more literary *Scotia: the Journal of the St. Andrew Society*, published in Edinburgh from 1907 to 1911.

The fifth of the quintet of nationalist journals before 1914 that survived for more than a few issues was the quarterly *Guth na Bliadhna: the Voice of the Year*, which appeared between 1904 and 1925, and was for a time supplemented by the monthly *An Sgeulaiche* (1909–11).[2] The proprietor of *Guth na Bliadhna* was the Hon. Stuart Erskine, second son of the fifth Lord Erskine, who began to style himself the Hon. Ruaraidh Erskine of Marr (Ruaraidh Arascain is Mhairr) in the early years of the twentieth century. Born in Brighton in 1869 and taught Gaelic by a nurse from Lewis, Erskine became a Vice President of the Scottish Home Rule Association in 1892 and was a minor literary figure in London and the Highlands until the turn of the century.[3] He then became passionately absorbed in the Gaelic revival, which had started with the formation of the Gaelic Society of Inverness in 1871.

During its early years the Gaelic revival had acquired a distinctly nationalist flavour as a result of the work of John Murdoch, who from 1873 to 1881 published a newspaper *The Highlander*, which was long remembered, and caused Murdoch to be regarded as one of the heroes of nationalism down to the 1920s.[4] But other longer-lived Highland papers had also something of a nationalist tone, notably the *Celtic Magazine* and the *Scottish Highlander*, which were owned and edited by the antiquarian Alexander Mackenzie, who was a Vice President of the Scottish Home Rule Association. The central interest of the Gaelic revival was Gaelic language and literature and the history of the

---

[1] *The Thistle*, IX (1917), 18–19. For Shinty see *Scottish Patriot*, III (1905–6), 10–11.
[2] *An Sgeulaiche* was succeeded by *Alba* (Stirling, 1920–1) which, according to an advertisement, stood for 'complete national independence, and the restoration to Scotland of her Celtic system of Government and her Celtic culture'. Both were written exclusively in Gaelic.
[3] There is no biography of him. But see Grieve, *Contemporary Scottish Studies*, pp. 244–50, and *Gairm*, No. 16 (Summer 1956), p. 367.
[4] There is an eloquent tribute by Erskine in *Guth na Bliadhna*, VI (1909), 165–6, and another by W. Gillies in *Scots Independent*, II (1927–8), 11–12.

Celtic peoples, but there was also a good deal of interest in Celtic music, art, dress and sports and in the development of a new economic basis for the Highlands. Here the lead was gradually assumed by An Comunn Gaidhealach, with its annual *Mod*, which was essentially concerned with entertainment rather than politics. The political side of the Gaelic revival had been represented by the Highland Land League and similar bodies, which were active between 1883 and 1895, but then petered out. After 1901 it became the object of Erskine of Marr to revive the political wing of the Gaelic movement in a new form, though he also took a keen interest in other aspects of the Gaelic revival and published a book about the kilt and the Celtic renaissance.[1]

The early years of the twentieth century seemed particularly timely for the creation of a Gaelic political movement. In Ireland the Gaelic movement was in full swing and Sinn Fein was taking shape, and it was natural that an attempt should be made in Scotland to follow the Irish example. The first volume of *Guth na Bliadhna* carried an article pointing out that Scotland must follow the example of Ireland, the second carried an article on education in the West of Ireland by P. H. Pearse, and the third included an article urging the creation of a Gaelic confederation: 'The drawing together of the Gaels of Scotland and Ireland is a natural consequence of the language movement in both countries. . . .'[2] Erskine claimed that he had himself invented the slogan 'No Language, no Nation',[3] but with variations it was the slogan of most national movements, including the Czech one, on which *Guth na Bliadhna* carried an article.[4] Erskine's ideas also reflected those of other nationalist language movements in being socially rather radical.

Erskine was not a Highland separatist. His object was to Celticize the whole of Scotland, building on the base created by An Comunn Gaidhealach and other Gaelic societies, but working outside them.

> We stand for Scotland and a Scottish State. No more dear-bought, hard-wrung, permission to cultivate, on sufferance, all that which, as a race, we hold most near and dear, will satisfy us—the progressive and militant forces of the Gaelic Movement. We aim at 'Scotland a

[1] The Honble. Stuart Ruadri Erskine [note the spelling], *The Kilt and How to Wear It* (Inverness, 1901).
[2] *Guth na Bliadhna*, III (1906), 11.
[3] ibid., IX (1912), 496.
[4] Count Lutzow, 'The Revival of the Czech or Bohemian Language', ibid., VIII (1911), 147–52.

Nation'.... The old cry of 'Alba! Alba!' and the more recent one of 'Sinn Féin a mhàin!' are our cries.[1]

Whether Erskine was behind the programme for a 'Scottish Party' announced by 'John, Earl of Mar' on 15th January 1907 is not clear. But, if not, it would be rather surprising, for the programme expressed some of his own views. It called for the restoration of a Gaelic-speaking community in the Highlands and for a compulsory qualification in Gaelic for every person in Scotland holding state office.[2]

As was to be expected, the programmes of the Scottish Party and of *Guth na Bliadhna* were not well received in the Lowlands, and even the courteous Theodore Napier was moved to protest that *Guth na Bliadhna* aimed to divide the Highlanders from the Lowlanders and 'to cause antagonism . . . instead of cultivating harmonious relations in order to effect in common the political and national freedom of *Scotland*'.[3] Nor was another Gaelic venture, the launching of a body called Comunn nan Albannach (Scots National League) in 1911, any better received. Though nationalists might approve the slogan 'Scotland free, Scotland Sovereign, Scotland a Nation once again', they were clearly scared of being tarred with the brush of Gaelic separatism.[4] It was only after these repeated ventures had failed that Erskine determined to come down from the hills of Aberdeenshire where he lived and to found a journal in the Lowlands, which would make a direct appeal to Lowland opinion. As he put it himself:

The Celtic culture takes its rise from the soil of Scotland, and bears the indelible impress of the collective genius of the nation. To the Anglicising tendencies of the new feudalism, it opposes a body of beliefs and aspirations which are drawn from the purest native sources. . . . Hitherto, what is called the 'Celtic Renaissance' has been confined to the Gaelic-speaking parts of the kingdom. It is now time for that movement to descend from the hills, and to endeavour to interest the English-speaking Celt of the plains in the manners and the customs of his pre-feudalised forefathers.[5]

---

[1] *Guth na Bliadhna*, VI (1909), 166.
[2] *Fiery Cross*, April 1907, p. 5.
[3] *Fiery Cross*, October 1907, p. 6. The *Fiery Cross*, January 1910, p. 6, however, gave a welcome to the Irish journal called *Sinn Fein*, which advocated similar ideas for Ireland.
[4] *Fiery Cross*, January 1911, pp. 6–7.
[5] *Scottish Review*, 37 (1914), 305–6.

The chosen instrument for this purpose was the *Scottish Review*, published from 1914 to 1920, which, along with its stable-mate *Guth na Bliadhna*, was to make a unique contribution to the development of nationalist ideas during the war years.

II

Theodore Napier once said that he regarded the Reverend David Macrae as 'the chief and leader of Scottish Nationalists' from 1897 until his death ten years later, and in a variety of articles other nationalists said much the same thing.[1] Macrae, however, is a difficult figure to place. The son of a United Presbyterian minister and himself a U.P. minister, he was in 1879 excluded from that church after a notable heresy trial in which he was accused of watering down the essential doctrines of orthodox Calvinism. He continued, however, to serve as minister in a church of his own, the Gilfillan Memorial Church in Dundee, where he had a large congregation until his retirement in 1897. In early life a noted temperance advocate and social reformer, he came to the fore as a nationalist in 1883 with a motion put before the Dundee School Board to the effect that school history books should be purged of their anti-Scottish bias and their misleading use of the national names. His views were taken up by T. D. Wanliss in a pamphlet,[2] and by W. K. Leask (subsequently Wanliss's coadjutor on *The Thistle*), who founded a Scottish National Rights Association in Dundee for 'purifying' school textbooks ('it is through School Books that this tide of Anglo-Mania has set in and through School Books we mean to crush it').[3] In 1901 Macrae became president of a new body called the Scottish Patriotic Association, of which John Wilson was a keen backer. The immediate reason for the creation of the Association was the desire to protest at the assumption by King Edward of the title 'King Edward VII' instead of 'King Edward I'. This 'renewed Edwardian aggression' united all nationalists, who agreed to stage a demonstration at the Borestone at Bannockburn.[4] The demonstration,

---

[1] *Fiery Cross*, July 1907, p. 4; *Scotia*, I (1907), 184–90; *The Thistle*, VII (1915), 70–6; *Scottish Patriot*, II (1904–5), 163.

[2] *Scottish Honour versus English Vanity: being the Report of a Speech by Rev. David Macrae at the Dundee School Board on 'The Misuse of our National Names', with an Introduction by Mr. T. D. Wanliss* (Dundee, 1886).

[3] Leask to J. S. Blackie, 15th May 1886. National Library of Scotland. MS. 2636, f. 219.

[4] *Fiery Cross*, August 1901, pp. 3–4. The Convention of Royal Burghs refused to back the protest by 65 votes to 6. ibid., April 1902, p. 8.

attended by 'several thousands of Scots'[1] became the first of a series staged on or about the 24th of June (Bannockburn Day) which were held every year down to 1914. One count put the number of those attending the 1912 demonstration at 15,000, and undoubtedly these demonstrations were very popular.[2] Furthermore, the Scottish Patriotic Association took up charitable work, and in 1914 its Scottish Flag Day raised over £3,000, much of which was used to relieve distress in the Western Isles and among the unemployed.[3]

The main interest of the Scottish Patriotic Association lay, however, in education—Macrae's chosen field. The Association spent several months in 1903 investigating the teaching of Scottish History in the schools and issued a statement expressing dismay at what was found.

> A close examination of the history books now in use has revealed the fact that a very large percentage of them are manufactured in England and are most offensive to Scotland. Now that the Scottish Patriotic Association has taken the matter in hand it is expected that our schools will be purged of those anti-Scottish books and the teaching of our national history will once again occupy the place it demands. It is noteworthy that those who have studied the matter are of opinion that the regrettable apathy of many Scots in regard to the affairs of their country has been brought about by this serious neglect of our history.[4]

The Association proceeded to lobby the Convention of Royal Burghs and the leading school boards on the subject, and secured their backing for a general campaign for the extension of the teaching of Scottish history.[5]

Macrae's death put a damper on the activities of the Scottish Patriotic Association in the educational field, though his successor was a headmaster, Charles William Thomson, but its work was soon supplemented by that of other bodies. One of the most important of these was the St. Andrew Society (Glasgow), which was founded in 1912 apparently as a counterpart to the Edinburgh body of that name which had published *Scotia*. Its members were said by *The Thistle* to be of a 'more Conservative cast' than those of the Scottish Patriotic Associa-

---

[1] ibid., August 1901, p. 3.
[2] *The Thistle*, IV (1912), 117–18.
[3] *The Thistle*, VII (1915), 132.
[4] *Fiery Cross*, October 1903, p. 7.
[5] ibid., October 1904, p. 3. See also the *Minutes* of the Convention of Royal Burghs 1904–7, *passim*.

tion,[1] but the President, the antiquarian George Eyre-Todd, who was editor of the *Scottish Field* and *Scottish Country Life*, had in fact produced the collected edition of the Rev. David Macrae's works and clearly regarded himself as working in the Macrae tradition. One of the first actions of the new body was to set up a Scottish History and Literature Committee, along with a National Names Committee and a Heraldry Committee.[2] Its labours in the field were soon supplemented by those of an Edinburgh-based body, the Association for the Promotion of Scottish History in Schools and Universities, of which Professor Richard Lodge of Edinburgh University was chairman.[3] And soon a full-scale campaign was under way, though there were those who feared that the Presbyterian enthusiasms of the supporters of Scottish history teaching would lead to the introduction of a new sort of bias, which might be as bad as the old.[4]

The Scottish patriotism associated with the Scottish Patriotic Association and related bodies, like the Scottish Rights Association of Greenock, was typical of its generation, and filled the pages of the *Fiery Cross, The Thistle* and the *Scottish Patriot*. It is fully reflected in a once well-known book, published by one of the main contributors to the *Scottish Patriot* who had succeeded Macrae as President of the Scottish Patriotic Association, Charles W. Thomson's *Scotland's Work and Worth*. Intellectually it was about as far removed from the heights of Gaelic intellectualism occupied by Erskine of Marr as it was possible to be. The standard nationalist 'programme', in so far as there was one, was that which John Wilson adopted for the *Scottish Patriot* in 1904.

The Cultivation of a Spirit of Patriotism.

The Defence of Scottish National Rights.

To Protest against the use of the terms 'England' and 'English' in place of 'Britain' and 'British'.

The Study of Scottish History, Music, Art and Literature.

Encouragement of Scottish Recreations.

Celebration of National Anniversaries. . . .

The Restoration of the Scottish Parliament.[5]

---

[1] *The Thistle*, IV (1912), 84.
[2] ibid., 83.
[3] ibid., 158–62.
[4] *Guth na Bliadhna*, VI (1909), 283–94.
[5] *Scottish Patriot*, II (1904–5), 178. A more detailed programme was given in ibid., I (1903–4), 4.

A similar 'programme' was promulgated by T. D. Wanliss in *The Thistle* in 1915:

1. To uphold the National Honour of Scotland.
2. To foster and encourage, as the chief means thereto, the patriotism of the Scottish people at Home and Abroad.
3. To secure for the Scottish people the entire control of their own Scottish affairs, under the aegis of the British Constitution. In other words, HOME RULE FOR SCOTLAND.
4. To expose, resent, and resist by every legitimate means the insidious and continuous encroachments that are made year by year, and day by day, by insolent, arrogant, and ignorant Englishmen on the National Rights and the National Honour of Scotland, as established by the Treaty of Union of 1706.[1]

Scottish nationalism for such men was essentially backward-looking and defensive, unless they found a constructive outlet, as Wilson did in the Scottish National Song Society. Nationalists were fond of quoting obscure phrases from ancient patriots like the Earl of Cromarty, who in the Union debates was believed to have said:

Scotland or England are words unknown in our native language. England is a dishonourable name imposed on Britain by Jutland pirates and mercenaries usurping on their lords.[2]

And they made use of a great repertoire of quotations from the 'national authors', notably Burns.[3] Theodore Napier's chosen Burns quotation was:

Alas! have I often said to myself, What are all the boasted advantages which my country reaps from the Union that can counterbalance the annihilation of her independence, and even her very name![4]

But each man had his favourite quotations, and the printing of little booklets of patriotic snippets seems to have begun at this time.

Scots patriots also made much play with newspaper clippings often from very unlikely sources. Some of these, such as one from *The Outfitter* of 30th August 1902, were simply oddities.

[1] *The Thistle*, VII (1915), 18.
[2] *The Thistle*, II (1910), 80.
[3] The best account of Robert Burns's nationalism is in *Scottish Review*, 38 (1915), 504–26.
[4] *Fiery Cross*, January 1912, p. 2.

The trouser-cum-frock-coat-cum-chimney-pot-hat is a costume not only artistically impossible, but essentially inelegant, and of absolutely no practical value, since it is no good in hot weather, no good in cold weather, and no good in wet weather. In short, it is precisely the costume that a gifted Celt might have predicted the stupid Saxon would produce. It is, of course, the trousers that make it so ridiculous and so deliberately indecent as it is.[1]

More often, however, Scots patriots, like their predecessors in the middle of the nineteenth century, were wont to quote passages from English newspapers of which they disapproved. *Punch* was often in trouble, and it was not only *The Thistle* which complained that *Punch* 'unjustly slanders the law-abiding and thrifty people of Scotland' and accused it of making 'Scottish thrift a butt for low and vulgar abuse' and 'attempting falsely to degrade the character of the Scottish people'.[2] Occasionally, however, patriotic Scots found something unexpected to please them in the English papers, such as an advertisement in the personal column of *The Times* in November 1914 which read

> Englishmen! Please use 'Britain', 'British', and 'Briton', when the United Kingdom or the Empire is in question—at least during the war.[3]

Patriotic societies were apt to pass resolutions like those which figured at the Bannockburn Day celebration at the Borestone in 1904. The President of the Rosebery Burns Club in Glasgow moved that

> This meeting appeals to Scottish patriotism and to English honour to cease the objectionable practice of using the sectional terms 'England' and 'English' as substitutes for the united and imperial terms 'Britain' and 'British'—a practice at variance with the truth of history and with the first and fundamental condition of union.

A minister, supported by the ex-provost of Greenock, then moved a resolution endorsing the policy of:

> having Scottish history taught properly in our public schools, securing suitable history books for the purpose, and books purged from the misuse . . . of our national names.

Another minister then moved a resolution deploring:

[1] ibid., October 1902, p. 6.
[2] *The Thistle*, III (1911), 117.
[3] ibid., VI (1914), 222.

the fact that in the midst of party conflict Scottish Members of Parliament, with a few exceptions, are shamefully neglecting Scotland's rights and honour as a nation.

Theodore Napier then moved a protest 'against the title "Edward VII" ', which was supported by a Mr. Crossthwaite 'in an original poem of nine verses'. And the meeting ended with the singing of 'Scots wha hae wi' Wallace bled' and 'Auld Lang Syne'.[1]

Patriotic speeches on such occasions were illustrated by references to particular Scottish grievances. The nationalist journals were also full of them. Some of the grievances turned on refusals of government expenditure in Scotland. Thus in 1912 *The Thistle* carried an article on Peterhead Harbour which began as follows:

> The unfairness of England towards Scotland, and the insolent way in which English officials disregard the rights of Scotland to a fair share in the expenditure of public money is well exemplified by the statement that the works at Peterhead for the construction of a harbour of refuge there are to be stopped by The Treasury.[2]

Other grievances were of longer standing. There was continued frustration at the failure of the government to understand that they must get their heraldry right—even though in some respects matters had greatly improved since the 1850s. There was a prolonged campaign against the use of the St. George's flag by the Royal Navy, which was associated with the name of John Alexander Stewart of Glasgow.[3] The Navy also came under fire because of its refusal to appoint full-time Presbyterian chaplains,[4] because it insisted on an English public school type of education, and because of its generally English point of view, which led Stewart to comment that 'the Royal Navy is for all practical purposes a preserve for the sons of wealthy English naval families'.[5] There was continuous pressure, both in the House of Commons and outside, for a change in the name of the Scotch Education Department to Scottish Education Department, which was at last successful in

---

[1] *Fiery Cross*, October 1904, pp. 2–3.
[2] *The Thistle*, IV (1912), 11.
[3] There is a useful summary of the issue in *The Thistle*, IV (1912), 62–6. All the nationalist papers carried regular features on the flags issue. There was, however, an anti-Stewart faction, which deplored his enthusiasm for the Saltire and championed the lion rampant. See ibid., IV (1912), 132–3.
[4] ibid., IV (1912), 70–1, 85–6, 98–9.
[5] ibid., IV (1912), 65.

1918.[1] There was a steady sniping at the officials of the department for their alleged attempts to 'denationalise Scotland' and for their refusal to speed the move of the department from London to Edinburgh, at the Scottish Universities because of the way in which they neglected Scottish History, and at lecturers in the universities who were unwise enough to express what were thought to be anti-national views. *The Thistle*, for instance, printed an article headed 'Unpatriotic Scottish Universities'[2] in 1912.

All this was often accompanied by unpleasant asides about Scots who had been so unpatriotic as to express views which did not fit readily into the nationalists' conception of what was patriotism. One target was Scotsmen educated in England. Thus *The Thistle* in December 1912, in an attack on Professor J. H. Millar, Professor of Constitutional Law and Constitutional History at Edinburgh University, a Tory who was the son and grandson of Scottish judges, wrote:

> There is a certain class of clever Scotsmen, who complete their education at the University of Oxford, with results not very creditable to themselves, or to the country of their origin. The Oxford influence and environment are too much for them; and their after career too often shows that though possessed of a good deal of intellectual power, they are devoid of much strength of character, and are possessed with an innate flunkeyism which leads them, not merely to bow down to and humbly accept Anglican ideas and Anglicising influences; but also with these, a desire to belittle the country which gave them birth, and to sneer at Scottish ways, Scottish literature, and Scottish history, as matters of a lowly and inferior type, quite unworthy of men who have 'been to Oxford'. We have on several occasions had to deal with anti-Scottish conduct of men of this stamp, and to point out and severely censure their unpatriotic and untruthful dealing with matters relating to Scotland, and to things which to Scotsmen generally, are very dear.[3]

Another target was Scottish historians of whom patriots disapproved, such as Sir Herbert Maxwell, who was described in *The Thistle* (in an article entitled 'The University of Glasgow Unpatriotic'), as 'the foul and gross libeller of the memory of Sir William Wallace'.[4] No doubt

---

[1] For this agitation see *The Thistle*, I (1909), 15–16, IV (1912), 101–2, 122–3, 130–2, X (1918), 132–6.
[2] ibid., IV (1912), 109–10.
[3] ibid., IV (1912), 197.
[4] ibid., V (1913), 180.

this rancour was in part simply a reflection of T. D. Wanliss's own distinctive point of view, or more generally of the type of censoriousness which comes so readily from old men with a grievance against the world. But it is also to be found in others, and is, alas, still a feature of nationalism today. Indeed, one of the many letters I received after *The Scotsman* had published a brief paragraph which reported my inaugural lecture at Edinburgh, was from a prominent nationalist who completely misunderstood what I had been trying to say, and whose words are reminiscent of those of Wanliss: 'You are merely wasting our Scottish money. . . . We don't want you here.'

III

Vaguely nationalist ideas were so common in Scotland at the beginning of the twentieth century that it was inevitable that there should be a demand for the creation of a nationalist party. Such a demand was first voiced in 1903—perhaps as a result of the stimulus provided by a short-lived paper started by Charles Waddie called *The Scottish Nationalist*. In April 1903 the *Fiery Cross* gave prominence to an appeal for the creation of a Scottish National Party:

> Why do not Scottish electors choose Scottish **Nationalists** as their representatives in Parliament, and thus create a **Scottish National Party** with a strong *Leader*—a Scottish Parnell?[1]

This was followed by a further article in July 1903 which argued that 'A Scottish National Party', having for its programme ' "**Scotland for the Scots** and the **Land for the People**", would be invincible'.[2] In October of the same year the *Scottish Patriot* carried a leading article which made the same point under a heading which read:

WANTED!
A SCOTTISH NATIONAL PARTY[3]

When nothing happened John Wilson of the *Scottish Patriot* decided to form a new organization single-handed. This was founded in May 1904 and was called the Scottish National League. Its objects were:

1. to secure proper attention to Scottish interests on the part of Scottish representatives in the British Parliament

---

[1] *Fiery Cross*, April 1903, p. 2.
[2] ibid., July 1903, p. 2.
[3] *Scottish Patriot*, October 1903.

2. where necessary to bring forward national candidates for Scottish constituencies

3. to agitate for and demand the establishment of a Scottish Parliament for the efficient conduct of Scottish affairs.[1]

But though Wilson worked hard to get an organization together it is clear that the Scottish National League never had any life of its own, though it secured a qualified backing from Joseph Dobbie, Liberal M.P. for the Ayr District from 1904 to 1906. By the middle of 1905 John Wilson was back at the old theme and advertising:

Important Appeal to Our Readers
Wanted!
Opinions regarding the formation of a thoroughly representative
Scottish National Association
For the Promotion of National Ideals and the Defence of
Scottish Rights[2]

There were a few replies, but to little point. The majority of Scottish nationalists clearly regarded the Liberal party or the Labour party as the natural channel for expressing political views.

In 1909 Theodore Napier tried again:

When will Scotsmen cease denominating themselves Conservatives, Unionists and Liberals, and become *Scottish Nationalists* instead? Ireland has shown us the way, yet Scotland has no *National* party in Parliament, but fatuously follow their party leaders. Until Scotland obtains a local Scottish Parliament in Edinburgh Scotland will continue in political serfdom to England. . . .[3]

But there was still no response. Nationalists had simply to follow the example of Charles Waddie and to demand specific pledges from the candidates of the existing parties that they would vote for the immediate implementation of Scottish Home Rule.[4]

IV

Nationalism first became a force to be reckoned with intellectually, and as something distinctive from the Liberal party with the publica-

---

[1] *Scottish Patriot*, II (1904–5), 82–3. Further references to the League are at ibid., II (1904–5), 138, 157, 166 and III (1905–6), 28.

[2] ibid., III (1905–6), 80.

[3] *Fiery Cross*, July 1909, p. 7.

[4] *The Thistle*, II (1910), 13–15.

tion of the *Scottish Review*. Though they never had a big circulation the *Scottish Review* and *Guth na Bliadhna* survived throughout the First World War and on until their work could be taken over by other journals in the twenties. They are two of the few major landmarks of early twentieth-century Scottish nationalism, along with the poems of Hugh MacDiarmid.

The *Scottish Review* had the great advantage over *Guth na Bliadhna*, which continued to appear as a Gaelic companion journal, that it could draw both on a wider range of authors and on the contributors to *Guth na Bliadhna*. Among those who wrote in early issues of the *Scottish Review* were the historian Robert Rait, the Liberal M.P. J. M. Hogge, the nationalist writer Lewis Spence, James Maxton of the I.L.P., and, as a regular writer on labour and economic questions, William Diack, an Aberdeen trade unionist. As with *Guth na Bliadhna*, there was an international flavour about a good many of the articles and the first number of the *Scottish Review* emphasized this internationalism by carrying articles on 'Ulster in Song' and 'France in the Remaking'. There was also a good deal of emphasis on Celtic traditions, including a well-illustrated series of articles by Charles Bell advocating a greater use of Celtic styles in Scottish architecture because 'the Celtic style of Architecture is so distinctive, and so well suited to the needs of the people, and the character of their land, that it should form the rudiments of a national style'.[1] The great strength of the *Scottish Review*, however, was the emphasis it gave to economic and labour issues. This not only distinguished it from its predecessors and contemporaries, it gave the anti-war section of the Scottish labour movement a serious platform. And it enabled unorthodox views to be discussed in a serious way. For instance, the *Scottish Review* was the first journal to carry a serious article (by H. C. Mac-Neacail) advocating the policy of Lockhart of Carnwath in the eighteenth century, that the Scottish M.P.s should withdraw in a body and reconstitute the Scottish Parliament which 'was not dissolved, still less abolished; it was merely adjourned'.[2]

History proves that action in Scotland is every way more potent for good than talking at Westminster. Let the future members for Scottish constituencies, pledged to the principle of the complete political Independence of Scotland, take up the discarded policy of

[1] *Scottish Review*, 38 (1915), 248.
[2] ibid., 40 (1917), 340.

Lockhart of Carnwarth; let them turn their backs on Westminster, and instead work, educate, and organise in Scotland.[1]

Both the *Scottish Review* and *Guth na Bliadhna* carried frequent articles by Erskine himself, many of them in Gaelic, which he was anxious to develop into an effective 'political' language. For him, indeed, the development of the language often seems to have been more important than the views expressed in it. What mattered for him was that by the end of the war a small body of journalists had come into being capable of writing articles on current problems in Gaelic. There was, therefore, a note of triumph in what he wrote when in 1918 he commented that 'The Gaelic language is a forcible, flexible, harmonious, extremely copious, and highly cultivated form of speech; and those who allege that it is unsuited to modern requirements, and is quite useless for cultural purposes, talk . . . fudge'.[2] Erskine's own writing in Gaelic has been praised by Hugh MacDiarmid (not a very competent judge) but is best summed up by the comment of a tactful Gael 'You have restored to us "Gentleman's Gaelic" '[3]—or in other words he used it as a well-bred non-native speaker would do.

The main feature of Erskine's thought was a sort of eighteenth-century rationalism which made him wish to create a new Scottish political system *de novo*. He had come to the conclusion that the existing system was a bad one, that the culture of the people had been debased, and that it must be re-created on a Celtic rather than an Anglo-Saxon basis. For exemplars he looked to Ireland, to Bohemia, and to Hungary, and he was by no means deterred by the apparent willingness of some members of the Gaelic movement in Ireland to resort to violence. He was an opponent of the First World War. He backed the 1916 rising in Dublin (though in guarded language because of wartime censorship).[4] He attacked Lloyd George as 'The Welsh Titus Oates' because of his attitude towards Ireland.[5] And he welcomed the Russian revolution with its declarations of universal brotherhood and support for national aspirations as warmly as any Arab nationalist.

Praise to the Bolsheviks! Honour to the Revolutionaries! It is the Russian Revolution that has set the Chancelleries of Europe by the

[1] *Scottish Review*, 40 (1917), 374.
[2] ibid., 41 (1918), 138.
[3] Quoted in Grieve, *Contemporary Scottish Studies*, p. 249.
[4] *Scottish Review*, 39 (1916), 354–74.
[5] ibid., 41 (1918), 272. This had not been his view in 1914. See ibid., 37 (1914), 80–1.

ears, and now bids fair to inscribe in large and indelible letters on the pages of the great Book of Universal National Rights certain priceless principles. . . . Self-determination for *all* Nations; no Annexations; and no Treaty-made premiums on after-war international enmity and greed. . . . The fabric of the old order is crashing about our ears. Over an angry sea of discord, strewn with the wreckage of foundered kingdoms and systems of rule, there rises, in splendid majesty, the sun of Democracy . . . Hail to Democracy! Let us cast from us our old wet and tattered political rags as we should do sodden garments, and bask in the warmth that the kindly luminary provides us with, rejoicing in the return of the day of Reason and of Right.[1]

Yet, in spite of all this Radicalism, Erskine was in some ways a traditionalist. His journals supported Highland Roman Catholicism and he himself was a monarchist, though he had a low opinion of monarchs and was quite happy to leave the issue of who was actually to be king of Scotland to the future.

The end of the war, and the Russian revolution seemed to Erskine to be the signal for a new type of activity. The Gaelic movement had to be democratized ('It has divided its attentions between the lairdocracy on one hand and the bourgeoisie on the other'),[2] perhaps through the medium of the revived Highland Land League, which was for a short time in close connection with the Labour party.[3] Moreover, the whole country had to be brought to terms with Marx 'the German Solomon'.

Until the people reign—until the Proletariat is everywhere in undisputed power—it were folly to expect enduring Peace, drastic Retrenchment, or honest and searching Reform. . . . It is possible, of course, that the Proletarian rule may disappoint in practise the glowing expectations formed of it by its friends, and may show itself to be as little dependable as *medicina animi* as Monarchy, Aristocracy, and government by the Capitalist class have proved themselves to be so . . . but . . . apart from the fact that real popular rule is as yet a practically unknown and untried force in political Europe, the Dictatorship of the Proletariat, how dismally soever it might

[1] *Guth na Bliadhna*, XV (1918), 97–8.
[2] ibid., 99.
[3] *Scottish Review*, 41 (1918), 544–7.

fail, could not possibly sin against humanity more deeply and unforgivably than the other systems of government have done.[1]

Holding such views it was natural for Erskine to seek out allies in the Labour party and the trade union movement. To them he therefore turned with an appeal that Scotland must be given independent representation at the Paris peace conference (the same claim that was successfully made by the British Dominions). With the aid of a mixed committee of left-wing Liberals, Labour men, and contributors to the *Scottish Review*, both the Labour Party's Scottish Council and the S.T.U.C. were persuaded to back a petition to the conference (in French), which made quite a stir on the continent.[2] And in 1919 the *Scottish Review* gave far more attention to labour questions than to any other subject. Readers were now assured by William Diack that whatever Erskine himself might owe to 'the crude materialism of Karl Marx' the Scottish Labour movement owed little: 'The Scottish Labour movement is of native growth; its roots go deep down into our national history.'[3] John Maclean and the Scottish Labour College were criticized for not giving a 'definite place for the study of Scottish history from the national and democratic point of view' and the work of James Connolly, who was 'heart and soul with the Gaelic revival in Ireland', was praised at length by way of contrast.[4]

None the less, Erskine soon found that John Maclean (by descent a Highlander from Mull) was a man whose views were in many ways similar to his own. Erskine had criticized him in 1918 for not arguing in the courts that a charge against him under the Defence of the Realm Act should be fought as a constitutional case in which the validity of the Act itself and the validity of the Union of 1707 might be tested.[5] And when Erskine asked Maclean to sign the memorial to the Paris Peace Conference, Maclean made it clear that though he was 'in favour of a Parliament or Soviet of workers for Scotland with headquarters in Scotland'[6] he cared nothing for the Paris Peace Conference or for President Wilson. As this was very much the case Erskine had himself been arguing in the *Scottish Review*, the two men seem to have come to

---

[1] *Scottish Review*, 42 (1919), 10.
[2] ibid., 40 (1917), 151–8; 41 (1918), 149–50, 417–30; 42 (1919), 12–25, 115–16, 232, 347.
[3] ibid., 42 (1919), 388.
[4] ibid., 42 (1919), 390, 400.
[5] ibid., 41 (1918), 268–9.
[6] Tom Bell, *John Maclean: a Fighter for Freedom* (Glasgow, 1944), p. 82.

some sort of *rapprochement*. Maclean signed as he was asked,[1] and thereafter steadily drifted further and further in a nationalist direction. He joined Erskine's National Committee late in 1919,[2] and like Erskine became identified with the view that the Scots should follow the example of the Irish, though in Maclean's case this was by following the example of the Irish labour movement rather than that of Sinn Fein. By the middle of 1920 this meant for him the creation of a 'Scottish Communist Republic as a first step towards World Communism, with Glasgow as the head and centre'.[3] In 1922 he stood as a candidate in the Gorbals division of Glasgow, and used the Irish-style argument that if elected he would not go to London but would 'stay in Scotland, helping the unemployed'.[4] This argument was further developed in the campaign which he started, but did not live to finish, in the Gorbals in 1923.

> I ... stand out as a Scottish Republican candidate feeling sure that if Scotland had to elect a Parliament to sit in Glasgow, it would vote for a working-class Parliament. ... the social revolution is possible sooner in Scotland than in England.... Scottish separation is part of the process of England's Imperial disintegration.... This policy of a Workers' Republic in Scotland debars me from going to John Bull's London Parliament.... Had the Labour men stayed in Glasgow and started a Scottish Parliament, as did the genuine Irish in Dublin in 1918, England would have sat up and made concessions to Scotland just to keep her ramshackle Empire intact to bluff other countries.[5]

What Maclean said about Labour candidates was equally true of the Communists who, under the leadership of William Gallacher, prepared to work within the framework of the Union of 1707.[6] And for this reason it was not possible for Maclean to be an orthodox Communist. But there were always a few members of the Communist party who held Maclean's views, as well as his small band of disciples outside

[1] *Scottish Review*, 42 (1919), 24.
[2] ibid., 447.
[3] Bell, *John Maclean*, p. 109.
[4] ibid., p. 121.
[5] ibid., pp. 123–4.
[6] William Gallacher, *Revolt on the Clyde: an Autobiography* (London, 1936), pp. 250–4; *Life and Literature of the Working Class: Essays in Honour of William Gallacher* (Berlin, 1966), p. 29. Gallacher was a disciple of Maclean's but had been won over by Lenin to the ideal of a unified Marxist movement in Britain. Maclean was, however, one of Lenin's heroes and acted as Soviet consul in Scotland: *V.I. Lenin on Britain* (Moscow, 1959), pp. 333, 360, 386.

the party (who are represented today by the Workers' Party of Scotland). And Hugh MacDiarmid, whether from within the party or without, has always championed Maclean's memory as that of 'in many respects the greatest proletarian leader Scotland has yet produced'.[1] As a result, Maclean's name is firmly rooted in Scottish left-wing folklore.

If Erskine lost one ally, even if he were an unpredictable and independent one, when Maclean died in 1923, he soon gained another in Christopher Murray Grieve, better known by his pen-name of Hugh MacDiarmid, with whom he was to work for a number of years.[2] Without being Highlanders by birth, they both had a passion for things Celtic. Erskine's slogan 'No Language, No Nation' fitted MacDiarmid's revival of 'Braid Scots' as a serious literary language just as well as it fitted Erskine's emphasis on the Gaelic revival. And both men shared the same desire to start things again from the beginning. As a result MacDiarmid's contributions to the *Pictish Review*, which Erskine started in 1927, read as a natural (though better-written) extension of Erskine's own earlier work. Moreover, these contributions include, I believe, much the most original of MacDiarmid's political ideas.

V

Erskine, Maclean and MacDiarmid were far too uncompromising for most nationalists who still clung to the Home Rule tradition. For a time after the war, however, there was a feeling of goodwill on the left which from time to time brought quite unlikely people together. This was clearly demonstrated when Ruaraidh Erskine got together a 'National Committee' late in 1919 to press not only for the recognition of Scotland by the Paris peace conference but also for other national interests. Its most prominent members were William Graham, M.P., and Robert Smillie, President of the Miners' Federation, but the other members of the committee included the 'Clydesiders' David Kirkwood and James Maxton, Thomas Johnston of *Forward*, John Maclean, Angus MacDonald of the Highland Land League, Joseph F. Duncan of the Farm Servants' Union, Aonghas MacEanruig who edited *Alba*,

---

[1] *Life and Literature of the Working Class*, p. 35; *Collected Poems of Hugh MacDiarmid*, ed. John C. Weston (2nd edn., New York, 1967), 242–3.
[2] For MacDiarmid's career see Duncan Glen, *Hugh MacDiarmid (Christopher Murray Grieve) and the Scottish Renaissance* (Edinburgh and London, 1964)

and the Liberal M.P. J. M. Hogge.[1] The *Scottish Review* in its final number made it clear just where Erskine now stood by launching a vigorous attack both on Asquithian Liberalism, because at Paisley Asquith had ranged it 'in opposition to the new ideals of Scottish democracy',[2] and on the 'Clynes and other Tadpoles that infest the English Labour "movement" '.[3]

One of Erskine's associates, Angus MacDonald of the Highland Land League, perhaps came nearest to Erskine's standpoint at the end of the war. The League itself was only a shadow of its pre-war counterpart, but it aspired to play in the Highlands the part played by the Labour party in the Lowlands, and its pretensions were formally recognized by the Labour party before the 1918 election. Though the Labour party soon tired of the League, and it quickly died, there was a time in 1920 when it claimed to be both a Labour and Nationalist party in the Highlands and issues a handbill which read as follows:[4]

SCOTLAND FOR EVER!
HOW IS SHE BECOME TRIBUTARY!
She that was Great among the Nations!

COMUNN AN FHEARAINN
(The Highland Land League)
(Air son Dachaidh agus Dùthcha).

Every Parish in Gaelic-speaking Scotland should have a Branch of the Highland Land League. The minimum membership subscription is 1/- per annum; and the objects for which the League exists are:—

THAT SCOTLAND MAY BECOME AGAIN AN INDEPENDENT NATION, AND THAT ALL LANDS, MINES, AND FISHERIES BE RESTORED TO THE SCOTTISH COMMONWEALTH.

Scotland, owing to her long subjection to England and English influences, is gradually losing the distinctive and most valuable features of her nationality. English Cabinets have always been principally composed of Saxon mandarins, whose reactionary and blundering rule over Scotland is mainly responsible for the sorry condition of our Country.

[1] *Scottish Review*, 42 (1919), 447. The other members were Duncan MacGregor Graham, M.P., Neil MacLean, M.P., John Robertson, M.P., Alexander Wilkie, M.P., and Erskine himself.
[2] ibid., 43 (1920), 44.
[3] ibid., 88. Clynes was a prominent Labour leader.
[4] ibid., advertisement pages.

It is indisputable that the political ability of the Scottish democrat is second to none, and the League appeals to all true patriots to work unceasingly for the freedom and independence of our country, so that ere long Scotland may be restored to her ancient proud situation among the nations of the earth.

SCOTLAND A FREE STATE AGAIN!

GOD SAVE SCOTLAND!

Both Erskine's National Committee and the Highland Land League soon disappeared. But Erskine did not despair, and in 1921 created a much more important organization to express his distinctive views, the Scots National League, with offices in Edinburgh and Erskine as Honorary President. Though advertisements claimed that the League was to be a federation of autonomous branches and that it was to be 'strictly non-party and non-sectarian and . . . open to men and women in favour of Scottish National Rights',[1] it consisted at first of a small core of fundamentalists both in London and in Scotland who would have no truck with the existing system of government. The chairman, Hugh Paterson, had, indeed, been associated with most of Erskine's Gaelic schemes, and was a fine actor in Gaelic plays. But the branches soon began to take on a life of their own and the basis of the party quickly broadened. By November 1926 the Scots National League was in a position to start a journal of its own, the *Scots Independent: the Organ of Scottish Nationality* in place of its leaflet called *Monthly Intelligence*. The editor was William Gillies, one of the leaders of the Highland Land League and a Gaelic playwright, the business manager was Thomas Gibson, and the leading writers were at first Angus Clark and Iain Gillies, although a number of the contributors to the *Scottish Review*, such as W. G. Blaikie Murdoch, President of the Edinburgh Branch of the Scots National League, H. G. MacNeacail and Erskine himself, also wrote for the *Scots Independent*.

The official policy of the League, adopted at a conference in January 1925, was quite uncompromising.

We hereby declare

(1) That Scotland, being a distinct nation, has the inalienable right to be recognised as such, and to be accorded that respect consistent with her dignity as a nation;

[1] *Guth na Bliadhna*, XIX (1923–4), advertisement pages.

142

(2) That Scotsmen acting nationally have the sole right to formulate and finally decide upon what scheme of self-government for Scotland shall be adopted, and that any other scheme submitted to the English Parliament for approval or modification or alteration shall be repudiated;

(3) That the relationship between Scotland and England must be mutually agreed upon between those nations acting upon mutual recognition of each other as an independent nation, and with equal powers;

(4) That the relationship between Scotland and the various countries within the Commonwealth of Nations must be a matter for adjustment with all the parties;

(5) That Scotland must be the sole judge of what part she shall take among the nations of the world, and that whether she shall, or shall not co-operate in this respect with other nations must be a matter for her to decide.[1]

Acting in the spirit of this policy the *Scots Independent* rejected the opportunity to take part in the National Convention staged by the Scottish Home Rule Association, and made use of the slogan 'Withdraw from Westminster!'.[2] Yet in the course of 1927 a great change came over the Scots National League. The name of the League was dropped from the title of the *Scots Independent* in March, and in June William Gillies was installed as a joint Honorary President along with Erskine. In the September issue Iain Gillies proclaimed 'Scotland's Need: a National Party' and for the next few months the *Scots Independent* championed the idea of a Scottish National Party free from all association with the other parties and urged the Scottish Home Rule Association to adopt its views. Delegates were appointed, at the invitation of Glasgow University Scottish Nationalist Association, to attend a conference with the object of creating a new national party. In April 1928 Roland Muirhead contributed an article to the *Scots Independent* which suggested that he was at last coming round to the League's point of view, and on 23rd June 1928 the National Party of Scotland held its inaugural meeting at Stirling, where Erskine, MacDiarmid and Hugh Paterson of the League were three of the six principal speakers. There was still some opposition to the idea of fusing the League with the National Party, notably in Edinburgh, but the majority of the League

[1] *Scots Independent*, December 1926, p. 6.
[2] ibid.

agreed to join the National Party, and the services of the *Scots Independent* were transferred from the League to the party as a matter of course.[1]

Though Erskine gave his blessing to the new party, he was the sort of person who never took kindly to organizations and did not care much for those who did not share his passionate dislike of things English. Moreover, he was more interested in ideas than in party machines. It is not therefore surprising that the shift of emphasis within the Scots National League in favour of co-operation with other nationalists, was accompanied by a new Erskine literary venture, the *Pictish Review*.

The *Pictish Review* (1927–8) was very largely written by Hugh MacDiarmid, who about the same time also became an active contributor to the *Scots Independent*. But Erskine's own articles show that his views had not mellowed with the passage of the years. It was a little unlike him to announce that the *Pictish Review* was owned by 'The Union of Picts and Scots'. But probably it was about this time that he began to drift out of nationalist politics. The emphasis of the new journal was on the development of a 'Scottish idea', on the fusion of the Scottish and Gaelic cultural groups in Scotland into a single whole, and on the common Gaelic background of both the Scots and the Picts. Hugh MacDiarmid set to work to distil from Gaelic culture what he regarded as the essence of the Scottish idea. This he defines in the following passage.

> The discipline of the Bardic colleges is what literature most needs to-day. The Gaelic Commonwealth suggests solutions to many of our major social problems. . . . The first step is to abolish the false Highland–Lowland distinction which has been the main obstacle to Scottish unity, and to restore a natural balance to Gaelic policy which has become Westernised and non-centripetal. In other words, the need is to stress the Pictish rather than the Gaelic elements in our Celtic culture.[2]

Because both Erskine and MacDiarmid held so strongly to Celtic traditions at this time, it was inevitable that they should find uncongenial the need to participate with very dissimilar people in the new National Party. MacDiarmid, as is well known, devoted himself to a strange mixture of Douglas social credit, communism and nationalism which took him in and out of the nationalist movements of the next

[1] *Scots Independent*, II (1927–8), 143.
[2] *Pictish Review*, December 1927, p. 14.

forty years.[1] Erskine, soon tiring of what he regarded as the 'collaborationist' tactics of the National Party of Scotland, denounced it in an article in the *Modern Scot* in 1930, and withdrew to the south of France. In what was to be virtually his farewell message he wrote of the National Party:

> I regret to say that instead of orientizing itself by turning its back to Westminster, it on the contrary executed the manoevre by turning its face to it. The existing Constitution is in some sort a reaffirmation of belief in the efficacy for national purposes of prayer and petition 'on the floor of the House'. The expression I doubt not will awaken memories at once melancholy and jocose. It was the favourite formula of the late Mr John Redmond, with whose political collapse one would have thought that it, and the policy that went with it, had perished for ever. . . . National Party circles . . . evidently still believe in the possibility of destroying the English ascendency in Scotland by sending members to the English Parliament. It is a child-like sort of faith to hold. . . .[2]

On this melancholy note we must part with one of the most consistent and able nationalists Scotland has so far produced. Though he lived for another thirty years, his home was usually abroad, and when he died in 1960 he was noted by *The Times* primarily as the writer of a somewhat arid book about the great men he had known, published in 1936.

[1] Major C. H. Douglas's social credit ideas, championed by a major literary periodical, the *New Age*, were taken up by many Scottish nationalists in the twenties and thirties, chiefly, it would appear, because Douglas was a Scot. Douglas's influence was, however, stronger in Canada than in his native land.

[2] *Modern Scot*, I (1930–1), 31.

CHAPTER SEVEN

The Rise and Fall of Literary Nationalism

I

There is a strong tradition of expository writing in Scottish church life which leads many parish ministers into journalism. For many years much the best known of these men was William Robertson Nicoll, who gave up his Kelso charge in 1886 and moved to London, where he was editor simultaneously of the *Expositor*, the *British Weekly* and the *Bookman*. The *British Weekly* soon became the chosen reading of thousands of Scots Presbyterians and English nonconformists, and Robertson Nicoll became himself an influential figure in British public life. A recognized ally of the Campbell-Bannerman and Asquith ministries he was knighted in 1909 and moved in the highest political circles. Nicoll was not a political nationalist, but he was a strong Scottish patriot when by his own fireside, and he preferred to find Scottish authors for the numerous serial articles which appeared in his papers and for the publishers with whom he was associated. As a result, Scottish writers found it easier to make their mark than at any time before or since. A little school of inferior writers—the Kailyard school as they were nicknamed by their detractors—secured a quite adventitious popularity.[1] And there was a seemingly unlimited market for the work of rather better writers like Norman Maclean, a minister in Edinburgh, so long as they wrote on Scottish topics. The Scottish story became a regular feature of English journalism and enjoyed the sort of vogue which Harry Lauder enjoyed in the English music hall. Furthermore, James Barrie, one of the writers associated with the Kailyard school, turned out to be a successful playwright. Scottish writing in this way became firmly established as a prominent feature of the British literary scene, and Scots back home felt a glow of patriotic pride in the achievements of their fellow countrymen.

[1] There are innumerable articles about the Kailyard school. For a general survey see George Blake, *Barrie and the Kailyard School* (London, 1951).

146

The Rise and Fall of Literary Nationalism

About the same time as Robertson Nicoll was building up his literary empire in London the character of the daily press was changing. The formal layout of the middle of the nineteenth century was giving way to the easy informality of the London letter, the contributed article, the banner headline, the pen and ink sketch and the photograph. A new type of journalist emerged, who was encouraged to express himself freely and develop a *rapport* with his readers—men like Wilfred Taylor, who today contributes a highly individual commentary on what he sees to *The Scotsman*. These men found a ready market both for books of reprinted articles and for hastily-put-together books on a wide range of subjects in which they expected their readers to be interested. The work of Neil Munro (1864–1930) has remained popular to this day—particularly his Para Handy stories—but the work of other writers, such as William Power of the *Glasgow Herald* and the *Scots Observer*, has been forgotten.[1] They were none the less an important social influence in Scotland, because under their guidance a whole generation grew up which took for granted as their cultural milieu a sort of romantic Scottish patriotism based on dialect stories, the cult of Bonnie Prince Charlie, Burns, and the 'characters' of Scottish towns and villages. Much of the writing of the time was akin to that of the Kailyard school, as was perhaps natural at a time when the writers for the daily press quite often contributed to the *British Weekly*, as well as to their own paper. But its purpose was more serious.

Even before the war of 1914–18 Scottish journalists began to dream of a Scottish cultural renaissance involving letters, painting, architecture and drama. In the years after the war when existing institutions were being challenged all over the world it was natural for journalists to suggest that at last the long awaited new era had come. Lewis Spence, who had worked for a time both for *The Scotsman* and the *British Weekly*, and seems to have made his living by writing travel books and adventure stories, contributed an article entitled 'The Scottish Literary Renaissance' to the *Nineteenth Century and After* in 1926,[2] which made much of the Scottish writers of the early twenties and was widely commented upon. In particular he drew attention to the emphasis placed by the new generation of Scottish writers on the use of Scots; 'The central fact regarding the Scottish Renaissance', he

---

[1] Power also wrote an autobiography, *Should Auld Acquaintance . . .* (London, 1937).
[2] *Nineteenth Century and After*, C (1926), 123–33.

wrote, 'is that the rising generation of Scottish poets are beginning to recognise that they must be bilingual'.[1] Most discussion about the 'Scottish renaissance', however, confused two things, the achievement of a small group of poets, of whom the best was Hugh MacDiarmid, and the existence of a great flood of publications collected from newspapers and magazines both in verse and in prose. Of much of this flood the best that could be said was that it helped to keep the authors alive or that it demonstrated that verse writing was not confined to any particular class. Indeed, even the Scottish farm servants produced a poet of their own[2] to place alongside such overrated versifiers as Charles Murray and James C. Welsh, the Lanarkshire miner.

The main importance of the 'Scottish renaissance' was that it created the illusion that a good many people in Scotland could live by their pens and that there was an economic basis for a national literary movement comparable with that which had occurred in various parts of Europe almost a century before. The Scottish newspapers, the reviews, the little magazines, became the equivalent of the Czech drawing-rooms before 1848 and of the literary salons for Young Ireland in the 1830s. It did not matter in the short run that the one real man of genius in the company, Hugh MacDiarmid, was ill adapted to secure the sort of popular success which fashion demanded. He was no Tom Moore, but a latter-day Carlyle writing in an environment in which Carlyle was utterly disregarded. Apart from MacDiarmid, the men who came to the top were sharp-penned 'literary gents' like Lewis Spence, good honest newspaper columnists like William Power, successful novelists like Compton Mackenzie and Eric Linklater (it looked for a time as though John Buchan might join in too) and that eccentric literary figure, part novelist, part romantic hero, R. B. Cunninghame Graham. Contemporary Scottish nationalism, in short, first became popular thanks to run of the mill literary handymen rather than as a result of the work of prophets like Ruaraidh Erskine, John Maclean and Hugh MacDiarmid. Even the picturesque Wendy Wood fits into the category of literary figures, since she is a prolific writer of articles and poems which are worked up into book form.

The first body to express the point of view of these literary men was a little group formed by Lewis Spence in Edinburgh in 1926 as a breakaway from the Scots National League, to which he gave the grandiloquent title of the Scottish National Movement. But the main outlet for

---

[1] ibid., 133.
[2] Andrew Dodds, *The Lothian Land* (Aberdeen, 1918).

literary enthusiasm was the National Party of Scotland founded in 1928.

What these literary men had to say was for the most part pretty conventional. Indeed, it is tempting to say of most of them that they merely expressed a nostalgia for the pre-1914 world with its calm expectation that Scottish national pride would receive its fillip in due course in the shape of Home Rule. In this sense Scottish writers were merely saying what the majority of Scottish M.P.s from 1906 to 1918 had been accustomed to saying. But there was also something peculiar to the post-war world: the emphasis on the need to develop a distinctively Scottish cultural movement—preferably based on Glasgow—which led among other things to the creation of a Scottish Centre of P.E.N. In addition some of the figures active in the Scottish renaissance had more down-to-earth interests and William Power, for instance, claims to have first suggested in the *Scots Observer* the creation of what afterwards became the Scottish National Development Council.[1] As against this, the Scottish literary world produced more than its share of extremists. Those who were prepared to believe that there was something important to be made of the national habit of singing Jacobite songs and of the wearing of the kilt, were relatively harmless. Enthusiasts like that could sometimes be put to use in bodies like the Scottish Watch which did valuable youth work, and in the movement to revive Scottish song and dance, but they were of very little value to Scottish nationalism as a political movement. But not all were so harmless. The development in Scotland of a small group of writers who delighted in attacking the demigods of Scottish popular culture in the manner of Lytton Strachey gave the Scottish literary renaissance a rather off-beat reputation. Catherine Carswell on Burns, Donald Carswell in a Stracheyesque series of essays called *Brother Scots*, George Malcolm Thomson in *Caledonia*, and a variety of writers in essays on Sir Walter Scott did their best to 'debunk' Scottish values.

One feature of this debunking was a growing habit of attacking Presbyterianism, so long regarded as the core of Scottish culture. In a little book of essays on the Scottish renaissance George Scott Moncrieff, for instance, wrote:

What has the Kirk given us? Ugly churches and services, identifying in the minds of churchgoers ugliness with God, have stifled the

---

[1] Power, *Should Auld Acquaintance*, p. 157.

Scottish arts almost out of existence. The cruelty similarly identified with the Deity has repressed the whole race. . . .

Always excepting the exceptions . . . the Scots minister if he is ardent has, owing to his misbegotten Calvinism, a mindful of pious sadism, combined, to do him justice, with a similarly pious masochism; otherwise he is lazy in his pride of being raised to the Ministry, 'almost a gentleman'.

The Kirk has failed. . . . It is a Defeatist Creed, and until the Kirk as it has been is dead Scotland will continue to be the Home of Lost Causes.[1]

While all this may have seemed true enough, it is just the sort of thing that alienates sober citizens with a strong sense of Scottish patriotism centred in their Church. As a result, there soon opened up a gulf between those Scottish writers who were influenced primarily by literary fashion, notably the writers for the daily papers, and the writers who regarded themselves as nationalists first and foremost. The cry that the nationalists were simply irresponsible poets and papists gained ground. And it remained the fashion in Edinburgh drawing-rooms right down to the time of the Covenant movement after the Second World War to sneer at nationalism as the last resort of crackpots.

II

The existence side by side of the different types of nationalist activity represented by the Scottish Home Rule Association, the Scots National League, and the literary men, notably Lewis Spence's Scottish National Movement, was clearly a nonsense. But for a time there seemed to be no way out. Roland Muirhead tried to bring all three groups together in a National Convention, but the Scots National League rightly pointed out that the Scottish Home Rule Association and the League stood for different things. The S.H.R.A. advocated devolution within the existing structure of the United Kingdom, whereas the S.N.L. stood squarely for breaking up the United Kingdom as soon as possible. It was not until a catalyst was found in the form of the Glasgow University Scottish Nationalist Association that the rival groups were prepared to come together to form the National Party of Scotland.

[1] D. C. Thomson, ed., *Scotland in Quest of Her Youth: a Scrutiny* (Edinburgh and London, 1932), pp. 71–2.

The Rise and Fall of Literary Nationalism

The Glasgow University Scottish Nationalist Association was the product almost of chance. In October 1928 there was to be a rectorial election in Glasgow University and a number of students were interested in making it a lively one. There was no student nationalist organization and in the ordinary course of events the election would have been fought by the nominees of the established political parties. There was, however, a vague feeling that the parties did not make the right sort of appeal to Glasgow students, and a small group of Labour students began to cast about for an unusual candidate. Their leader was John MacCormick, a law student who was working in a solicitor's office as well as attending classes at the university, who has since told the story of the campaign in his *The Flag in the Wind*.[1] MacCormick and his friends were at first at a loss for a suitable candidate, but they eventually lit on the name of Cunninghame Graham, and persuaded him to become their candidate. They then turned for help to Roland Muirhead, but found that instead of offering assistance he expected them to take part in the work of his National Convention. In fact it soon became clear that the students alone had the enthusiasm, the dynamism and the capacity for hard lobbying which a nationalist movement needed, with the result that the rectorial election campaign provided the background for the formation of the National Party of Scotland.

The rectorial election campaign turned out to be something of a *tour de force*. Nationalism and the magic of Cunninghame Graham's reputation were reinforced by brilliant heckling and speaking. Indeed, the students seem all unknowingly to have repeated many of the ploys employed by nationalists in Glasgow rectorials in the 1850s from which some posters survive in the Mitchell Library. But the main feature of the campaign was the attention it attracted in literary circles. Hilaire Belloc and G. K. Chesterton promised to speak, and when they could not were replaced by Compton Mackenzie who had recently settled in Scotland.[2] Hugh MacDiarmid also wrote and spoke in favour of Cunninghame Graham and for the first time became a well-known platform speaker.[3] But it was the students who demonstrated to a surprised Scottish public that nationalism was a force to be

[1] J. M. MacCormick, *The Flag in the Wind: the Story of the National Movement in Scotland* (London, 1955).

[2] Compton Mackenzie, *My Life and Times: Octave Six* (London, 1967) includes an account of his part in the election.

[3] For MacDiarmid's trenchant views of the candidates see *Scots Independent*, II (1927–8), 115–16, 169–70.

151

reckoned with among the young. For at the close of the poll Cunning-hame Graham was only sixty-six votes behind the Prime Minister, Stanley Baldwin, for whom a runaway victory had been predicted.[1]

The sense of euphoria created by the Glasgow rectorial election was an important factor in the creation of the National Party of Scotland. But it was not the only one. The actual suggestion that nationalists of all schools should come together in a single party was apparently made by T. H. Gibson of the Scots National League, who subsequently became one of the most influential members of the Scottish National Party. He seems to have been able to draw on a general feeling that it was time nationalism ceased to be a literary movement and began to fight elections. The Glasgow rectorial election had revealed that there was popular enthusiasm for nationalism among the young. The strength of the Scots National League was such that it looked as though a nationwide nationalist movement would be viable. And the Home Rulers were temporarily in eclipse because parliamentary devolution seemed to have been shelved by the existing political parties. In April 1928 it was agreed that a new party should be formed, on 23rd June 1928 it celebrated its inauguration at a Bannockburn Day celebration at Stirling, and shortly afterwards the names of four parliamentary candidates were announced: Roland Muirhead in Renfrewshire West, J. M. MacCormick in Glasgow–Camlachie, C. M. Grieve (Hugh MacDiarmid) in Dundee,[2] and Lewis Spence in an undefined Midlothian constituency. And at the end of the year the party held its first conference at which Cunninghame Graham was elected President, Roland Muirhead Chairman, Lewis Spence Vice-Chairman, and John MacCormick, Honorary Secretary.

Curiously enough, it was left to Lewis Spence to explain the new party's aims and objects in the *Edinburgh Review*.[3] Very much a moderate himself he announced that the party would 'function through parliamentary representatives at Westminster, as well as by means of propagandist effort on Scottish soil'. This was clearly an attempt to ward off the likely criticism that it was an anti-parliamentary body like the Scots National League. The objects of the party Spence described in terms of the draft constitution as 'self-government for Scotland with

[1] The voting was S. Baldwin (Unionist) 1,044, R. B. Cunninghame Graham (Nationalist) 978, Sir Herbert Samuel (Liberal) 396, Rosslyn Mitchell (Labour) 226. *Scots Independent*, III (1928–9), 16.

[2] MacDiarmid ceased to be a candidate when he moved to London in 1929.

[3] 'The National Party of Scotland', *Edinburgh Review*, CCXLVIII (1928), 70–87.

independent national status within the British group of nations, together with the reconstruction of Scottish national life'. But the main emphasis of Spence's article was on the cramping effects of Whitehall control over Scotland and on the numerous problems confronting the Scottish economy.

The great weakness of the National Party during its first few years was the lack of experience of most of its members of the day-to-day business of conducting a political party. Parties can put up with a good deal of internal dissension and disagreement about their objectives, provided that they have a well-organized set of branches capable of standing on their own feet, and enough workers to do the amount of house-to-house visiting which is necessary before the electors are prepared to believe that a party means business. Lord Beaverbrook was undoubtedly right when he told John MacCormick that the National Party should have started by contesting municipal elections, where organization counts for less than in parliamentary elections, in order to help build up a grassroots organization.[1] But the leaders of the National Party all had a horror of machine politics, and preferred to pit eloquence against organization. This led in January 1929 to a crushing defeat in North Midlothian and Peebles, where Lewis Spence stood as a candidate at a by-election, and then to two rather poor results in the 1929 general election, before the party learned its lesson.

The success of the Glasgow rectorial election and the fact that the National Party had begun to fight elections caused a good deal of hasty rethinking in the established political parties. The Unionist Party in Scotland for the most part stood firmly behind the Union, although a few nationalist noises were made in various parts of Scotland. But the Liberal Party hastened to resurrect a Home Rule scheme drawn up by the Scottish Liberal Federation in 1924, to which Sir Herbert Samuel gave his blessing in the course of the North Midlothian and Peebles by-election. And a good many individual Labour M.P.s and Labour supporters renewed old pledges of support for Home Rule. This had the effect of dividing Home Rulers from Nationalists (the Duke of Montrose, for instance, supported the Liberal candidate in Midlothian against Lewis Spence), and of creating a certain amount of confusion among the electors. Nationalists, as a result, found themselves driven to readjust their time scales. Hence we find Compton Mackenzie writing in March 1929 that 'To my mind it would be better to wait for thirty years and die at the end of it with every dream unfulfilled than

[1] MacCormick, *The Flag in the Wind*, p. 61.

accept such a parody of a nation's life' as was offered by the Liberals and Labour.[1]

More important, the discovery that the path of the National Party was going to be a rough one produced an immediate demand for a purge of the party. Lewis Spence after the Midlothian by-election wrote bitterly:

> The general movement in favour of a national rebirth has attracted some of the finest and most generous spirits in Scotland—and many of the greatest cranks in Christendom. . . .
>
> I am all for the new nationalism, but at the moment it presents to me a maelström boiling and bubbling with the cross-currents of rival and frequently fantastic theories, schemes and notions, riotous with tumultuous personality and convulsive with petulant individual predilection. . . . If Scotland is to survive as a nation a strong curb must be put upon the blatant egotism of many of her protagonists. . . . Every month produces its harvest of new 'poets', critics, and theorists, political and literary, until the mind reels before the kaleidoscopic confusion displayed by their multi-coloured and frequently absurd doctrines.
>
> We have people who want all Scotland to speak the Gaelic, and who hate Braid Scots, people who continue the Old Language and clatter out a gutter Scots with an English basis of syntax in the sad belief that it is the genuine article. Some hark back to the hope of a sixteenth-century Scotland regained, others suggest a national approchement with France, still others a Jacobite restoration. A certain group sees in the expulsion of all the English and Irish in Scotland the country's only chance of survival. Some look to Labour, others to Liberalism, others, and these the most national, to a Scottish National Party which would send representatives to Westminster for the hope of securing self-government. Some desire the ruin of the Empire, others to strengthen it. Some are zealous and well-equipped propagandists; others the very reverse, the mouthing orators of small mutual admiration societies. Certain circles cry out for the settlement of every acre of deer forest by all and sundry, irrespective of agricultural experience or ability. We are informed by one school of critics that only if Scotland returns to the Catholic fold shall she be able to rekindle the fires of her art, by another, equally absurd, that the Presbyterian faith alone is the true guiding star of Scottish

---

[1] *Scots Independent*, III (1928–9), 59.

artistic effort. The members of the Kailyard genre still blaze up occasionally, and the new poets and critics stamp rather ostentatiously and unnecessarily upon its half-quenched cinders. All is hubbub, outcry, chaos. There is no chart, no plan, nothing approaching a serious, practical Scotsman-like policy in either art or politics.[1]

It is impossible not to sympathize with Spence's outburst and with his cry that 'Those of us who were [the Scottish renaissance's] first and, I think, its reasonable protagonists, now find ourselves hemmed in on the one side by the grey-beard Kailyarders, spluttering anathemas in the bad Scots of the Poet's Corner, and the hysterical youngsters who write and speak of us as if we were already moss-grown antiquities'. But the sad truth was that neither Spence nor the other literary men in the National Party had the interest or the talent to organize a political party.

Erskine of Marr, clear-sighted as ever, recognized that once the literary men joined forces with those whose primary interest was in winning elections, the literary men (who were for him the true nationalists) would be thrust on one side. In an article in the same number of the *Scots Independent* as that in which Spence's article appeared, he argued that, while there was a strong case for greater discipline, it could only be secured by abandoning the policy of sending members to Westminster. Purity of principle should come first, and this meant building up a movement undistracted by the business of fighting elections. For fighting elections involved a serious risk of nationalists being outbidden by the Labour and Liberal parties and of constant internal tension in the nationalist movement.

For most nationalists, however, there was no going back on the decision of 1928, which meant that the National Party of Scotland became increasingly dependent on its one man with a talent for electoral organization, John MacCormick. MacCormick was a young man and an ambitious one. He was determined to make the National Party a success, and he accordingly placed his primary emphasis on those things that were likely to lead to success. By background and temperament he was disposed to regard Home Rule rather than independence as the more acceptable goal for the party. And he was clearly concerned that the Scottish Liberal Federation's 1924 Home Rule policy was not so very different from what he himself wanted. He

[1] ibid., III (1928–9), 65–6.

therefore inaugurated the policy, with which he was to be identified for the next twenty years, of emphasizing the reasonableness and moderation of the National Party.

With such a man as its organizer the National Party was unlikely to hold together for very long. But for a time events conspired to give the party a certain unity. The Local Government Act of 1929 which emasculated the smaller Scottish local authorities, was very unpopular in Scotland (it still is) and brought Home Rulers and fundamentalists together because both regarded it as a clear breach of the Treaty of Union. MacCormick talked for a time of no longer acknowledging the authority of the United Kingdom parliament and of refusing to pay taxes. And William Gillies, as editor of the *Scots Independent*, was able to keep the fundamentalists in line.[1] Old-style Home Rulers began to talk of withdrawing from Westminster and fundamentalists were willing to tolerate a campaign to win parliamentary elections. Party membership began to grow (it was moving up towards 4,000 by May 1930)[2] and all seemed to be going well. There was no money in the party coffers, but that did not seem to matter, except to the party organizers who were disappointed that they simply could not afford to send speakers into the villages. Moreover, in 1931 the National Party received a great boost to its morale when Compton Mackenzie was triumphantly elected Lord Rector of Glasgow University.[3] In retrospect John MacCormick was to speak of it as a Pyrrhic victory, because the enemies of the party made much of Mackenzie's Roman Catholicism, and even spread it abroad that MacCormick was an Irish Catholic.[4] But this was to take the usual undercurrents of political nastiness too seriously. Occurring as it did in the middle of the 1931 general election the rectorial victory gave a much-needed boost to nationalist morale.

In parliamentary elections the National Party made sufficient impact on the voters to show that it counted, and gradually came to be accepted by the press and by parliament as a significant feature of Scottish life. The first venture at North Midlothian and Peebles pro-

---

[1] ibid., III (1928–9), 83.

[2] ibid., IV (1929–30), 100.

[3] The result was Compton Mackenzie (Nationalist) 849, Sir Robert Horne (Unionist) 762, Professor Gilbert Murray (Liberal) 581, Thomas Johnston (Labour) 110, Sir Oswald Mosley (New Party) 21. For Mackenzie's account of the matter see his *My Life and Times: Octave Seven* (London, 1968), pp. 19–44 *passim*.

[4] MacCormick, *The Flag in the Wind*, pp. 51–3.

duced only 842 votes in January 1929, and at the general election of 1929 John MacCormick secured only 1,646 votes in Glasgow–Camlachie and Roland Muirhead 1,667 in West Renfrewshire. But thereafter things quickly improved. J. M. McNicol obtained 2,527 votes at a by-election in Glasgow–Shettleston in June 1930 and Oliver Brown obtained 4,818 at East Renfrewshire in November 1930, the first nationalist candidate not to lose his deposit. Moreover, the party's share of the vote rose steadily—4·1 per cent in North Midlothian and Peebles, 4·8 per cent in Glasgow–Camlachie, 5·0 per cent in West Renfrewshire, 10·1 per cent in Glasgow–Shettleston and 13·0 per cent in East Renfrewshire—and the party membership began to grow quite rapidly until by May 1931 it had nearly reached 8,000. Once the party had begun to do reasonably well at elections it became a steady votegetter, down to the general election of 1935, though naturally enough some constituencies were more reluctant to take nationalism seriously than others. What was most significant about the seats fought by the National Party was that, apart from a side show based on Inverness after 1931, they were all in urban areas—the mining area of Midlothian, Renfrewshire East and West, Glasgow–Camlachie, –Shettleston and –St. Rollox, Dunbarton, East Edinburgh, Montrose Burghs, East Fife, Kilmarnock and Greenock. The National Party was committed to tackling the Scottish heartland rather than the Celtic fringe.

One of the odder features of the National Party's election campaign was that they from time to time received a good deal of quite fortuitous outside support. The *Daily Record* was very sympathetic, so was the B.B.C., and so was the *Daily Express*. On one occasion Lord Beaverbrook wrote a favourable article in the *Express* about Scottish Nationalism (14th July 1932) and he also offered the support of his Empire Free Trade campaign to National Party candidates who gave appropriate pledges.[1] One consequence of this outside interest was that the National Party leaders became conscious that there was a good deal of support to be had from outside the National Party if only the National Party adjusted its appeal to bring in a wider range of people. The first Glasgow rectorial campaign had brought a number of Conservative students into the Party, including Miss Elma Campbell, who fought Glasgow–St. Rollox at a by-election in 1931 and again at the subsequent general election. The problem was how to appeal to the much greater number of Conservatives and Liberals with nationalist leanings who were still in the Unionist and Liberal parties.

[1] MacCormick, *The Flag in the Wind*, pp. 50, 57–78.

III

The 1931 general election was the last occasion on which the various segments of the National Party co-operated reasonably harmoniously. The Scottish literary renaissance was enjoying its last major flourish in the *Modern Scot*, the best nationalist journal of opinion since the *Scottish Review*. Public opinion was generally sympathetic to the demand for greater devolution of administration from London to Edinburgh. The economic depression and the unemployment that went with it did not yet seem to present a real threat to nationalism as a point of view. And many of the newspapers were vaguely sympathetic. Moreover, John MacCormick had hit upon a propaganda device, The Covenant, which seemed capable of holding the nationalist movement together by drawing it into a revivalist campaign. The Covenant itself, the nationalist equivalent of the temperance pledge, was intended to reawaken echoes of the past in Presbyterian hearts and to persuade men of goodwill that nationalism was a viable policy. But it was so worded that it was not needlessly offensive to the fundamentalists. Launched at a great demonstration at Stirling on 21st June 1930 it read:[1]

THE COVENANT

We, the undersigned, holding a high ideal of our nation's destiny, believe in the urgent necessity of Self government for Scotland. In the faith that a regenerated Scotland will take a leading place among the nations of the world in all peaceful progress, we solemnly pledge ourselves to do everything in our power to restore the independent national status of Scotland.

We bind ourselves to act on our belief that the mandate of a majority of Scottish citizens is sufficient authority for setting up an Independent Parliament in Scotland.

MacCormick and his immediate circle were anxious to broaden the base of the party and to win public recognition for it as a serious movement on a par with the other major political movements in Scotland. They saw it as a sort of crusade to educate and coax the public into supporting the creation of a Scottish parliament. Because the public was unlikely to respond to coaxing by the National Party if

[1] *Scots Independent*, IV (1929–30), Suppl. to July 1930 issue.

the party was associated with such people as Hugh MacDiarmid, who was widely suspected of being a dangerous man, there was a growing tendency for MacCormick to grow impatient with the more Radical literary men in the party, whom he regarded as little better than saboteurs. But for a time nothing happened. Then MacCormick saw his chance. In June 1932 there was a revolt in the Unionist Association in the Cathcart Division of Glasgow, which declared itself in favour of Imperial Federation and Scottish Home Rule—the Milner programme of the pre-war years with a dash of Lord Beaverbrook added. The revolt was generously reported in the Glasgow *Daily Record* and it soon spread to other parts of Scotland and to Scots working south of the border. Kevan McDowall, the leader of the revolt, was an enthusiast, and with the aid of such recruits as the Duke of Montrose, Sir Alexander MacEwen of Inverness, and Andrew Dewar Gibb, later Regius Professor of [Scots] Law at Glasgow University, he determined to found a moderate nationalist party ('the Moderates'), which eventually took shape as the Scottish Party. The programme of this new party was largely drawn up by Sir Alexander MacEwen, who took the precaution of consulting John MacCormick in advance, so that it would not be needlessly offensive to the National Party.[1] As a result there was from the first every chance of the Scottish Party amalgamating with the National Party.

The Scottish Party was just the sort of party MacCormick approved of. It boasted a great name (the Duke of Montrose), a notable public figure (Sir Alexander MacEwen), a patriotic lawyer (Andrew Dewar Gibb) and a first-rate organizer (Kevan McDowall). It had good press connections. And its policy was a gradualist one that pointed to Home Rule rather than independence. The opportunity for broadening the base of the National Party had come and MacCormick was determined to make the most of it. He therefore launched a debate about the future of the National Party, designed to lead to a change in the aims and objects of the party.

MacCormick's aim was to bring the policy of the National Party into line with that of the Scottish Party, and to secure acceptance of the principle that the National Party should seek a broader base by amalgamating with the Scottish Party and other suitable organizations should they exist. The change of policy was openly discussed in the *Scots Independent*, with the majority of the party executive taking MacCormick's view and Hugh Paterson, the former chairman of the

[1] MacCormick, *The Flag in the Wind*, p. 66. MacEwen was a Liberal in politics.

159

Scots National League, advocating a stiffening of the party line by reverting to the policy of the Scots National League. For a time it looked as though MacCormick might be beaten. At a delegate conference in Glasgow on 27th May 1933 there was heated opposition to the change of policy and the conference very nearly broke up. A revised policy statement was carried by 69 votes to 45, but the proposal that the executive council should be empowered to negotiate with the Scottish Party and other bodies was defeated late in the day by 47 votes to 40.[1] Neither side could claim a victory and MacCormick's position was now intolerable. He, therefore, proposed the drastic step of a purge of the party which took the form of the expulsion of the South-East Area Council, based on Edinburgh, and the London Branch. At a special conference on 1st July which met in secret session MacCormick was trounced by Angus Clark, a native Gaelic speaker, who spoke out for Erskine of Marr's policy, but he had the big West of Scotland battalions on his side. The expulsions were agreed to by 72 votes to 57[2] and at a stroke the party lost somewhere about one-fifth of its membership. Soon afterwards the National Party and the Scottish Party co-operated at a by-election at Kilmarnock, and on 20th April 1934 the two parties merged to become the Scottish National Party.

IV

The purge of 1933 (sinister date) gave control of the National Party to those whose aim was that of the Scottish Home Rule Association's Bills of 1926–28—Home Rule within the British Commonwealth—and who eschewed romantic literary flourishes. There was now no place in the National Party either for Erskine of Marr and the Gaelic militants of the Scots National League, or for most of the wild young literary men. They were driven into the wilderness, from which they bitterly watched what appeared to be a revival of the Kailyard—above all in the Scottish newspaper press—and a conscious turning away from the venturesome optimism of the twenties. At the same time they were forced to realize that the nationalism which they cherished did not hold the answer to the problem of world economic disorganization and world poverty. Nationalism, by contrast with Communism and Fascism, seemed a puny thing—yet it was more humane, more liberal, more desirable than either. A nationalist

[1] *Scots Independent*, VII (1932–3), 135.
[2] *The Scotsman*, 4th July 1933.

version of Douglas social credit offered some sort of outlet, but it was always a minority cult, and lacked the prestige of Marxism.

Finally, there was the great literary war between Edwin Muir and Hugh MacDiarmid, which finally destroyed such unity as there had been in the Scottish literary camp. Muir, an Orkney man, had watched the rise of literary nationalism in the twenties from abroad. He avowed himself a nationalist, became one of the spokesmen of the Scottish centre of P.E.N. which had been started by MacDiarmid, and took up the cause of the Scottish renaissance. But Muir was never an enthusiast. In 1927 he wrote to his brother-in-law:

> When we were in Scotland last time we heard a lot about Scottish Nationalism from C. M. Grieve who wrote *A Drunk Man Looks at the Thistle*. It seems a pity that Scotland should always be kept back by England, and I hope the Scottish Republic comes about: it would make Scotland worth living in. Grieve is a strong nationalist, republican, socialist, and every thing that is out and out. He thinks that if Scotland were a nation we would have Scottish literature, art, music, culture and everything that other nations seem to have and we haven't. I think that would probably be likely; but I feel rather detached . . . because after all I'm not Scotch, I'm an Orkneyman, a good Scandinavian. . . .[1]

As the years went by Muir became less and less hopeful about the prospect of a Scottish national revival. And in 1935 and 1936 he finally did to Scottish letters what John MacCormick had done to the National Party—he endeavoured to conduct a sort of intellectual demolition job. In *Scottish Journey* (1935) he wrote that:

> Though Scotland has not been a nation for some time, it has possessed a distinctly marked style of life; and that is now falling to pieces, for there is no visible and effective power to hold it together. . . . The impulse of Scottish Nationalism at its best comes from a quite sincere conviction that the course of Scottish history needs to be changed; but it is probable that the change can come only from outside, from a change in the structure of civilised society in general, by means of which all nations will be given a new start and all peoples taken into a new federation.[2]

[1] P. H. Butter, *Edwin Muir: Man and Poet* (Edinburgh and London, 1966,) pp. 111–12.
[2] ibid., pp. 146–7.

And in the following year he launched a concealed but obvious enough attack on Hugh MacDiarmid in *Scott and Scotland*, where he argued that Scottish writers should abandon the use of Scots for English. This was an attack on the 'No Language, No Nation' school of thought with a vengeance and it destroyed what little was left of the dreams of the Scottish renaissance. The Kailyard rejoiced, safe in the employment of the daily papers, and applauded Muir. MacDiarmid could now be excommunicated with a good conscience.

Erskine of Marr was safely out of the way in Mediterranean lands, but for MacDiarmid this was the final betrayal. His own work was going through a difficult phase, torn apart by the fact that while he preached the writing of Scots he was himself writing in English. His finances, never in good shape, were in a bad way, and he, too, retreated —to Shetland. In his *Literary History of Scotland* published in 1903 John Hepburn Millar (the man so reprobated by T. D. Wanliss) had rejoiced that 'The conditions of Scottish life and society seem almost to preclude the possibility of the existence of a distinctive literary class or caste in Scotland' and that there was no danger 'that the practice of literature should be reserved for a self-elected coterie of experts'.[1] The Scottish literary renaissance had stood for the principle that the Scottish nation needed a Scottish literary class to give meaning and depth to its culture and to put Scotland on the map of Europe. John MacCormick and Edwin Muir alike preferred to opt for a purely provincial Scotland managed by local politicians without any sense of a higher national purpose. Celtic Scotland was not to follow Celtic Ireland into independence, but was to opt for second-class status within the United Kingdom, with its literary standards set by the *Glasgow Herald* and *The Scotsman* or by the English press, rather than by the national poets.

[1] J. H. Millar, *The Literary History of Scotland* (London, 1903), pp. 682–3.

CHAPTER EIGHT

The Scottish National Party

I

The Scottish National Party started life in 1934 with a well-established base and a Home Rule policy. Though Cunninghame Graham was still Honorary President, the chief officers of the party, apart from John MacCormick himself, were drawn from the Scottish Party. The Duke of Montrose was first President and Sir Alexander MacEwen the first Chairman. Moreover, the policies of the party were a public guarantee that the S.N.P. had broken with its past. The 1928 policy of the National Party had emphasized the *independence* of Scotland—'Self-government for Scotland with Independent National Status within the British Group of Nations'—very much in terms of the 1926 Imperial Conference definition of dominion status ('Autonomous communities equal in status and in no way subordinate to one another in any aspect of their domestic or external affairs'). This might mean different things to different people, but could reasonably be construed, as it was construed in 1933, as 'The aim of the National Party of Scotland is to restore to the ancient Scots Nation and People their former Freedom to govern themselves'.[1] By contrast the S.N.P. programme emphasized the desire of the Scots to be treated as equals in the United Kingdom and to retain their share in the management of the empire. Indeed, it is not too much to say that the programme chiefly reflected the views of Andrew Dewar Gibb of the Scottish Party, whose books emphasize the Scottish contribution to the development of the empire and the need for the English to adopt more Scottish ideas into their law and life. The actual wording of the original programme was as follows:

> The object of the Party is Self-Government for Scotland on a basis which will enable Scotland as a partner in the British Empire with the same status as England to develop its National Life to the fullest advantage.

[1] *Scots Independent*, VII (1932–3), 92–3.

The Policy of the Party for the achievement of that object is that—

(a) There shall be established in Scotland a Parliament which shall be the final authority on all Scottish affairs including Taxation and Finance.

(b) Scotland shall share with England the rights and responsibilities they as Mother Nations have jointly created and incurred within the British Empire.

(c) Scotland and England shall set up machinery to deal jointly with these responsibilities and in particular with such matters as Defence, Foreign Policy and Customs.

(d) The Scottish National Party shall be independent of all other political Parties.

The Party shall pursue the achievement of its objects by all such methods as shall be determined by the Party assembled in National Conference or by the National Council from time to time, and in particular the Party shall contest Parliamentary elections, and shall present a programme of national re-construction.

MEMBERSHIP

All persons who signify their adherence to the Objects and Policy of the Party shall be eligible for membership of the Party. The Party shall be non-sectarian.[1]

This policy was essentially of MacCormick's making, and was to be the prelude to a *rapprochement* with the other political parties committed to Home Rule and to a membership drive on a large scale. The proof of the new pudding was to be its success in attracting new sources of support. Accordingly, the party looked forward to the 1935 general election in the expectation that S.N.P. candidates would do better than National Party candidates had done. But when it came to the crunch the S.N.P. did worse in its traditional urban heartland than before. The only compensation was that Sir Alexander MacEwen's accession to the party was a help in the far north. The figures given by the *Scots Independent* in order to underline the S.N.P. failure were as follows:

	1935 percentage	Previous election percentage
Greenock	3·34	—
Kilmarnock	6·24	16·88 (1933)
Dunbarton	7·79	13·45 (1932)

[1] *Scots Independent*, May 1934, cover.

East Renfrewshire	10·43	13·91 (1931)
West Renfrewshire	11·30	10·96 (1931)
Inverness	16·09	14·01 (1931)
Western Isles	28·06	—

By the beginning of 1936 the *Scots Independent* (now an independent journal)[1] had plucked up the courage to publish an article which suggested that the chief reasons for this failure were connected with the fusion of 1933, which in retrospect now seemed to have been a mistake:

> The tampering with the wording of the Object and Policy of the Party which began in 1932 and culminated at the fusion of the National Party of Scotland with the Scottish Party, must be held as being chiefly responsible for the weakening of the enthusiasm of its members.
>
> Some immediate results of this were the resignation from the Party of a number of hard-working and enthusiastic Scottish Nationalists, the expulsion of others and the incoming into the S.N.P. of some very moderate Nationalists.
>
> But more damaging to the Party was its act in putting at its head a member of the Scottish nobility, that relic of the past, an action distasteful to the democracy of Scotland.[2]

There was clearly strong feeling in the party that something must be done, and John MacCormick gave way under pressure with the result that at the 1936 conference of the S.N.P. the party officers were changed (R. E. Muirhead became Honorary President, Sir Alexander MacEwen President and Professor Andrew Dewar Gibb Chairman), though the key officers were still chosen from the Scottish Party. The party Objects were also revised to read:

Object: Self-Government for Scotland;
Policy: The establishment in Scotland of a Parliament which shall be the final authority on all Scottish affairs;
The Party shall be non-sectarian and independent of all political parties.

These changes, however, were mere window dressing. MacCormick was as determined as ever to get his own way, and his object now was a

---

[1] The *Scots Independent* ceased publication in January 1935 as a publication of the S.N.P., and resumed life under the imprint of the Scottish Secretariat in September 1935. It was restored to the S.N.P. in October 1939.
[2] *Scots Independent*, February 1936, p. 1.

grand coalition of all the Home Rule elements in Scotland. At a special conference in October 1936 he was authorized to open negotiations and during the next three years he established links with the Liberals through Sir Thomas and Lady Glen-Coats and with Labour through the Rev. James Barr. The climax was to have been a Scottish National Convention in the City Hall, Glasgow, in 1939, for which a programme of resolutions was drawn up.[1] This programme included all the features of the post-war covenant movement, but it was destined to be still-born because of the war.

II

The war was to have profound consequences for the Scottish National Party. From 1936 onwards party conferences were continually agitated by the possibility of war and by the dangers represented by the rise of Nazism in Germany and (more alarmingly) in England. The party rank and file came out extremely strongly for 'unswerving opposition to all forms of undemocratic government' in 1937 and has remained hostile to fascism ever since. But the party found it more difficult to decide how it should react if war were to break out. While war seemed still a long way off in 1937 the annual conference resolved that:

> This Conference declares that the Scottish National Party is strongly opposed to the manpower of Scotland being used to defend an Empire in the government of which she has no voice, and all male members of the Scottish National Party of military age hereby pledge themselves to refuse to serve with any section of the Crown Forces until the programme of the Scottish National Party has been fulfilled.

But when war came the overwhelming majority of the S.N.P. ignored this resolution and supported the war. There remained, however, a strong undercurrent of feeling in favour of the original resolution of 1937, and when Douglas Young refused conscription because he did not recognize the right of the British government to call him up, and was sent to prison in 1942 for his temerity, he became for the time being a popular figure.

After the outbreak of war the S.N.P. was not affected by the electoral truce which prevented the major parties from contesting seats held by

[1] Scottish National Convention, *Draft Resolutions* . . . (Glasgow, 1939).

their opponents. As a result, the few S.N.P. candidates who had the opportunity of standing had the chance to collect a great many protest votes. This was shown first in Argyll in April 1940 when William Power succeeded in securing 7,308 votes as against 12,317 for the Conservative candidate. But there were few constituencies like Argyll, where the S.N.P. could be sure of gaining the left-wing vote and there was a shortage of suitable candidates. As a result, tempers began to rise in the S.N.P. over by-election strategy and in particular there was a lot of ill-feeling about the arrangements made for fighting Glasgow–Cathcart in April 1942. Worse still, members of the party were very irritated that the party leaders did not take a stronger stand on industrial conscription. From May 1941 onwards the *Scots Independent* was full of complaints that Scots girls were being forced to go south to England because there were no jobs for them in Scotland. Perhaps Sir Alexander MacEwen could have done something about the problem, but he died in the middle of 1941. The *Scots Independent* was still appearing with banner headlines on the subject ('Scots girl conscripts, why forced labour in England?')[1] a year after complaints had started. Furthermore, the editor of the *Scots Independent*, by now again an official party paper, made the sense of frustration worse when in a leading article in June 1942 he attacked Douglas Young's opposition to conscription, although Young was the only nationalist who seemed to many of the rank and file to be doing anything to carry out the principles of the party. There was, therefore, a great deal of discontent in the party by the time it met for its 1942 conference.

John MacCormick was well aware that things were not going well, although in his annual report he made much of the fact that the Labour and Liberal parties seemed to be stronger on Home Rule than they had been for a long time. He therefore announced at the beginning of the 1942 conference that he proposed to retire from the secretaryship after fifteen years' service. In normal circumstances such a declaration would have drawn the sting of the critics. But at the 1942 conference the dissidents in the party were exceptionally strong, and they chose to fight a battle about the way in which the party should be going. As one of them put it, they resented 'the control of the movement . . . falling more and more into the hands of a small Glasgow group under the leadership of Mr. MacCormick . . . resulting in a gradual freezing of enterprise, bewildering opportunism and a lack of courage in facing

[1] *Scots Independent*, April 1942, p. 1.

national issues fair and square'.[1] They therefore nominated Douglas Young for the chairmanship in opposition to MacCormick's candidate, William Power, and turned the election into a brutal slogging match. Tempers became roused and when Young was elected by 33 votes to 29, MacCormick, Power and their allies resigned on the spot and seceded to form a new organization which they at first called the Scottish Union.

The choice of Douglas Young as the dissidents' standard-bearer was the direct result of the publicity he had secured over his refusal to accept conscription. Born in Fife in 1913, and educated at Merchiston Castle School, Edinburgh, St. Andrews University and New College, Oxford, he had been a nationalist since as a schoolboy he had backed Lewis Spence in Midlothian in 1929. While Assistant to the Regius Professor of Greek at Aberdeen University he had become active in the S.N.P. and was secretary of the Aberdeen branch. He was already quite widely known in Scotland as a promising poet, scholar and writer, and his impressive personal appearance (well over six feet and bearded), and manifest integrity, gave him a certain air of distinction which commanded respect. He was not himself an extremist by temperament. Indeed, he seems in general to have held views rather similar to those of MacCormick. But he had become a symbolic figure round whom the opposition in the S.N.P. chose to group itself. The reports of his various trials, printed by the Scottish Secretariat, were widely circulated among the younger nationalists and there were sufficient of them to keep his name to the fore as a symbol of Scottish resistance to English exactions throughout the war.[2] When his initial attack on military conscription was rebuffed by the courts, he was sent to prison for twelve months, of which he served the usual eight months. When he came out of prison he returned to active nationalist politics, and contested a by-election in the Kirkcaldy burghs in February 1944, when he received 6,621 votes against 8,268 for the Labour candidate. The poll created something of a stir, and soon afterwards the authori-

---

[1] *The Scotsman*, 2nd June 1942. For an account of the conference see *Scots Independent*, July 1942, p. 2, and *The Scotsman*, 1st June 1942.

[2] *A Scot's Free Fight: Statement delivered in Glasgow Sheriff-Court on April 13, 1942* . . . (Glasgow, 1942); *The Free Minded Scot: trial of Douglas C. C. Young in the High Court, Edinburgh* (Glasgow, 1942); *British Invasion of Scottish Rights —Douglas Young's trial in Paisley Sheriff-Court on June 12, 1944* (Glasgow, 1944); and *An Appeal to Scots Honour by Douglas Young: a Vindication of the Right of the Scottish People to Freedom from Industrial Conscription and Bureaucratic Despotism under the Treaty of Union with England* (Glasgow, 1944).

ties gave Young the chance to stage a further protest. He was charged with non-compliance with the industrial conscription regulations, which he challenged on the ground that:

> Since 1940 the British Government in London has been imposing on the people of Scotland a system of industrial conscription, whereby the British Ministry of Labour has transported many thousands of Scots working folk, including young girls, far away from their homeland to forced labour in a foreign land.[1]

The courts were once again treated to a carefully argued constitutional homily, and once again they refused to listen, though this time they were less friendly to Young. Young himself was once again imprisoned, and again secured some of the advantages of political martyrdom: wide publicity and a good deal of popular sympathy.

The result of the 1942 split was virtually to divide the nationalist movement into two camps, which corresponded roughly, but not exactly, to the old division between the Home Rulers and the fundamentalists. MacCormick and his friends had argued at the 1942 conference that the S.N.P. should change its function and become an agency for promoting an agreed measure of Scottish Home Rule. The new organization which they now formed, called first the Scottish Union[2] and then the Scottish Convention, became as a result very similar in its objectives to the old Scottish Home Rule Association, while the S.N.P. now occupied rather the same position as the Scots National League. Indeed, the *Scots Independent* began to sound for a time very like the *Scottish Review* and *Guth na Bliadhna*, though its accents were much more shrill. Those expelled from the National Party in 1933 began to drift back to the S.N.P. and it began to look as though something like the old National Party was to be re-created, since many of its more prominent members, including Roland Muirhead, had not seceded with MacCormick.

III

Losing control of the S.N.P. was a heavy blow for John MacCormick, but he never lost hope of building an alternative organization. The Scottish Convention speedily obtained over 1,000 members and was able to set up several branches, but wartime conditions

---

[1] *An Appeal to Scots Honour*, p. 1.
[2] *The Scotsman*, 1st June 1942.

prevented it from making much immediate impact. Moreover, Mac-Cormick chose to commit the Convention to securing a consensus in Scotland as to the need for Scottish Home Rule, rather than to fighting for changes. The object now was to bring people of all parties together to discuss the governmental, social and economic problems of Scotland from a non-party point of view. The fighting of parliamentary elections was renounced, and membership of the Convention was thrown open to all. MacCormick, indeed, demonstrated that he had entirely abandoned the quest for an independent nationalist party by joining the Liberal party and standing as a Liberal parliamentary candidate at the 1945 election. And he was joined in his move to the Liberal party by two prominent members of the I.L.P., Dr. John Macdonald, who had edited the *Scots Independent*, and Robert Gray, who had been a nationalist candidate on several occasions.

It was 1947 before anything much was heard of the Convention. Then it summoned a 'Scottish National Assembly' to meet in Glasgow in March 1947, issuing invitations to every local authority, every Church of Scotland presbytery, every trade union, chamber of commerce and trade association, and a variety of other bodies as well. The idea (which had been discussed by the Convention of Royal Burghs in 1914) caught the public imagination and the Assembly gave the Convention just the sort of publicity it wanted. For the 600 delegates were emphatic in denouncing government from London and in demanding that a Scottish parliament should be set up to handle Scottish affairs. As MacCormick put it later, 'Scotland after so many years of sleep, had at last come back again to vigorous life'.[1] The Assembly appointed a committee which spent a year in producing a 'Blue-Print for Scotland', which was adopted at a second meeting of the Assembly on 20th March 1948. In this way MacCormick succeeded in getting a good deal of Conservative support for a measure of devolution, and also kept the Liberal party firmly tied to its Home Rule traditions.

The weakness of MacCormick's policy was that it gradually alienated the Labour party, because the attacks on 'London government' made in the Assembly and in Convention meetings were often indistinguishable from attacks on the Labour government of Clement Attlee. Worse still, MacCormick himself stood as a 'National' candidate with Conservative support at a by-election in Paisley at the beginning of 1948, and for a time looked as though he might win it from Labour (the result was Labour 27,213, MacCormick 20,668). It is

[1] MacCormick, *The Flag in the Wind*, p. 116.

170

not therefore surprising that, though the Scottish Convention included some Labour men (like William Gallacher of the S.C.W.S.), it was regarded by the Labour Secretary of State for Scotland, Arthur Woodburn, as a political movement aimed at overturning the Labour government. Nor was there any chance in the conditions of 1948, when the Labour government was fighting for its life in the first of the big post-war economic crises, of the Labour party being prepared to spare the energies and the parliamentary time necessary if it was to go thoroughly into a scheme of Home Rule.

The Scottish Convention, as a result, became a purely propagandist body. Its major object was now to secure public adhesion for a new Scottish Covenant (an old theme of MacCormick's) which was widely circulated. This read:

> We, the people of Scotland who subscribe this Engagement, declare our belief that reform in the constitution of our country is necessary to secure good government in accordance with our Scottish traditions and to promote the spiritual and economic welfare of our nation.
>
> We affirm that the desire for such reform is both deep and widespread through the whole community, transcending all political differences and sectional interests, and we undertake to continue united in purpose for its achievement.
>
> With that end in view we solemnly enter into this Covenant whereby we pledge ourselves, in all loyalty to the Crown and within the framework of the United Kingdom, to do everything in our power to secure for Scotland a Parliament with adequate legislative authority in Scottish affairs.[1]

The signing began with a third session of the Scottish Assembly attended by 1,200 delegates, which met in the Church of Scotland Assembly Hall on 29th October 1949. The idea quickly caught on; 50,000 people signed within a week, and within six months the million mark was in sight.

Home Rule was now a demonstrably popular cause. But the underlying weakness of MacCormick's methods was soon apparent. Town councillors might sign the covenant by the thousand, but their signatures were quite irrelevant to the ordinary political process. This was made explicit by James Stuart as chairman of the Scottish Unionist M.P.s when he wrote to MacCormick:

[1] ibid., p. 128. For the 1930 Covenant see p. 158 above.

If the people of Scotland were ultimately to decide in favour of a Scottish Parliament no one could gainsay them.

We do not, however, hold the view that such extremely complex matters can properly be determined either by plebiscite or by reference to the number of signatures affixed to any document. The constitutional methods by which the people in our democracy can make their wishes known and effective are well understood, generally respected, in constant use, and available to all shades of opinion.[1]

Or, in other words, MacCormick's supporters must either capture the nomination of Conservative, Liberal and Labour M.P.s, or put up candidates of their own. The Covenant as an effective political instrument was dead.

For MacCormick himself there was one final and appropriate apotheosis. He was elected in October 1950 Lord Rector of Glasgow University, where he had started the Nationalist Association over twenty years before. It was the great achievement of his career and gave him the sense of fulfilment he was to need in his retirement. For though the covenant movement still went on, and more than two million signatures were eventually secured (some of them, alas, bogus), the rest was anti-climax. A Royal Commission on Scottish Affairs was appointed in 1952 (the Balfour Commission), there was an interesting court case relating to the royal style and titles, and there was the curious episode of the removal of the Stone of Scone (otherwise the Stone of Destiny) from Westminster Abbey to Scotland,[2] which appealed to MacCormick's undergraduate heart. And then there was the writing of MacCormick's autobiography which appeared in 1955. The Scottish Convention movement simply faded away, although it was never formally wound up, giving pride of place in the 1960s to the revived S.N.P.

IV

The Scottish National Party without MacCormick was a very different party. But it soon found an alternative leader in Dr. Robert D. McIntyre, then of Edinburgh and later of Stirling, and it was soon well on the way to total reconstruction. At the end of the first year after

[1] ibid., pp. 139–40.

[2] MacCormick was associated with the frolic, for which see Ian R. Hamilton, *No Stone Unturned: the Story of the Stone of Destiny* (London, 1952).

the split McIntyre claimed that the membership of the party had increased by 60 per cent and the sales of the *Scots Independent* by 13 per cent.[1] And at several by-elections towards the end of the war the S.N.P. did very well—notably at Kirkcaldy where Douglas Young was the candidate, and at Motherwell in 1945 where Dr. McIntyre was actually elected. Though Motherwell was lost again to Labour at the general election the very fact of having even one ex-M.P. in the ranks of the party was a big gain in terms of morale.

Dr. McIntyre gave an entirely new direction to the policy of the S.N.P. A patient man, he did not demand quick results. He argued simply that the S.N.P. must decide what sort of party it was and should then stick to its decision. It was he who took the initiative in drawing up the comprehensive policy statement which the party adopted in 1946 (Appendix). And it was he who saw to it that the party adopted a new constitution in 1949. Douglas Young was much too much the intellectual, much too much in the Home Rule tradition, to provide an alternative leadership, and resigned from the S.N.P. in 1948 when it excluded members of other parties.

Dr. Robert McIntyre is one of those distinctively Scottish figures whose whole pattern of thought derives from Scottish presbyterianism. His father, the son of a minister, was a United Free Church minister well known in his day for his sympathy for the anti-war movement during the First World War. His mother was a minister's daughter. He himself became a tuberculosis specialist working in the public health field, where there was ample opportunity to do valuable work among the poor. His education was entirely Scottish[2] and he has rarely been out of Scotland for any length of time. Like many Scottish ministers' sons in the 1930s he flirted with the ideas of Trotsky and the other fashionable creeds of his day, but he abandoned his student socialism, because he had come to believe that the possession of property was an inalienable human right and because he thought that the future was on the side of the nationalists.

Dr. McIntyre's ideas are very similar to those of the small-town democrats of the prairie provinces of Canada and parts of the United States. He has a passionate belief in economic freedom, which he believes can only be assured if all men possess some property (in this

[1] *Scots Independent*, July 1943, p. 4.
[2] Robert Douglas McIntyre was born in December 1913 and educated at Hamilton Academy, Daniel Stewart's College in Edinburgh and Edinburgh University. At the time of his election as M.P. for Motherwell he was aged 31.

sense he is a neo-Lockean populist who believes in a property-owning democracy). His ideal is to see property so widely distributed that even urban man has something to fall back on—whether it is a workshop in the backyard or a croft in the Highlands. Since the amount of land is limited, he is prepared to accept that there must be some limitation to the amount of property in land which any individual may own. He envisages the Scotland of the future as a body of autonomous self-dependent individuals, regulated by a state which is a judge and law-giver rather than an over-mighty centre of power. The state is to be the inspirer and developer of individual initiative through autonomous state agencies like a land bank. But the individual must also be pro-tected against the state. All individuals are to be regarded in terms of Reformation theology as equal in the eyes of God and to be enabled to achieve their potential. Privilege is to be gradually whittled away. The new democracy is to be a democracy of self-respecting factory workers, shopkeepers, farmers and providers of professional services. Above all it will be a new and liberating spiritual experience.

> To the Scottish realist the issue is not between the materialist creeds of state socialism and private enterprise. . . .
> The Scottish National Party policy shows that the Scottish radi-cals have transcended that now sterile and empty conflict. . . . The world wide struggle of the age we are now entering is for the human rights of man.[1]

The party had been toying with ideas of this sort since before the war, when Douglas social credit was a force to be reckoned with in Scotland, both as a homespun philosophy and as an intellectual creed promulgated in the *Free Man*. The party programme adopted in October 1936, had, indeed, laid down as the S.N.P. programme: (1) national control of credit by means of a state bank; (2) national control of transport; (3) national control of power; (4) decentralization and ruralization of industry; (5) 'those who work the soil to acquire ownership'; (6) the systematic development of Scottish fisheries. But this was the sort of programme which might be read either in the libertarian terms of the *Free Man* and the social crediters or in the mildly socialist terms of Douglas Young. Now, however, the party was

---

[1] *Scots Independent*, May 1947, p. 1. McIntyre's ideas are also set out in the first three chapters of a pamphlet called *Whose Country?* and in *Some Principles for Scottish Reconstruction* (S.N.P., Glasgow, 1944).

committed to an entirely new departure—a complete policy statement on libertarian lines.

The new party policy was drawn up, reportedly at two long sessions, by a small group of people meeting in the house of George and Mary Dott. The meeting place was a significant one, because the Dotts had been associated for many years with the movements from which the new S.N.P. drew many of its ideas. George Dott was a slow-spoken, deliberate Scot, who liked thinking things out for himself, and as a mining engineer had knocked around the world a good deal. He had learned about guild socialism and social credit from the *New Age*, he had picked up a little populism, a little Henry George, and a little New Deal Liberalism in America, and he was one of the ardent social crediters who bought and ran the *Free Man*. His libertarianism fitted in well with that of McIntyre, especially after McIntyre had read Peter Drucker's book *The End of Economic Man*, of which he approved.

Anyone who reads the S.N.P. 1946 policy statement (which is still official S.N.P. policy) will recognize that he is reading an unusual document. For it deliberately sets out to offer something quite different from the offerings of other parties. The nearest parallels are with the social credit movements in Canada and New Zealand and with the populism of the United States and Scandinavia. There is much the same emphasis on the little man, and on building up small-town democracy, as in these parallel movements outside Scotland. And there is the same mixture of influences at work—Henry George, Douglas Social Credit, Christian Socialism, anarchism, political Radicalism—everything except a frank acceptance of the modern state and of modern bureaucratized industrial, political, trade union, and commercial empires.

The most significant single feature of the new S.N.P. policy was the total omission of a section on Scottish culture. The S.N.P. was to be a party fighting for the small man to whom culture was something that he had already. Writers are read by the sort of man the S.N.P. programme was intended to win only when they write about his culture convincingly and sentimentally (the *Sunday Post* published in Dundee catches the tone exactly). When they write about things beyond the ken of small-town man they are not read at all. Education is a technique instilled like other forms of training as a preparation for life. It is not regarded as contributing to real life, because the intellectual, the writer, the scientist are men who do not work in the small-town environment. Writers like Hugh MacDiarmid who come up with incomprehensible nostrums are a nuisance. They are irrelevant to the great fight to protect the small man against the state—that swindling dictatorship which takes away a man's goods and gives him nothing in return.

Ideas of the sort found in the S.N.P. programme are usually confined to fringe movements in which anarchy and internecine warfare are endemic. What is unique about Dr. Robert McIntyre is that he combines populist ideas with a strong sense of discipline. For him the obvious way of doing things is to follow the example of the Presbyterian churches which combine a high degree of organization with a high degree of participation by ordinary members of the church. The co-operative housing association, the credit corporation, the burgh council, and the agricultural bank provide the sort of committee machinery through which McIntyre thinks that men find it natural to work. On the same analogy he is inclined to think of political parties as coherent and relatively tightly knit bodies like a church, whose function it is to achieve definite ends. He dislikes the atmosphere of confusion and anarchy which is associated with fundamentalists, whether in religion or in politics, and prefers to win tangible gains (like seats on town councils) rather than intellectual victories. It is characteristic of him that he appears to derive great satisfaction from the work which he has been able to do as Treasurer and subsequently Provost of the Burgh of Stirling.

The adoption of the new S.N.P. policy led logically to a revision of the party constitution and a general tightening up of party discipline. The 1948 S.N.P. conference resolved that no member of the S.N.P. might in future belong to any other political party and the decision was confirmed in the following year. A number of persistent troublemakers were suspended from membership, and a number of other members resigned because they disagreed with the new trend of party policy, among them Douglas Young who thought that the S.N.P. should allow people like himself to remain members both of the Labour party and the S.N.P. But the new emphasis on unity gave greater coherence to annual conferences after 1947, and Dr. McIntyre as party chairman from 1947 to 1956 proved to be very businesslike in the chair, much in the manner of a moderator of the General Assembly of the Church of Scotland. As a result, since 1947 there has never been any successful attempt to divert the party from the course upon which it then embarked.

The campaign strategy of the S.N.P. during the late forties and fifties was to keep up the momentum of the party by concentrating on municipal elections and by fighting parliamentary elections only in places where the party was already well established. There were to be no more rash gestures that would cost the party money it had not got. There was simply to be a continuous stand for the truth—nationalist policy—until such time as the country had come round to the S.N.P. point of view. In local politics this strategy was soon successful. The first nationalist provost of a burgh was elected in 1949 (at Alva)[1] and thereafter there was a steady trickle of nationalist victories in local elections—chiefly in small towns. And many of the more prominent party leaders were soon members of their local town councils. In parliamentary elections the S.N.P. made only modest ventures. There had been eight S.N.P. candidates of rather varying views at the 1945 general election:[2] in 1950 there were only four (though there were a number of other Home Rule or nationalist candidates of different colours including an Irish Anti-Partition League candidate in the Gorbals division of Glasgow whose slogan was 'Ireland United and Scotland Free'),[3] and in 1951 and 1955 there were only two. The S.N.P. preferred to husband its resources and wait for a suitable chance to make a really big splash.

V

The narrowing of the sights of the S.N.P. and the gradual dropping out of many of the older nationalists led to the creation of a number of splinter movements outside the S.N.P., most of them with only a small membership. The most important of these was the Scottish National Congress started by Roland Muirhead in 1950 (when he ceased to be President of the S.N.P.). At 82 Muirhead was still a formidable and persistent figure. He started a new journal, *Forward Scotland*, and he attracted to his Congress many of the nationalist firebrands of past nationalist movements. Muirhead's sympathies still lay with the old I.L.P., and his Congress, therefore, had something of a left-wing flavour, which it retained after his death. But Muirhead became more and more interested in the technical problems of constitution-making,

---

[1] *Scots Independent*, June 1949.
[2] For their campaign see R. B. McCallum and Alison Readman, *The British General Election of 1945* (London, 1947), pp. 120–3.
[3] Chrimes, ed., *The General Election in Glasgow: February, 1950*, p. 101.

and his final gesture was the creation in 1962 of a Scottish Provisional Constituent Assembly to draft a constitution for an independent Scotland.

A Constitution for Scotland by Matthew F. Somerville, Catherine P. Snodgrass and John D. MacLean, was published in 1964 and was the last of Muirhead's publishing ventures (he died later in the year).[1] It is the sort of constitution that a group of Radicals with high ideals might be expected to draw up. That is, it takes it for granted that a Scottish constitution would be very like the present British constitution, but endeavours to improve on it by the inclusion of a list of fundamental rights and a number of exhortations. The monarchy is retained, but the use of titles is banned. ('The title "Lord" shall cease to be used in relation to all offices within the nation. No personal or hereditary titles or privileges shall be recognised other than those of Princes and Princesses of the blood royal within the immediate succession. There shall be no party-political honours or decorations.') Scotland is declared to be 'a free, independent, democratic nation, the power to rule being vested in the Scottish people and exercised by them through a National Assembly'. The Church of Scotland is recognized as the national church, but 'All citizens have freedom of religious belief and worship and there shall be no discrimination on grounds of religion'. The right of Gaelic speakers to use Gaelic in courts of law and government offices is guaranteed. So is the right to refuse to bear arms on conscientious grounds. Government is to be in the hands of a Prime Minister and a body of Secretaries of State. But it is prescribed that the state 'shall remain the servant of the citizens and shall be subservient to their fundamental rights'.

The Scottish National Congress was not the only splinter group formed by seceders from the S.N.P. A good many individual nationalists created little groups of their own, among them the irrepressible Wendy Wood, long a favourite with the press, whose Scottish Patriots continue to meet regularly in Edinburgh and to conduct a campaign against the petty pinpricks of English domination. The importance of the Scottish National Congress was that it was a hold-all like the old National Party of Scotland, and when it gradually went into decline after Muirhead's death there was obviously a need for a similar organization to be created. During 1967 and 1968 this was provided by the 1320 Club, which started as a fundamentalist movement, lurched

[1] There were tributes to him from all sorts of nationalists in the last number of *Forward Scotland* for September 1964 (Vol. II, No. 9).

towards the S.N.P. and respectability, and then turned back to funda-
mentalism of the 'have no truck with the English' variety.

Splinter groups like the Scottish National Congress, the Scottish
Patriots and the 1320 Club offered no real threat to the S.N.P. The
fundamentalists on the nationalist fringes have always been too
divided among themselves, too devoted to crotchets, to matter. But the
rivalry of John MacCormick's Covenant Movement was much more
dangerous. For the Covenant appealed to the same group of people as
the S.N.P. and seemed to offer a short-cut to success. Hence there was a
good deal of sniping by members of the S.N.P. at the covenant movement and by members of the covenant movement at the S.N.P., though
there was also a fair degree of co-operation in some places. The
Covenant was constantly in the news, the activities of the S.N.P. were
rarely reported, and when they were reported it was usually because
some vocal fundamentalist member of the S.N.P. had been suspended
from the party or had resigned. Worse still, student nationalists tended
to sympathize with the heroics of the Covenant rather than with the
steady campaigning of the S.N.P., with the result that the S.N.P. was
deprived of a good many promising recruits.

VI

The great achievement of the S.N.P. from 1942 to 1964 was simply to
have survived. But its survival has been based entirely on a very limited
conception of nationalism. By shunning intellectuals, by concentrating
on the small man, it has deliberately set out to win over the rank and
file of the older political parties, rather than their leaders. It has
become emphatically the party of the little man, and its philosophy has
just the right ring to make a direct appeal to the ordinary man in the
street who has never taken an interest in politics. The S.N.P. is a
grassroots political movement or it is nothing.

Yet there are dangers in narrowing a party's sights so much. Not
only are the intellectuals—the founders of nationalism—disaffected.
The party is forced to rely upon men who are by definition hostile to
the state and incapable of understanding how it is run and what it is
trying to do. Such men are well enough *en masse* at public meetings,
but as town councillors or parliamentary candidates they are often
incredibly inept. It is greatly to the credit of the S.N.P. that it has tried
to extend popular participation in the democratic process by enlisting
the aid of such people. But the television maintenance man and the

fitter snatched away from their workshops are no substitute for an experienced local leadership. Moreover, the higher ranks of the party lack flexibility of approach. The party has had an excellent expositor of its programme for twenty years in Arthur Donaldson. But the ideas of the party have changed but little since 1946. The S.N.P. has its Westminster confession and is determined to stick to it.

American and Canadian experience has shown that it is possible for parties like the S.N.P. to achieve power and to provide competent, if uninspired leadership when in power. But a Scotland run by the S.N.P. would be a simple agrarian or small-town democracy without any frills. It might experiment, as Saskatchewan has experimented with state medicine, but it would not be in any sense an intellectual force. So far as the S.N.P. is concerned the Scottish renaissance might never have occurred.

CHAPTER NINE

The Lion Clamant

I

How Scotland should be governed became a live political issue during the last years of the series of Conservative administrations that lasted from 1951 to 1964. After a period of *laissez faire*, the Conservative government was in process of developing an enthusiasm for planned growth and regional development, and in Scotland a series of reports were produced which seemed to promise great things for the future. The Toothill *Report on the Scottish Economy* prepared for the Scottish Council (Development and Industry) in 1960–1 was published in 1962. The government White Paper *Central Scotland: a Programme for Development and Growth* was published in November 1963. And the great Forth Road Bridge started in 1958 was completed in 1964. But the outstanding feature of the period was the gap between the expectations of the people and what was actually happening. Led to expect prosperity, most Scots found instead that they were little better off, or that they were actually worse off. For although new industries were planned, or had actually been started, as was the case with the new Scottish motor industry, there was a time lag. Old industries were everywhere closing down—mining, shipping, iron and steel—but there was for many people no obvious replacement. Moreover, in many parts of the country the closure of railways and the decay of small-scale agriculture were affecting the character of rural and small-town life. The whole economic basis of the Highlands and the Borders seemed to be threatened. And emigration, always an important indicator of Scottish morale, seemed to be on the increase. It was true that conditions for many people were much better than they had been in the immediate past, but ordinary working people were oppressed by a sense of anxiety about the future.

The first sign that the politicians had that things were not well was a falling-off of support for the Conservatives. In 1955 the Scottish

181

Unionists had secured an absolute majority of the Scottish vote (50·09 per cent) for the first time this century, though their total vote was lower than in 1951. Conservative prosperity seemed to be working. Then came the fall. A Conservative vote of 1,349,298 in 1951 had been cut to 960,654 by 1966, an extraordinary slide by recent standards. Moreover, it was a slide that had a dramatic effect on the number of Conservative seats, which fell from 36 in 1955 to 20 in 1966. To some extent the fall must be attributed simply to the Liberals putting up more candidates. But there was clearly also a considerable swing from the Conservative to the Labour and Liberal parties. The Liberals in particular did unexpectedly well, with four seats in 1964 and five in 1966.

But that was not the end of the story. With Labour back in office after 1964, the Labour vote also began to erode. As with the Conservatives, there was a plethora of proposals, notably in the White Paper *The Scottish Economy, 1965 to 1970: a Plan for Expansion* published in January 1966. But once again action seemed to be as far away as ever. Indeed, the contrast between the picture of the modern technological society that Labour would create painted by Harold Wilson in 1964 and the economic facts of 1966 and 1967 was startling in the extreme. All over Britain there was a flight from Labour, which in Scotland assumed surprising proportions and culminated in the loss of one of the safest Labour seats in the House of Commons at Hamilton in 1967 and in an unprecedented clear-out of Labour town councillors in 1968. Nor was the Liberal vote safe. By 1968 it was quite clear from the public opinion polls that in most of Scotland support for the Liberals was falling off too. Clearly the existing party system was under attack from the grass roots, and something like a wave of national protest was sweeping the country. *The Scotsman* came out in support of a federal system for Britain as the only way of securing a Scottish economic and social revival to match the expectations of the people,[1] and all the political parties hastened to re-examine their policies.

II

In electoral terms just what had been happening is easily told. First, there was a straightforward switch from the Conservative party to one of the two alternative Westminster parties, which was accentuated by

---

[1] *How Scotland should be Governed: The Scotsman states its Policy on Self-Government* (Edinburgh, 1968).

the fact that, where the Liberals were likely to win, a good many Labour voters voted Liberal in order to keep out a Tory, and where Labour was likely to win, there was sometimes a Liberal switch to Labour.[1] Then there was a much more general shift of allegiance, which often had curious local effects. Sometimes voters simply abstained from voting, sometimes they shifted their support to one of the minor parties, sometimes they voted nationalist. One of the most interesting cases is that of West Lothian, where the Conservative break-up happened early and dramatically, and where the Labour party apparently did unexpectedly well almost entirely because the electorate was steadily growing in size. The voting was 1959 Labour 27,454, Unionist 18,083; 1962 by-election Labour 21,266, S.N.P. 9,750, Unionist 4,784, Liberal 4,537, Communist 1,511; 1964 Labour 24,933, S.N.P. 15,087, Unionist 8,919, Communist 610; 1966 Labour 26,662, S.N.P. 17,955, Unionist 5,726, Communist 567. In this case quite a big Unionist vote, and a by-no-means negligible Liberal vote, have now been virtually wiped out, and it only requires a national swing away from Labour at a general election to accentuate these trends and to give the S.N.P. an excellent chance of winning the seat.

At the general election of 1959 the nationalist vote was still of very little account. There were only five nationalist candidates, and they obtained only 21,738 votes between them (·81 per cent of the Scottish vote). And of this vote a very substantial proportion (9,637) was secured by Dr. R. D. McIntyre, former M.P. for Motherwell, in Perth and East Perthshire. At the 1964 general election the number of nationalist candidates grew to fifteen, who secured between them 64,044 votes (2·43 per cent of the Scottish vote). But the nationalists were still not in the same class as the Liberals, who with twenty-six candidates obtained 200,063 votes (7·6 per cent) and won four seats. But it was encouraging for the nationalists that in addition to the remarkable result in West Lothian (30·5 per cent of the vote), seven other candidates secured 10 per cent or more of the votes cast. During the 1964 parliament the only by-election of note was that in Roxburgh, Selkirk and Peebles, which was won by the Liberals (a Scottish nationalist persisted in standing but he was disowned by the party). The 1966 general election was much better for the S.N.P. With twenty-

---

[1] This phenomenon is shown clearly in Roxburgh, Selkirk and Peebles where the voting was: 1959 Unionist 22,275, Liberal 12,762, Labour 9,336; 1964 Unionist 18,924, Liberal 17,185, Labour 7,007, S.N.P. 1,093; 1965 by-election Liberal 21,549, Unionist 16,942, Labour 4,936, Independent 411.

three candidates the party secured 128,476 votes (5·03 per cent) which was getting somewhere near the, by this time smaller, Liberal vote of 172,429 (6·8 per cent) for twenty-four candidates. Moreover, sixteen of the S.N.P. candidates got over 10 per cent of the vote in their constituencies, of whom four got over 20 per cent. This was not a breakthrough, but it indicated that at last the S.N.P. was a serious political force.

What was most significant about the twenty-three S.N.P. candidates in 1966 was their distribution. Most of the constituencies they fought were situated in the industrial heartland of the country, where nationalists had traditionally fought in the past: two in Dunbartonshire, three in Stirlingshire, four in Fife, five in Glasgow, plus the individual constituencies of West Lothian and Rutherglen. In addition there were two contests in Perthshire, an isolated one in the north in Aberdeenshire East, one in Edinburgh, and one in the south at Dumfries. In only two of the twenty-three constituencies fought was there a Liberal candidate, and in only one of these two was the Liberal party a strong political force. There was, in other words, a clear tendency for the Liberals and the S.N.P. to share out the work of being a third party. In the 71 Scottish constituencies, 21 were fought by the S.N.P., 22 by the Liberals, and 2 by both parties—leaving the major parties to fight it out, with or without Communist or other intervention in the remaining 26.

A number of surveys made during the period 1964 to 1966 indicated that these election results did not reflect the real strength of the Scottish National Party in the country. It was already much more active in municipal affairs than in parliamentary, and it was building up the framework of a new organization. Branches were constantly in process of formation, and it was clearly going to be some time before the party was fully equipped to fight elections not as a second Liberal party but as a serious rival to the Labour and Conservative parties. Because the nationalists put up so few candidates in 1966 it was not, indeed, possible to know where electoral discontent with the other parties was strongest. But the campaign in Midlothian was some pointer to what might happen in such places if only the electors were given a chance to say what they thought. Midlothian had not been fought by a nationalist since the abortive campaign by Lewis Spence in 1929, yet an enthusiastic campaign by a band of young nationalists headed by students in 1966 secured 7,974 votes (16·3 per cent). Furthermore, canvassers discovered that the S.N.P. would have got more votes had they been able to show that the nationalists were a serious alternative to Labour and the Conservatives as a parliamentary party.

Nationalist strength increased dramatically as soon as the Wilson government showed clearly that life with Labour meant a curbing of real incomes and a curtailing of public expenditure. As under the Conservatives there was a marked reaction from the Scottish electorate to the deferment of hopes. With further pit and railway closures announced, the National Plan abandoned, the Highlands and Islands Development Board apparently stultified, many of those who had voted Labour in 1966 were now prepared to vote S.N.P.

Yet at first the S.N.P. found the going heavy. There were not enough by-elections to enable it to give its electoral machine a thorough airing, and finding candidates of suitable quality for municipal elections was a tantalizing problem. But the party did make headway. At a parliamentary by-election in Glasgow–Pollok on 9th March 1967 the S.N.P. did less well than it had expected, but with 10,884 votes (28·2 per cent) the S.N.P. knocked out the Liberals (735 votes) and came quite near the Labour vote, 12,069. Then came the unexpected at Hamilton, a safe Labour seat. In 1966 the voting at Hamilton had been Labour 27,865 (71·2 per cent), Conservative 11,289 (28·8 per cent). In a by-election on 2nd November 1967, however, there was an astonishing turnround, the result being:

Mrs. Winifred Ewing (S.N.P.)	18,397 (46·0 per cent)
Alexander Wilson (Labour)	16,598 (41·5 per cent)
Iain Dyer (Conservative)	4,986 (12·5 per cent)

The result of the Hamilton by-election was one of those dramatic events that attract the attention of the whole country by its unexpectedness. But what was really important about it was that it so strikingly registered trends of opinion apparent long before. To those of us who were watching from the sidelines there was a sort of inevitability about what was happening, though we did not expect quite such a big drop in the Labour vote. The S.N.P. had not contested the seat since 1959, but there was the nucleus of an S.N.P. organization, and it was possible for the nationalists to bring in workers from all over central Scotland. Moreover, in Mrs. Winifred Ewing, a Glasgow solicitor, they had a quite exceptionally good candidate, who coped remarkably well with the ordeal of trial by television which is a feature of modern by-elections. By contrast, the local Labour leaders behaved as though Hamilton were a snug and safe Labour bailiwick. In place of their old member, Tom Fraser, who had been a prominent figure in the House of Commons and Minister of Health, they chose a pleasant local party stalwart, who was acceptable to the National Union of Mineworkers, the traditional Labour overlords of the constituency. They apparently did not stop to consider that he might prove to be a dumb dog at press conferences and on television. Moreover, the Hamilton constituency Labour party made it clear that it could manage the election on its own with a minimum of outside support. The result—the competent Conservative candidate did not count— was a confrontation between those who demanded a new approach to politics and the problem of Scottish prosperity and those who championed the cosy old ways of the Scottish trade union branches. It was scarcely surprising in the circumstances that many electors who would normally have voted Labour were tempted to vote S.N.P. as a sign that they were tired of the old system and of the Labour government.

Hamilton is in many ways typical of modern central Scotland. Once the seat of the Duke of Hamilton and still the judicial centre for much of Lanarkshire, it was long the centre of a coal-mining district and just across the valley from it lie the great steel mills of Motherwell. But Lanarkshire is no longer what it was. By the time of the by-election all mining had ceased. The town of Hamilton was being modernized. There was a regular electric-train service to Glasgow, and since the by-election a new motorway on the edge of the constituency has formed a fast new road-link with Glasgow and other neighbouring industrial towns. Hamilton is being slowly sucked into the new industrial system of greater Glasgow. Meanwhile, it is an area which is visibly in course of transition from the nineteenth-century cottage life of the coalfield to the twentieth-century life of working-class suburbia. Inevitably, the old loyalties are slackening. The claim of the miners to dominate the constituency Labour party no longer makes economic sense. And the old mining communities no longer vote Labour as a matter of course now that their mines have closed. Hamilton is still the sort of place that requires a jolt before it will cease to vote Labour as a matter of course, so that Mrs. Ewing's seat is not a safe one, but it is no longer the sort of place it was in the old days.

The Hamilton by-election gave a tremendous fillip to nationalist morale. The opinion polls began to show a significant hardening of support for the S.N.P. And at the municipal elections in the following May the nationalists secured a run-away victory. They did not do quite as well as they had done at Hamilton, but as a Conservative paper put it:

> The Scottish burgh election results confirmed the pattern of the Hamilton by-election.
>
> There is a massive swing against Labour in Scotland, as elsewhere in Britain. In England this swing is to the Conservatives. In Scotland it is largely to the S.N.P.[1]

This paper gave the following as the results of the May 1968 municipal elections:

	Gains	*Losses*
Conservatives	15	—
Other Right-wing	18	13
Independents	9	33
Socialists [i.e. Labour]	4	88
S.N.P.	103	2

Nor was this the end of the S.N.P. triumphs. In June 1968 the S.N.P. won control of the first town council elected in the new burgh of Cumbernauld—the most adventurous of the Scottish 'New Towns'—taking 18 of the 21 seats (the other three went to Labour). Cumbernauld, like Hamilton, had hitherto been regarded as a Labour town, so that once again the S.N.P. was making inroads into an established Labour vote.

One thing which emerged clearly from all these election results was that the S.N.P. was making ground fastest in Labour areas outside the big towns. It made big gains in Glasgow, but it did less well in Edinburgh, Dundee and Aberdeen, though its performance was still remarkably good by pre-1967 standards. In the big New Towns where the modernization of Scotland has gone furthest—Glenrothes, East Kilbride and Cumbernauld—the 'new working class' is clearly prepared to experiment. Sometimes, as at Glenrothes, this may mean voting for a Conservative. Usually it means voting S.N.P. Moreover, in these New Towns the S.N.P. organization is unusually strong. In older industrial areas like Hamilton and West Lothian, where new factories have begun to transform the pattern of employment and mining has died out, there is a remarkable readiness to switch to S.N.P. Elsewhere the S.N.P. has taken a big bite out of the Labour vote, but has not usually made much impact on the Conservatives.

[1] *New Scotland,* June 1968, p. 6.

187

The results of a 1968 survey in Dundee conducted by J. M. Bochel and published in *The Scotsman* give a good idea of the pattern of S.N.P. support early in 1968 outside those areas where it fought parliamentary elections in 1966.[1] A sample of electors asked how they would vote gave the following responses:

	Voting intention 1968	Result of 1966 parliamentary election
	%	%
Labour	24	55
Conservative	36	40
S.N.P.	25	—
Others	7	5
Don't Know	8	—

This indicates clearly that the S.N.P. has still a long way to go to catch up with Labour and the Conservatives at parliamentary elections but that its strength in 1968 was such that it should have been capable of making a good show in some wards at municipal elections—and particularly in those where the Conservatives were not strong.

Equally interesting, the Dundee poll showed that the S.N.P. was attracting a large proportion of the younger voters. The voting intentions of the main age groups were as follows:

	21–44 years	45 years and over
	%	%
Labour	21·5	27
Conservative	29	43
S.N.P.	34	15
Others	7·5	7
Don't Know	8	8

This finding confirms what has been clear from observation at elections, where S.N.P. supporters seem markedly younger than their opponents.

Finally, the Dundee poll gave an indication of the occupations of the supporters of the various parties. It made clear that the S.N.P. was socially much more representative of the population as a whole than either of the other two parties, though it was weak in the professional, managerial and clerical spheres.

[1] *The Scotsman*, 8th July 1968.

	Professional and managerial %	Other non-manual %	Skilled manual %	Other manual %	Miscellaneous %
Labour	8	10·5	27·5	38	15·5
Conservative	67·5	58	26	17·5	54
S.N.P.	17	14·5	29·5	28·5	30·5
Others	5	8·5	8	6·5	—
Don't Know	2·5	8·5	9	9·5	—
	100	100	100	100	100

As *The Scotsman* pointed out: 'It must be worrying for Labour to learn that it has the support of only just over one quarter of skilled manual workers, the largest occupational group in the electorate.'

III

Since the war, two United Kingdom parties at different ends of the political spectrum have taken a keen interest in Scottish Home Rule, the Liberals and the Communists. The Scottish Liberals have always been very conscious both of their party's long Home Rule tradition and of the strength of Home Rule sentiment in Scotland, and since the Scottish Covenant movement of the late 1950s the Liberals have received a good deal of support from people active in the covenant movement. Moreover, the small band of Liberal M.P.s after 1964 has included several enthusiasts for Scottish Home Rule. They argue—rightly—that whereas the opinion polls have long shown that national sentiment is strong in Scotland, the people of Scotland are not agreed as to what should be done about the future government of Scotland. Hence a phased move towards Home Rule would be the sort of scheme which would appeal to the Scottish people, as well as making for good government. One of the main points made by Liberal speakers during the Liberal revival at the 1964 election was that the Liberals alone wholeheartedly championed Home Rule, and the party made much of a booklet published by the Scottish Liberal Party and called *Scottish Self Government*.[1] The case has since been restated in a later Liberal pamphlet by William Riddell, *Towards Scottish Home Rule* (January 1968).

[1] This pamphlet, first published in 1962, 3rd edn. 1964, was a development of an earlier one with the same title.

The Liberal position has been neatly summarized in a 1968 leaflet entitled *Self Government* which sets out to distinguish the Liberals alike from the Conservatives, Labour, and the S.N.P. This reads as follows:

LIBERALS TALK SENSE ON SELF-GOVERNMENT

WE KNOW WHAT'S WRONG
Unemployment is always TWICE the U.K. average.
Housing lags far behind the rest of the U.K.
Wages are below the U.K. average.
Emigration is rising (up to 47,000 per year).

WE KNOW WHY THIS HAPPENS
Because Westminster has no time to discuss Scottish problems.
Because Scotland doesn't get the different treatment she needs.
Because London doesn't care and isn't interested in Scotland.
Because there is no financial control in Scotland.

WE KNOW WHAT TO DO
Scots should run their own affairs.
This means a Scottish Parliament controlling all Home Policy *including* taxation.
Leave Westminster to run Foreign Affairs, Defence and Commonwealth affairs. It's stupid to duplicate expenditure.
Build up a Federal system in Britain.

WHAT HAVE WE DONE?
We introduced a Bill for Scottish Self Government which for the first time said clearly how a Scottish Government could be set up.
This Liberal solution is what millions of Scots supported in the Covenant of the 1950s.
All plebiscites and polls have shown clearly that this is what the great majority of Scots want.

WHAT IS THE ALTERNATIVE?
Tories and Socialists are being forced to talk of more devolution.
For example, Heath's Scottish Assembly proposals just tinker with the problem and *still wouldn't bring decision* to Scotland.
The SNP want complete separation from the U.K. with a separate army, navy, air force and foreign embassies. They are prepared to see customs posts on the Cheviots.

Not only do people in Scotland not want this, but it would not solve
their problem.

Complete separation hasn't made Eire rich. The average wage is
£11 9/- compared to £19 15/- in Scotland. If Britain devalues, so
does Eire. If Britain joins/stays out of the EEC, so does Eire.
We need to co-operate about matters of common interest.

ONLY LIBERALS TALK SENSE ON SELF-GOVERNMENT

Two Liberal M.P.s have made the question very much their own.
Russell Johnston, M.P. for Inverness, introduced a Scottish Self-
Government Bill on 30th November 1966 in an attempt to revive the
pre-1927 habit of putting forward Home Rule bills at regular inter-
vals.[1] And David Steel, M.P. for Roxburgh, Selkirk and Peebles, has
devoted a well-argued pamphlet to suggesting that the most useful
change that could be made at the moment would be the introduction of
a piecemeal system of legislative devolution.[2] In particular, he has
argued that a Select Committee on the work of the Scottish Office
should be established, that parliamentary questions should be asked in
the Scottish Grand Committee, that the Scottish Grand Committee
should be confined to the Scottish M.P.s, and that the Scottish Grand
Committee should meet more frequently, its meetings to be held every
second Monday in Edinburgh. Moreover, the United Kingdom
Liberal Party has been showing an increasing interest in devolution.
The party leader, Jeremy Thorpe, proposed a measure of Home Rule
All Round called a Federal Government Bill in the House of Commons on 21st February 1968, and when the Liberal Party Assembly
and the Scottish Liberal Party held a joint meeting in Edinburgh on
17th–21st September 1968 much of the business was concerned with
measures of devolution.

The great weakness of the Liberal party position has been that,
though the Liberals favour Home Rule, they had not been able to
suggest any way in which they might be able to secure it, until David
Steel made his 'piecemeal' proposals in February 1968. Furthermore,
they have been handicapped by the distribution of their voting strength
in Scotland itself. The Liberal M.P.s elected in 1968 all represent
predominantly rural constituencies, several of them with relatively

[1] 737 H.C. Deb., 5 ser., c. 456–9.
[2] David Steel, *Out of Control: a Critical Examination of the Government of Scotland* (Scottish Liberal Party, Edinburgh, 1968).

small populations.[1] The Liberal party for a time in the early 1960s also had a substantial backing in the suburbs of the big towns, notably among the young. But now its strength in the towns is confined to a few pockets, of which the most important is Greenock, where it controls the town council. It cannot therefore expect to make any significant advances, though it may win back Caithness and Sutherland, which had a Liberal M.P. from 1964 to 1966. Worse still, many Liberal seats would be endangered if the S.N.P. were to put up a candidate against the sitting Liberal M.P. The S.N.P. could not win them, but it could ensure that the Liberal was defeated by the Conservatives or by Labour. It is, indeed, a curious fact that the party which has thought most about Home Rule, and whose policy most closely reflects the views of the Scottish electorate as shown in public opinion polls, should be the least capable of doing anything about implementing it.

The Communists offer a striking contrast to the Liberals. During the 1920s, when the Liberal party had already been committed to Home Rule for over thirty years, the Scottish communists under the leadership of William Gallacher, though generally favourable to Scottish devolution, committed themselves to resisting Scottish separatism, which they associated with the revisionist views of John Maclean. The Communist Party of Great Britain, as a result, became a highly centralized body, with a number of influential Scots in key positions in its London headquarters in King Street. Because its members after a time dominated the Scottish area of the National Union of Mineworkers, Communist influence in the industrial field was very strong in Scotland and between the wars this strength was used for anti-nationalist purposes, though the Communist party usually professed to favour devolution. This was not just a matter of tactics. It arose from the genuine feeling that the international solidarity of the working class must come first, a policy which had ample justification after the rise of Mussolini in Italy and Hitler in Germany had given sinister overtones to nationalism. Even so, it looked for a time during the thirties as though the party might be contemplating a relaxation of its centralist policy, but after a long debate in 1937 and 1938 the party reaffirmed its old position by expelling Hugh MacDiarmid for nationalist deviation.

After the war the Communist party began to reassess its position. Though still strongly centralist in principle, it began to recognize that

[1] The constituencies are Orkney and Shetland, Ross and Cromarty, Inverness, West Aberdeenshire, Roxburgh, Selkirk and Peebles.

economic conditions in Scotland were very different from those in England, and that this was reflected in the greater strength of working-class Communism in Scotland. The Labour government's policy of nationalization was welcomed, but the party recognized that the highly centralized structure of the new nationalized industries—coal, electricity and gas in particular—might lead to considerable practical difficulties both for Scotland and for Communists in the Scottish trade union movement. A Scottish Coal Board, for instance, might well have come under Communist influence, whereas a United Kingdom one would not. As a result, the Scottish Communists gave a great deal of attention to the distinctive problems of the Scottish economy, and John Gollan in *Scottish Prospect: an Economic, Administrative and Social Survey* (Glasgow, 1948) made a thorough, and on the whole convincing, study of the question, which can still be read with profit today. The party also began to recognize that it must make some concession to nationalist feeling. The result was an increasing flexibility which was reflected in the party's general election manifestoes. The 1951 manifesto simply declared that 'There must be full recognition of the national claims of the Scottish and Welsh peoples, to be settled according to the wishes of these peoples'.[1] But at subsequent general elections Communist policy for Scotland became more and more elaborate, until it became committed to a policy of devolution by stages, which would make possible a smooth transition to Scottish self-government.[2] Indeed, in 1957 it was actually possible for Hugh MacDiarmid to rejoin the party. This evolution has largely been brought about by a change in the policy of the Scottish Area of the National Union of Mineworkers which now favours a separate Scottish parliament. But though the Communist party in Scotland is now firmly committed to Scottish self-government, what this means for Scotland is not very clear, because the Communist party in Scotland has been a declining force in recent years.

Of late the Communist party has also had to cope with a rival organization, the Workers' Party of Scotland (Marxist–Leninist), which has set itself up in opposition to the Communist Party of Great Britain as the expression of pro-Chinese feeling, as against the Moscow-oriented line of the C.P.G.B. Though extremely small in numbers, the Workers' Party of Scotland has attracted a good deal of attention

[1] *The British Road to Socialism* (Communist Party, London, 1951), p. 11.
[2] Gordon McLennan, *Demand a Future for Scotland* (Communist Party, Glasgow Committee, n.d.).

by deliberately trying to model the party on the movement started by John Maclean before 1923 and by playing down its Chinese connections (which are few). This has meant that the W.P.S. has been militantly nationalist in tone, and has often gone well beyond the S.N.P. in the vehemence of its nationalism: indeed it speaks of 'The "Partial" Self-Government Proposals of the S.N.P.'.[1] It is not always easy to take the W.P.S. very seriously because its publications have an endearingly amateur flavour about them: *Scottish Vanguard*, for instance, which uses the name of John Maclean's old paper, carries slogans which seem to belong to the 1930s:[2]

> Take DIRECT action;
> Create a HEALTHY UPROAR;
> Indulge in REBELLION!!!!!!!

But there is no doubt of the W.P.S.'s nationalism. Much is made of William Wallace, Robert Burns and John Maclean, and the declared objective of the party is a 'Socialist Republic of Scotland'.[3]

The main contribution by the members of the W.P.S. to the nationalist cause hitherto has been the foundation of the John Maclean Society. This was inaugurated on 31st March 1968 in the Grand Hotel, Glasgow, and exists to publish the works of Maclean. (Those of Connolly, another hero of the W.P.S., have already been published in Ireland and all that remained to do for him was to erect a plaque marking the place of his birth in Edinburgh.) The sponsors of the society include old men who had known Maclean, like Emanuel Shinwell and Emrys Hughes, orthodox left-wingers like Lord Provost John Johnston of Glasgow, the churchman George Macleod (the Right Rev. the Lord Macleod of Fuinary), orthodox Communists like Abe Moffatt, unorthodox Communists like Hugh MacDiarmid, and a number of prominent members of the S.N.P. Little is likely to come of the society, however, though it has already led to some rather nasty right-wing jibes at the S.N.P. in the *Glasgow Herald*, under the headings 'S.N.P. Leaders' contact with Far Left' and 'Communists who like S.N.P.'.[4]

---

[1] *Scottish Vanguard*, Vol. 2, No. 1 (January 1968), p. 1.

[2] ibid., Vol. 2, No. 3 (March 1968), p. 12. Another slogan is 'To hate is meritorious'.

[3] The party's policy is set out in a Manifesto of 24th May 1967 published in *Scottish Vanguard*, Vol. 1, No. 2 (1967), pp. 11–14.

[4] *Glasgow Herald*, 25th June 1968. Reprint available from the Conservative Party.

IV

The Conservatives have been much more flexible in their attitude to the challenge of the S.N.P. than has the Labour party. This is largely, one suspects, because the Conservative party has been doing so badly in the last few years that it cannot sit back and hope that with the swing of the pendulum all will come right again. Whereas the English Conservatives benefited from the swing away from Labour after 1966, the Scottish Conservatives have benefited but little. There are those who regard the growing strength of the S.N.P. as a passing phase and who argue that all will come well if the party only sits tight, but unless they can point to some evidence that things will soon get better they will not be listened to. Already there are Conservative ginger groups at work, notably the Thistle Group, which are determined to give the Scottish Conservatives a more distinctly Scottish flavour.[1]

The Scots Conservatives have suffered from the great handicap of not having fought municipal elections as a matter of course. Municipal affairs have been left to separate organizations called at one time Moderate and now Progressive. Most Progressives are Conservatives, but the local Progressive associations also attract a significant amount of support from those who argue that national party politics should be kept separate from local politics. Since most Progressives are not known to be active in the Conservative party, this means that the Conservative party has been effectively deprived of one of the usual means of creating an urban party leadership. Local Conservative associations have therefore tended much more than in England to be officered by hereditary Conservatives who have no desire to be mixed up in local politics. Hence the complaints so frequently heard from Young Conservatives about the stuffiness of their elders, their unwillingness to do the hard work necessary to keep a party going, and their hostility to the selection of parliamentary candidates from outside the traditional group of professional and landed families. Certainly it seems to be harder in Scotland than it is in England for a pushful young man to get himself elected to Parliament. The Conservative leaders are aware that something must be done, but the business of engineering a Conservative entry into municipal politics has proved an exceptionally difficult one. This is partly because in the four big cities the Progressives did well at the May 1968 municipal

[1] *The Thistle Group*, pamphlet No. 1 (Edinburgh, [1967]).

elections, when they benefited from the swing against Labour where the S.N.P. had not yet established itself. Partly it is because there is real opposition from the Progressives to Conservative encroachments. The relatively few Conservatives who have offered themselves as avowedly Conservative candidates have not done notably well in municipal elections except in unusual circumstances.

Frustrated, the Conservatives are apt to turn upon one another. The newspapers during 1968 were full of reports of dissatisfaction with the party leadership in Scotland among (unnamed) prominent Conservatives. The ostensible causes were said to be dissatisfaction with individual Conservative leaders, dissatisfaction with the image the party presents in Scotland, dissatisfaction with the way the party goes about its business, and hostility to the policy statement outlined by Edward Heath as party leader at the Scottish Conservative conference in May 1968.

Edward Heath's policy statement arose from the report of a group of leading Conservatives ('the Scottish Policy Group') who were appointed by Heath to consider 'the machinery of government north of the border'. Aware that Conservative voters in many parts of the country had already deserted to the S.N.P. or were thinking of doing so they wanted to give ordinary Conservatives the sense that the party was going somewhere and to prevent them from deserting their ordinary allegiance. On the basis of the old maxim, if you can't beat them join them, they also, no doubt, hoped to win over those waverers (especially among those who had voted Liberal in 1964 and 1966) who felt that the Conservatives were not sufficiently Scottish in their orientation. They therefore prepared the outline of a Conservative scheme of legislative devolution, which became the basis of Mr. Heath's speech.

The main argument put forward by Mr. Heath was that whereas in the United States, in the European Economic Community and elsewhere, the tendency of modern mass society was all towards larger units, whether they took the form of larger markets, larger industrial firms or federal rather than state governments, people everywhere were demanding that government and the decision-making process should become less impersonal, less remote.[1] Hence, it was at one and the same time natural to think in terms of Britain joining the common market and in terms of taking government to the people, whether this

[1] The text of the speech is contained in Conservative Central Office News Service Release 402/68.

was done by regional governments in England or by national governments in Wales and Scotland. The object of the Conservative party should be on the one hand to remain 'the Party of the Union' ('Our fundamental belief is in the destiny of the United Kingdom. This . . . was reinforced by the Liberal Unionists who joined us in the 1880s and added the name of Unionist to our Party') and on the other hand 'to see power more widely diffused within the framework of a united country'. For Scotland this dual policy provided an opportunity to 'give a lead in new developments in the way in which she is governed'. Federalism was ruled out because it would mean a fundamental change in the constitution of the United Kingdom. So too was the Northern Irish system, which had been adopted in Ulster simply *faute de mieux*. Both systems might involve Scotland in taking on expenditure which it could not afford. For Scotland was not an area of high prosperity but one that needed development expenditure. The right answer was to experiment with a Scottish legislative assembly. This would be a single-chamber body meeting in Scotland which would 'enable purely Scottish legislation to be handled at certain stages in Scotland'. In addition there should be further administrative devolution.

These proposals were all made in an extremely tentative form on the understanding that details would subsequently be worked out by a constitutional commission. But they immediately provoked a good deal of opposition. Those in the Conservative party who were associated with the Thistle Group thought an ill-defined Scottish assembly a poor substitute for a constructive social and economic policy. Those who disliked any tampering with the *status quo* were outraged. A group of Conservative M.P.s announced that they had never liked the plan.[1] And much central opinion was cynically convinced that nothing would or could come of the proposed Scottish Assembly. It had, they remarked, all the worst characteristics of many botched-up colonial constitutions of the period before independence in Africa, and would be unworkable in practice. Nor was their scepticism reduced by the appointment of the promised constitutional committee. The committee got off to a bad start. It included a judge, Lord Avonside, who subsequently resigned when he found his position an impossible one, and its composition was attacked because, whereas it included an Australian lawyer and an American one, both working in England, an English lawyer who is a professor in a Scottish university, and an English ex-Lord Chancellor, it included no Scottish lawyer. Further-

[1] *The Scotsman,* 11th July 1968, and *The Times,* 8th July 1968.

more, there was a good deal of criticism behind the scenes, both from those who disapproved of the whole thing, and from those who thought that the composition of the committee was such that it was unlikely to reach any worthwhile conclusions, about the way in which the committee had been appointed.[1]

Mr. Heath clearly intended to give a lead to the Scottish Conservatives, which would enable them to cope with the challenge of the S.N.P., but the vagueness of his constitutional ideas seems in fact simply to have provided additional ammunition for his enemies. The one thing that can be said for Mr. Heath's policy statement is that it was a warning to Scottish Conservatives that they might find themselves some day living in an independent Scotland, unless they were prepared to make some concession to nationalist sentiment.

The Labour party's attitude towards the rise of the S.N.P. has been for the most part one of irritation and contempt. Nationalism seems to most Scottish Labour leaders a romantic absurdity, far removed from the day-to-day problems of bread and butter. And they resent the fact that a party of what they like to think of as 'tartan Tories' has been winning support from Labour voters. As the party in power since 1964 the Labour party has, therefore, tended simply to batten down the hatches and to hope that the time will come when the Labour government will do something for Scotland of which the Labour party can be proud. The record of the Labour Secretary of State, William Ross, has been a good one in United Kingdom terms. Most of Scotland has been declared a development area; the effects of the selective employment tax have been moderated; a new aluminium smelter has been authorized for erection at Invergordon; and the austerities of the post-1966 period have hit England harder than Scotland. But from a Scottish point of view things look very different. The Labour government has prevented things from getting worse, but it has little to show in terms of positive achievements. Mr. Ross has consistently said that the Union has been of advantage to Scotland, in that industry has been directed from England to Scotland and that the level of social security expenditure is set by southern English standards. But little notice has been taken in Scotland. Conditions under Labour are little different from those under the Conservatives, and, if anything, the Labour party seems less tender towards Scottish sensibilities. Both the selective employment tax and the Transport Act, 1968, drawn up with English conditions in mind, have had to be adapted for Scottish purposes

[1] *Sunday Telegraph*, 18th August 1968.

painfully and inadequately. The Labour government's transport policy, with its provisions for the taxation of road transport, was indeed wholly inappropriate for Scottish conditions, where distances are great and the population is relatively small.

The attitudes of the Scottish Labour leaders stem largely from the inter-war period. During that time the Scottish trade union movement gradually shifted from support for Home Rule, strongly backed in 1918, 1920, 1921 and 1922, to hostility towards it signified at the 1931 Congress of the S.T.U.C. Indeed, the speeches made by the opponents of self-government for Scotland in 1931 might well be made today.

> Mr. T. Barron (Amalgamated Society of Woodworkers) suggested that the motion might create difficulties that would be very hard to get over in the future. That had happened in the building trades in Ireland since the Free State was set up. The very breath of their spirit was internationalism, and this sort of thing would do their movement a great deal of harm.
> Mr. J. M'Clounie (National Union of Railwaymen) opposed the resolution, and pointed out they had made no headway in the railways until they got away from the old Caledonian, G. & S.W., Lancashire and Cheshire, Great Western and so on unions. This resolution represented a parish pump outlook, and it was significant that it emanated from an organisation [the Scottish Horse and Motormen] which could only think in terms of the parish pump. Workers should look upon themselves as workers, and not as Scotsmen or Englishmen. Let them be honest and get back to the ideals of international Socialism.[1]

There was still, however, a feeling both in the Labour Party and in the Scottish trade union movement that more local autonomy for Scotland was desirable—at least in the administrative field. As many as 39 per cent of the Labour candidates at the general election of 1945 favoured the creation of a Scottish parliament,[2] and in 1947 the S.T.U.C. voted to explore the possibility of establishing 'a Scottish body, with special powers in order that problems peculiar to Scotland, which arise from time to time, can be expedited'. The champions of the motion were again the Scottish Horse and Motormen, but their attitude was now no longer regarded as parochial, as it had been in 1931. Other unions after 1945 began to toy again with the idea of greater

[1] S.T.U.C. report for 1931.
[2] McCallum and Readman, *The British General Election of 1945*, p. 104.

autonomy for Scotland, among them the National Union of Mineworkers, Scottish Area, which found that it had gained little or nothing from the creation of the National Coal Board beyond a change of alien masters. Hence in the first flush of surprise at the Hamilton by-election it is scarcely surprising to find the Mineworkers coming forward to the 1968 S.T.U.C. with a straight nationalist resolution:

> That this Congress, recognising the desire of the Scottish people for a Scottish Parliament, calls upon the Government to introduce legislation to establish a Parliament for Scotland, the ultimate form and powers of which should be determined by the Scottish electorate.[1]

Other unions (notably N.A.L.G.O. and the Foundry Workers) hastened to emphasize their support for the Union of 1707, and the General Council of the S.T.U.C. stepped in quickly to prevent either a nationalist landslide or a unionist demonstration. The General Council maintained that 'any argument for total separation in economic terms of Scotland from the United Kingdom' was 'totally irrelevant to Scotland's pressing economic problems', but also argued that it was impossible entirely to ignore the rise of nationalism. Hence it suggested a general inquiry into the whole matter of how Scotland should be governed to be undertaken on behalf of the General Council. Backed by strong unionist speeches by visiting politicians (including Harold Wilson) this policy was accordingly adopted. And in August 1968 the S.T.U.C. accordingly announced the appointment of a seven-man committee to look into the question.[2]

Within the Labour party leadership, Home Rule (as distinct from nationalism which has little backing) has been a bone of contention. Most Scottish M.P.s appear to be fervent unionists, but some favour the development of a form of regional devolution for Scotland, among them John P. Mackintosh, who has written extensively on the subject in the newspapers. Moreover, there seems to be a good deal of support for a further measure of Scottish devolution from English M.P.s who support regional devolution in England. A Scottish parliament, they argue, would be no different from the regional parliaments they hope to get for England. But the logic of Labour statements points towards further measures of administrative devolution rather than the making of a rash step towards Home Rule. One move towards further devolu-

[1] From the S.T.U.C. conference papers.
[2] *The Scotsman*, 6th August 1968.

tion was the announcement in July 1968 that the Labour government favoured permitting the Scottish Grand Committee to meet occasionally in Edinburgh, as from the beginning of the 1968–9 parliamentary session.[1] Other moves under discussion involve further devolution of administrative responsibilities from Whitehall departments and agencies to the Scottish Office. But the whole subject was referred late in 1968 to a Royal Commission on the Constitution, whose report is unlikely to be ready in time for the government to act on it before the next general election.

Fundamentally, the great difficulty for the Labour party of making any dramatic move towards Home Rule is that it takes a pessimistic view about the prospects for the Scottish economy. Labour calculations suggest that in the 1960s Scotland, because it is a relatively backward region of the British Isles, has been quite heavily subsidized from United Kingdom resources. As a development area Scotland receives tax incentives and subsidies for the building of new industries. As a low-income area Scotland pays in less to the United Kingdom Treasury than on a *per capita* basis she might be expected to do. And Scotland receives a great deal in the way of indirect subsidies, as a result of government pressure to move industries to Scotland. There would be no nuclear power station at Dounreay, no aluminium smelter at Invergordon, no Post-Office Savings Bank at Glasgow, no international airport at Prestwick, no Scottish motor industry, if it were not for the Union of Scotland and England. Furthermore, it is argued that the considerable number of American companies which have established factories in Scotland have done so because they will have free access to a unified United Kingdom market. Moreover, when Scottish Labour leaders think of 'independence' they think of the low-wage Republic of Ireland, not of prosperous Denmark. They fear that an independent Scotland would simply be an impoverished state on the periphery of Europe, to whose people emigration would appear more attractive than ever before. Labour ministers find the need to counter the nationalist threat a useful stick with which to beat their English colleagues (who are supposed to be afraid of losing the backing of the Scottish Labour members in the House of Commons). But there is also a good deal of anxiety in the Labour party lest the talk of nationalism should encourage the government at Westminster to take a little-England point of view and spend the bulk of tax income where it is raised—in England.

[1] *The Scotsman*, 24th July 1968.

The economic rights and wrongs of these Labour arguments are difficult to disentangle because there are no adequate Scottish financial and economic statistics on which to base a serious evaluation. Such attempts as have been made to produce a balance sheet (notably those of Dr. Gavin McCrone),[1] tend to suggest that it is almost certainly true that England does subsidize the Scottish economy and that industry would not be attracted so readily to an independent Scotland as to the Scotland of the present day. But there are real difficulties about just what these conclusions mean. Comparisons with the Republic of Ireland and with Denmark seem on closer investigation to be unhelpful because the Scottish economy is a very different sort of economy. The Republic of Ireland has only recently established a modern industrial base and the economy of Denmark is geared to a highly efficient and specialized agriculture. Scotland, by contrast, is an old-established industrial country. In so far as there is any parallel to it in Europe it is probably Belgium—or rather a Belgium with parts of Norway tagged on. Certainly, on the basis of such figures as are at present available, Scotland would be a very much wealthier and economically stronger country than the Republic of Ireland.

It is rash to hazard a guess in the absence of adequate statistics, but it looks very much as though the Labour Party is right to argue that a country like Scotland or Belgium badly needs outside help during the period of readjustment following the decline of staple industries (Scotland gets this help from England, Belgium from the European Community). However, the balance of advantage may well be different once old industries have been run down. In an era of state-fostered industry a 'national' government might well be more ready to develop an across-the-board range of modern industries and to provide a sound basis for further economic growth than a United Kingdom government which thinks primarily in terms of sharing out industries to the various regions of the country. The wider the range of growth industries the less the risk of undue dependence on obsolescent industrial giants and the greater the chance of participation in promising new industrial ventures. As things are, a country like Scotland which appears to be geographically remote (largely because of the long road-hauls involved) tends to attract only specialized branches of big international firms. These are liable to closure in the event of an economic crisis or a shift in consumer demand because they are peripheral to the interests of the parent firms. And they are usually not involved in

[1] Gavin McCrone, *Scotland's Economic Progress, 1951–60* (London, 1965).

development work: they simply carry out routine procedures laid down by the development engineers of the parent firm. What is wanted in Scotland is a much wider range of up-to-date Scotland-based industries. These need not necessarily be Scottish owned: some of them may well be divisions of big international firms: the important thing is that they should employ a complete range of industrial talent—managerial, scientific and technological—so that there is created in Scotland the right sort of intellectual climate for fostering growth industries.

The argument used by the Labour party in combating the case for 'national' economic development is that it has already started, that the fostering of an across-the-board range of Scottish industry is part of a long-standing governmental policy going back to the war years, and that regional development policies, whether called 'national' or not, form an essential part of the development economist's stock in trade, whether he is working in the United Kingdom or an independent country. What is at stake is, therefore, according to the Labour Party, merely a matter of opinion, since some argue that the present system works well, some that a system of Home Rule would make for faster economic development, and some that only national independence will lead to balanced economic growth. The problem is essentially one of assessing risks. The greatest risk of things going wrong would be run if independence were granted: the least risk is to be run by sticking to the present system. The logic of the situation is, therefore, to concentrate on improving and developing the existing system. As for nationalist sentiment, it must be regarded as irrelevant.

This is, of course, no answer to those who say that the present state of relative inertia in the Scottish economy is intolerable and that they are prepared to make sacrifices to get things going again, provided that they have something to sacrifice themselves for. The post-1967 governmental emphasis on consumer restraint and getting the balance of payments right offers no higher goal to the electors. They are simply to tighten their belts and hope that things will come right in the end, though they know that if things do come right Scotland will get less of the good things that are coming than will the south of England. If sacrifice is to be called for; sacrifice in order to build a new nation, in order to release the energies of the people, is much more meaningful than sacrifice in order to save the pound. In this sense nationalism is not just an irrelevant sentiment, as Labour speakers so often regard it, but an important economic incentive. And so long as the Labour party refuses to use it as a tool of economic policy, the S.N.P. seems likely to gain support.

V

Where stands the S.N.P. in 1968? In terms of numbers it has never been stronger. In 1962—a bad year—it had only 2,000 members, but after the Labour government took office in 1964 the number began speedily to grow: 42,000 in November 1966, 50,000 in March 1967, 100,000 in April 1968. Likewise the number of individual branches has grown astonishingly: in 1962 there were 20, by 1967 there were around 400, and by mid-1968 there were over 500. Many of the new members are too young to vote and it has been necessary to impose a minimum age limit for membership, but all the same this is an astonishingly good record.

No systematic survey of S.N.P. membership has so far been conducted, but to the outside observer it seems that the S.N.P. has appealed particularly strongly to the considerable body of people in Scotland who have been hitherto outside party politics altogether. The active branch members tend to belong to occupations which lay a great deal of stress on individual initiative. There are numerous shopkeepers, mechanics, engineers in the Post Office and other big organizations, small businessmen, teachers, photographers and minor business executives. But there is also a not-inconsiderable minority of trade unionists—especially miners and ex-miners—and of other refugees from the Labour party. To these must be added a fluctuating body of students and young shop assistants who are useful at elections and are good for keeping up party morale at social gatherings.

At times in the past the S.N.P. has often appeared to be primarily a university graduates' party, because student nationalism was so much stronger before 1966 than was nationalism in the country as a whole. Graduates who had been student nationalists and went into teaching or law were spread about the country both before and after the war in such a way that they became the nucleus for all sorts of nationalist activities—sometimes in the S.N.P., sometimes in the Scottish Convention, and sometimes in the Liberal or Labour party. Since 1966, however, the graduate element in the S.N.P. has been reinforced by a host of other activists and it would no longer be true to say that the S.N.P. is dominated by its graduates. It is now much more a populist party appealing to all those who feel that the present system fails to offer them the sort of opportunities they would like to have.

Conservative propaganda has tried to suggest that the S.N.P. is a left-wing party with dangerously socialistic tendencies. Labour propaganda, by contrast, has tried to suggest that the S.N.P. is a right-wing party with Poujadist leanings. The S.N.P. itself argues that the claims that the S.N.P. is either 'reactionary tory' or 'doctrinaire socialist' cancel one another out, and that 'they illustrate the democratic non-sectarian nature of the National Party'.[1] It would do better to argue that these claims merely illustrate how tied the Conservative and Labour parties are to their own terminology. For the S.N.P. is simply not like other parties in membership or policy. In its origins the S.N.P., as has been shown, was connected with the Left. But its members are for the most part drawn from what might be called the centre. A survey of a sample of S.N.P. members in Edinburgh at the end of 1967 showed that their views were almost dead centre on an attitude scale running from left to right. And it seems unlikely that members in other parts of the country would be different. In so far as the S.N.P. members have distinctive views they seem to be those which are held by many people who live in small or medium-sized towns and expect the government to do something for them. The nearest parallel is perhaps to be found in Australia and New Zealand, where the concept of what used to be called 'state socialism' is firmly rooted in Labour and non-Labour parties alike, and governments are expected to do something positive for every section of the community by way of state trading and industrial corporations and other national enterprises.

For the ordinary member of the S.N.P. the nationalism of its appeal is fundamental. He rallies to the S.N.P. slogan 'Put Scotland First' and the ideas that go with it.

> The National Party stands for the nation; all sections, all people in it; welded in a common purpose; devoted, dedicated to the social and economic improvement of all. The SNP stands for pride in a courageous and adult Scotland, and for confidence in a future guided by your hands and by the hands of your children. Our slogan is 'Put Scotland First'—a slogan of which we are proud—a slogan which no other politicians can use because the National Party is the only Scottish political party.
> Why PUT SCOTLAND FIRST ?
> We want prosperity for our nation. We want bread for our people.

---

[1] *SNP & You: Aims & Policy of the Scottish National Party* (3rd edn., S.N.P., 1968), p. 25.

But we want dignity too. For we know that bread is not enough to sustain the lives of men. We want health for our cities. But we want more than that—graciousness and breadth and beauty too.

We turn envious eyes upon the spacious cities of the little lands which ought, by all the arguments of the Westminster politicians, to be poor and wretched. We think of Stockholm and Copenhagen, Oslo and Amsterdam. And then compare Glasgow and Edinburgh and other places which have wretched slums. And we look south to England where wages are so much higher and wealth so much more plentiful, at our expense, for there is no doubt that we subsidise England, under unionist rule—Tory or Labour; and that we help to keep London and Birmingham rich and help to keep unemployment there down to a quarter the Scottish rate.[1]

But behind all this rhetoric lies a series of well-thought-out policies which have been gradually evolved from the programme adopted by the party conferences of 1944 and 1945. The starting point is that, with over half the population of the United Kingdom living within 125 miles of London, Scotland is now a peripheral part of the United Kingdom which the Labour and Conservative parties can ignore if they so choose. Had Scotland had the same rate of unemployment as England from 1951 to 1968 Scotland would have 500,000 more Scots living and working in Scotland than there are today. The only hope of preventing a still further draining away of people is to create a Scottish economic renaissance, which is entirely Scottish in its orientation. This means establishing an entirely new set of institutions, starting with a Scottish parliament.

The emphasis now placed on a Scottish parliament by the S.N.P. is less strong than it used to be, partly no doubt because of the ill repute into which parliamentarianism has temporarily fallen. The S.N.P. will continue to send M.P.s to Westminster to vote and work 'in the interests of the people of Scotland' and 'in support of legislation which is in accord with the S.N.P. policy'.[2] However, when the S.N.P. has secured a majority of the Scottish seats in the House of Commons the party's M.P.s 'will ask the UK Parliament to set up a Scottish Legislature'. Failing that, 'the SNP M.P.s and any other Scottish M.P.s who care to join them, will form a Scottish government, loyal to the crown'. This government will then prepare a constitution for sub-

[1] ibid., pp. 2–3.
[2] ibid., p. 7.

mission to the electorate and call a general election. The S.N.P. will continue in being after independence, but the party recognizes that 'other parties will develop in opposition'.[1] The members of the party, as of other independence movements, are divided as to whether the party which achieves independence will survive for long or not, but they are content to leave the resolution of the problem to the future.

The main reason why the S.N.P. can afford to be a bit vague about constitutional issues is that its chief emphasis is now on economic development. This is sometimes a cause of dismay to those who put patriotism first and cannot make head or tail of economics. But it is an emphasis that accords well with the mood of the country as a whole. For publicity purposes the party puts its chief emphasis on fuel, transport and power, because these are the subjects that have caused most bitterness in post-war Scotland. It argues that recent government policy on coal pits is 'economic murder' and that Scottish pits have been much harder hit by closures than those in England (33 per cent in Scotland, 2 per cent in the rest of the U.K.). It would stabilize Scottish coal output at fifteen million tons a year and put 'an end to destroying whole communities, forced flittings and unreasonable travelling distances', until such time as there were alternative new industries to employ the miners.[2] It would halt the closure of main railway lines and introduce a co-ordinated transport system, including new coastal shipping and air services. And it would create a fuel policy specifically geared to Scottish needs which would take no account of general United Kingdom policy. Such a policy would give some scope for private enterprise, but would chiefly involve the use of public corporations. ('The S.N.P. believes in the public ownership of coal and other minerals and in public control of an adequate transport system to serve the interests of the Scottish people.')[3]

The main feature of the S.N.P.'s economic policy is the use of public credit-granting bodies and of an industrial development corporation as the means of promoting economic growth. An independent Scottish government would create a Scottish central bank and continue the existing policy of building factories and making grants and loans to industry. It would also put great emphasis on small-scale industry by 'providing risk capital through a Development Corporation for groups of people to own and run "workshop factories" for the development of

[1] ibid., p. 7.
[2] *Action Now: Coal & Power*, S.N.P., March 1968.
[3] *S.N.P. & You*, p. 8.

new enterprises, especially in areas where new industry is badly needed'.[1] And it would encourage 'Credit Unions and other Co-operative enterprises by appointing qualified men and women to stimulate this kind of social and economic growth'. There would be a Council for Land Use to undertake a survey of land and natural resources and a Land Development Board to carry out the policies suggested by the Council by purchasing, developing, selling or leasing estates and farms. There would be marketing boards for meat, cereals, potatoes and eggs controlled by farmers; and producer-controlled co-operatives to manage government-owned abattoirs, grain stores and other communal rural enterprises. The fishing limits would be extended to fourteen miles and extensive state aid would be made available for reshaping the fishing industry. And there would be better social services.

All these policies are very similar in conception to those pursued in other advanced small countries, such as Israel and Norway. Finance would be found partly by restricting defence expenditure to £100m. at 1968 prices (compared with an estimated £200m. in 1968), partly by the use of state credit facilities, partly by changes in the balance of taxation. Just what tax changes would be needed is a matter for dispute. The optimists in the S.N.P. are inclined to think that the saving from no longer having to subsidize England (which is what they believe Scotland does at the moment) would be sufficient to enable some taxes to be reduced. The pessimists are inclined to think that Scottish taxation might have for a time to be much higher than at present (as it is in Norway), at least until such time as the Scottish economy is booming again.

On one important matter the S.N.P. is adamant. At the 1967 conference a resolution on British membership of the Common Market laid down that the S.N.P. would:

> not countenance any negotiations to take Scotland into the European Economic Community without separate consultation of the People of Scotland, and states that an independent Scottish Government will not accept any Agreement which London makes, and will repudiate any Agreement under which Scotland has no separate National representation.

As in the discussions before 1939 on British entry into the war, the argument was that the party must stick to its principles through thick

[1] ibid., p. 10.

and thin. It was particularly galling to the pride of members of the S.N.P. that had the United Kingdom joined the Common Market Luxembourg would have had a vote (though it has a smaller population than Edinburgh) but Scotland would not. But the real argument at issue was an economic one. The official S.N.P. point of view is that United Kingdom membership of E.E.C. would markedly worsen Scotland's economic position and accentuate the tendency for Scottish industry to decline and for Scots to emigrate.[1] A Scandinavian-style solution to the economic problems of Scotland might work: E.E.C. membership without safeguards for Scotland would be intolerable, because it would make the present bad situation worse.

The cultural policy of the S.N.P. now bears little relationship to the case for a literary renaissance made by the literary men of the 1920s and 1930s. Culture is seen almost as an adjunct to economics. Education is spoken of as a costly process which must be geared to the production of the sort of skilled people the new Scotland will need. Much play is made with university statistics which undoubtedly show that an excessive number of English students are studying in Scottish universities and keeping out qualified Scots. And there is a policy for a reallocation of educational expenditure which, says the S.N.P., should be transferred from the local authorities to the central government. A good deal of eloquence is expended on the goals of education—'Our children must learn how to appreciate not only knowledge but one another. They must be taught about their country and its history, geography, literature, art, music, etc.'[2] But it is a curious feature of the S.N.P. that in the quest for political success it has shed most of the few notable Scottish writers and literary men from its membership and that its membership among Scots on the staff of the Scottish universities is tiny. An over-exposure to poets seems to have made the S.N.P. almost hostile to modern Scottish culture.

This came out clearly during 1967 and 1968 over the case of the 1320 Club. This club was founded in Glasgow in an attempt not merely to keep alive the memory of the Declaration of Arbroath (signed in 1320) but to develop the cultural side of Scottish nationalism which had been neglected by the S.N.P. To this end it sponsored a journal, *Catalyst*, and appealed for help to nationalists of all sorts, whether they were members of the S.N.P. or not. As a result, the 1320 Club looked for a time like a nationalist rival to the S.N.P., since it aimed to bring

[1] *No Voice No Entry* (S.N.P., 1967).
[2] *S.N.P. & You*, p. 16.

together dissident nationalists like Wendy Wood, Oliver Brown, Hugh MacDiarmid, Douglas Young, and the Workers Party of Scotland, and a wide variety of other persons interested in Scottish self-government, to discuss such questions as the future government of Scotland and the future of Scottish culture. In the light of past experience this was perhaps a rather rash thing to do, because nationalists have never spoken with one voice, but it was an interesting experiment. The S.N.P., however, promptly declared the 1320 Club a prohibited organization and ruled that any member of the S.N.P. who joined it would be expelled from the party. One sympathizes with the leaders of the S.N.P. in their desire to prevent the party being tarred with the various brushes wielded by the nationalist lunatic fringe. But the episode leaves one with the impression that some of the leaders of the S.N.P. rank neat party statements above the sort of free discussion that the other parties have fostered at their summer schools. Student nationalists are often on excellent terms with a wide range of non-nationalists and their societies discuss a great variety of topics. But the S.N.P. itself does not make a feature of gatherings, such as the Conservatives have long held, at which party members have the chance of discussing their problems with distinguished outsiders. And the S.N.P. literature service does not include any works of serious analysis. On the evidence available at the moment the S.N.P. seems to be as different from the old National Party described by Lewis Spence in 1929 as a party well can be.

The S.N.P.'s position on relations with England is a deliberately cautious one. Because the party now emphasizes economics as much as patriotism it has been forced to recognize that the fact that the vast majority of Scottish trade is with England (about 80 per cent according to one estimate) means that independence would not mean complete severance from England. There would need to be some sort of partnership, such as there is between the United Kingdom and the Republic of Ireland, at least during the transitional period after independence. And the S.N.P. are clearly prepared to think in terms of institutionalizing the economic links between Scotland and England. The monarchy would provide one such link and there would also be joint authorities to administer common services. For instance, the S.N.P. seems to have little enthusiasm for a customs barrier between England and Scotland and would apparently prefer some sort of specially negotiated customs union. Independence would be indicated chiefly by the existence of a Scottish national government devoted largely to the development of the Scottish economy, by Scotland opting out of the United Kingdom's defence commitments and closing down foreign bases on Scottish soil (why, it is asked, should Scotland have a nuclear submarine base as a target for enemy attack when England does not have one?), and by Scotland establishing diplomatic relations with the other European states. There might in the end have to be a customs barrier at the border with England, but it will be the result of English intransigence, not of S.N.P. policy.

VI

Much ingenuity has been devoted (chiefly by opponents of the S.N.P.) to the question, would the S.N.P. policy work? But this is the wrong question to ask. Independence has been made to work in dozens of countries which are less strong economically and less united than Scotland. Even such an unlikely event as the closing of the border between Scotland and England would not be an insuperable obstacle to success. It might, indeed, spur the people of Scotland on to hitherto undreamed of feats of economic prowess. The important question is, what sort of independent Scotland does the S.N.P. envisage?

The answer seems to be a Scotland based initially on current institutions. The Scottish Office will be divided into a series of separate ministries. A Scottish cabinet and parliament will be created. Scotland will join the United Nations and will have its own diplomatic representatives abroad. But otherwise the emphasis is all on fairly routine administrative devices such as all newly independent countries adopt —the creation of a central bank, a development corporation and all the other mechanisms for promoting economic growth. There are all sorts of populist themes in the S.N.P. programme (just as there are in the Conservative programme) about setting the people free and about giving the people greater control over administration, but these are notoriously difficult to develop in practice. They are the overture to an opera yet to be written and it may reasonably be doubted whether the opera will ever be written at all unless the style of government is radically changed. Whether there will ever be a radical change in governmental style depends on two factors about which it is too early as yet to say anything—the tone of the new Scottish parliament and the way in which the new Scottish administration would be constructed. Even if there were no positive steps towards popular control over administration, the very fact that the Scottish civil service is a relatively small one would have some effect on its style. It is noticeable at the present time that Whitehall is less approachable, because of its size, than is St. Andrew's House, and that St. Andrew's House is less welcoming than the administration of countries with a smaller population than Scotland, such as New Zealand. Presumably the very fact of dividing the Scottish Office into separate departments of modest size would tend to make for a less formal style of government and one more susceptible to popular pressure.

The great argument in favour of an independent Scotland is that it might release energies and enthusiasms that would not be tapped even by a system of Home Rule. At the height of its popularity the Union was inspired by a sense of purpose. Scots felt that they were sharing in a great imperial venture and took pride in the achievements of Scots all over the world. Now that the Empire is dead, many Scots feel cramped and restricted at home. They chafe at the provincialism of much of Scottish life and at the slowness of Scottish economic growth, which is related to that provincialism. To give themselves an opening to a wider world the Scots need some sort of outlet, and the choice appears at the moment to be between emigration and re-creating the Scottish nation at home. An independent diplomatic service would widen Scottish horizons as nothing else would. There might even be a chance of a political *rapprochement* that would enable an independent Scottish government to make use of the talents of such able men as Jo Grimond and David Steel, who seem at the moment doomed to a life of frustration on the back benches of the House of Commons. But, once again, it is hard to say anything positive about what the sense of liberation that would come with independence would lead to in practical terms.

It follows, I think, from this analysis that the independent Scotland envisaged by the S.N.P. would be very like the present Scotland, except that it would be better governed and have a focus of national loyalty. In this sense the S.N.P. must be regarded as a much more conservative body than its critics on the left and the right are inclined to make out. The nearest parallel is to be found in the old colonial empire, where dominion status or independence simply meant a transfer of power to a new group of politicians, while the structure of the state and of society was but little changed.

Statement of Aim and Policy of the Scottish National Party, adopted 7th—8th December 1946[1]

AIM OF THE NATIONAL PARTY

The People of Scotland, as members of one of the oldest nations in Europe, are the inheritors, bearers and transmitters of an historic tradition of liberty. They have in common with the peoples of all other nations an inherent right to determine their own destiny in accordance with the principles of justice accepted by the social conscience of mankind. The aim of the Scottish National Party is therefore 'Self-Government for Scotland. The restoration of Scottish National sovereignty by the establishment of a democratic Scottish Government whose authority will be limited only by such agreements as will be freely entered into with other nations in order to further international co-operation and world peace.'

POLICY OF THE NATIONAL PARTY

I. CONSTITUTIONAL

1. Central Government

In a self-governing Scotland the establishment of a representative Parliament is indispensable. Only such a body, elected by and responsible to the Scottish people, can make the Scottish people's will effective in action and can have the knowledge, experience and authority to develop to the full the rich resources of the country, both human and material, for the benefit of the whole community and thus ensure for all a standard of living as high as in any other self-governing country.

(1) On the election to the British Parliament of a majority of Scottish National members from Scotland, a Scottish Constituent Assembly shall be summoned either (a) in virtue of an Act of Parlia-

[1] Printed from the *Scots Independent*, January 1947.

ment passed by agreement with the English members or (b) failing such agreement, by the Scottish National members acting in terms of the authority conferred upon them by the Scottish electorate.

(2) It will be the task of the Constituent Assembly in framing a Constitution for Scotland to determine such problems as the relationship of a self-governing Scotland to the other countries of the British Isles and Commonwealth; the composition and powers of the legislature; the method of electing representatives; and the desirability of introducing the referendum and initiative. The Constitution so framed will be submitted to the Scottish electorate for approval.

(3) It is clear, however, that in order to ensure effective democratic representation there must be an increase in the number of directly elected members of Parliament and that area as well as population must be taken into account in the consequent redistribution of constituencies.

(4) Since Scotland forms a convenient unit of government in area and resources the creation of the centralized administrative machinery essential in the modern state need not lead to the growth of an irresponsible bureaucracy. A comparatively small executive and Civil Service will be adequate as shown by current examples from abroad.

(5) The existing Privy Council shall have no powers or competence whatsoever in Scotland. The functions of the Crown in Scotland will be exercised during the residence of the Sovereign in and through a Scottish Privy Council and in the absence of the Sovereign by a Council of State appointed from the Privy Council.

(6) Legislation will be enacted by Parliament as a whole and the delegation of legislative powers to Ministers or others strictly limited. Where such delegation is deemed essential in the national interest orders made in pursuance thereof will not have the force of law until laid before Parliament and, if approved, brought effectively to the public notice.

2. Local Government

Scottish Nationalism is based primarily on spiritual values, on the recognition of the needs of the individual and the right to express himself fully and freely within the framework of a community knit together by the ties of an enduring tradition.

(1) Since effective democratic Government depends on an alert, informed and enlightened public opinion it is of prime importance to create and maintain a healthy interest in local affairs and so enable the

ordinary citizen to play a responsible part in running his own country.

(2) A redefinition of the functions, powers and areas of local authorities is now imperative with the object of retaining as much power and initiative as practicable with the local body. Such bodies as the Convention of Royal Burghs and the Association of County Councils should be developed as effective instruments of local opinion particularly in the spheres of social welfare and economic development.

3. Judiciary

The system of law must be the safeguard at once of the rights and liberties of the people and of the authority of the government, thus constituting the essential and enduring bond that reconciles the interest of the State and of the individual. To equate practice with principle there is need in Scotland of a complete overhaul of the machinery for the administration of justice; of legislative reform in many spheres; and of a new approach to legal education.

(1) Jurisdiction within Scotland must be exercised exclusively by Scottish Courts.

(2) Since liberty is insecure whenever the functions of judicature and administration overlap, all legal rights conferred and duties imposed upon the citizen must be open in the last resort to vindication in the law courts.

(3) Judicial appointments must be made on a basis that ensures a judiciary independent of the executive. They must not be rewards for political services.

(4) Decentralization is required to make the Civil Courts readily accessible to all. The Court of Session should therefore be reconstituted as the final Court of Appeal with provision for Circuit Courts as in the case of the High Court of Justiciary and its originating jurisdiction transferred to a reformed Sheriff Court.

(5) The administrative functions of the Sheriffs Principal are unnecessary and their appellate jurisdiction indefensible. The office should therefore be abolished and an equally inexpensive and expeditious mode of appeal substituted.

(6) In all Courts, all judicial functions shall be exercised by properly qualified salaried magistrates and officers of the State.

4. Religion

Freedom of conscience and the free profession and practice of

215

religion must be guaranteed to every citizen. No disabilities will be imposed nor any discrimination made by the State on the ground of religious profession, belief or status.

5. International Relations

A Self-Governing Scotland would, in accordance with long established tradition, work to establish close and friendly relations with all other countries and participate fully in all movements for the preservation of world peace based on respect for the principle of the equal rights of nations large and small. It is recognized that if civilization is to survive the emphasis must be placed less on the concept of exclusive national sovereignty and more on the development of international co-operation and mutual obligations between peoples.

(1) A particularly intimate relationship with the other countries of the British Isles is enjoined by geographical and economic considerations. The creation of joint arrangements for the discussion and settlement of matters of mutual concern would be a measure at once natural and beneficial.

(2) The ties of kinship and the influence of history require the closest direct political and economic relations with the self-governing Dominions.

(3) Scotland's geographical situation and record in history combine to offer to the Scots an unique opportunity of forming a link between the peoples of the New World and the Old. Equal representation with other countries in the U.N.O. and on all other allied or subsidiary bodies concerned with solving world problems is therefore an essential element in self-government.

II. PLANNING

1. General

Planning must be forward-looking and creative, and in Scotland it should be directed towards a better distribution of work and people as between the industrial belt and the rest of the country, than exists today. It should aim at ensuring the fullest use of natural resources consistent with the welfare of the community and the maintenance of family life. There must therefore be close co-ordination between Economic and Social policy. Accordingly, the central administrative machine should be designed to facilitate the closest co-operation between departments dealing with Industry (including Research and

216

Agriculture), Education and Physical Environment (town and country planning, and Housing, and Health Services).

2. Town and Country Planning

(*A*) *Regional.* Provision should be made for permanent Regional Planning bodies, consisting of representatives of Planning Committees of Counties and Burghs, grouped in the following manner:— (1) Clyde Valley, Ayrshire, Dumfries and Galloway; (2) Forth and Tweed; (3) Tay and Central; (4) N.E. Counties; (5) Highland Counties and Islands. Their function would be to conduct Research, to ensure regular consultation between the constituent authorities on matters of common interest such as the location of industry, transport and afforestation and resettlement, to ensure a closer relationship between town and country, to advise on the siting of new towns and villages and on the strengthening of the older burghs where suitable for new developments. Government Departments should send representatives to ensure co-ordination between central and local governments on matters of general policy, and provision should also be made for regular consultation with Trade and Cultural bodies. These Regional Planning bodies would be financed partly by the State and partly by the constituent local Authorities. While they would act for the Ministry in passing local Authorities' housing proposals, their general character would be Advisory.

(*B*) *Local.* The function of local planning should be to ensure formulation of planning policy *in matters of detail* connected with Transport, location of both Industry and Housing, and the proper use of Land. The local planning authorities should be the City, the Burgh and the County, assuming certain revision of present anomalous boundaries in relation to area and population. The planning of small burghs should be evolved in close co-operation between county and burgh, requiring the consent of the burgh which should not be unreasonably withheld either party having right of appeal to the Minister. Provision should be made for regular consultation with Trade and Cultural bodies.

III. ECONOMIC

The land and all natural resources and accumulated wealth rightly belong to the people of Scotland from whom they may not be alienated. Every citizen has the right to a share in the national inheritance and to own property. Such rights will be upheld by the State. The ownership of property will however be limited to prevent infringement of the legitimate freedom of any citizen. Individual freedom must extend to the economic sphere to permit freedom of choice to the citizen as a worker to select his occupation and as a consumer to satisfy his needs according to his inclinations.

The economic safeguard of democracy lies in the diffusion of economic power. The concentration of economic power in the hands of either private or State monopolies is inimical both to the freedom of the individual and to the proper functioning of democratic government. In order to ensure democratic control of the economic structure of the State it is essential therefore either to eliminate or to subject to strict supervision all private monopolies and to restrict State monopolies to the minimum. It is in the national interest to increase the technical efficiency of small and medium sized production units in every way as, for example, by encouraging co-operation for research and marketing. Where, however, technical efficiency requires very large productive units and thus monopoly or virtual monopoly such monopolies must be State-owned.

As the standard of living of the people depends on the distribution as well as on the amount of the national income and national wealth, it is desirable that economic activity should be distributed throughout all parts of the country and that there should be no great inequalities in individual wealth and income. The essential needs of the Scottish people should be met as far as possible out of Scottish resources. Intensive development of these resources is therefore necessary in order to raise the standard of living.

1. Natural Resources
A. Land

Land as a strictly limited resource must be utilized in the interests of the community as a whole. Radical reform of the system of land ownership and tenure and of the semi-feudal land laws is long overdue.

(1) A national survey is required both to determine whether it is in the national interest to develop land for agriculture, afforestation, industry, housing or recreation, and to indicate the areas most suitable for improvement and reclamation.

(2) An upper limit must be placed on the size of individual and corporate holdings varying with the type of country.

(3) This involves immediate measures to end the evils of absentee

landlordism, the progressive break-up of existing large estates and their replacement by owner-occupier farms of economic proportions.

(4) Access to hills and mountains must be free where there is no interference with agriculture or forestry. Sporting rights must be brought under national or local control.

(5) Access to rivers, streams and lochs for fishing shall be available to all on an equal basis, and pollution and obstruction to free movement of fish must be effectively prevented.

B. Minerals

As all minerals are wasting assets, it is imperative that they be owned by the nation and their development controlled by the State in the public interest. Where there is economic inducement for private enterprise, that enterprise should work under licence from the State covering orderly development and price control; where economic inducement is lacking but it is in the public interest that the mineral should be worked, the State should do so by contract as in the present case of opencasting for coal. Where there is a conflict between surface and mining interests, the mineral should except in exceptional circumstances be first worked out.

(1) *Coal.* It is improbable that the coal industry could ever again be confided to private enterprise. But while in this as in all nationalized industries, policy must be laid down at the centre, actual management must be in the hands of district committees familiar with local conditions and including not only miners and mining engineers but representatives of local authorities.

1. THE MINERS. As the miners' work is at once particularly hazardous and uncomfortable and of great value to the community the State is under obligation to make provision for a vast improvement in working conditions and environment and for the generous treatment of the disabled and their dependents. It is essential that men should be encouraged to become miners and mining engineers. They must therefore have steady work at good wages and their working and living conditions must be the first concern of the controlling authority. Arrangements must be made for the transference of miners to less arduous duties when it is considered that they are unfit for coal face work, irrespective of age.

2. COAL UTILIZATION. The national coal policy should be directed to obtaining the maximum value out of every ton of coal by scientific methods. A long-term policy should be initiated with the object of

replacing raw coal by processed fuel for domestic and industrial use.
3. EXPORT. Scottish coal has always been a valuable export and thus
has permitted useful imports. When practicable, therefore, the export
trade should be encouraged. But, as in pre-Union Scotland, the State
must ensure that the interests of the home consumer come first.
4. HEAT, LIGHT AND POWER. All the available hydro-electric power
in Scotland would not in itself be sufficient to supply the requirements
of the country for electrical energy. Coal must therefore continue to be
used for electrical generation. The key to the economic generation of
gas or electricity is to place the generating station beside the coal, to
eliminate haulage costs and permit the use of low-grade fuel. The ideal
solution is the erection of combined power stations and processing
plants at suitable points throughout the coalfields. For purely heating
purposes gas is more economical than electricity and should be used
for that purpose by the laying of gas grids or by the use of surplus blast
furnace gas where available.

(2) *Other Minerals.* Scotland is the most favoured part of the British Isles in minerals, such as shale, which are richer than coal in
valuable by-products. These should be developed in an endeavour to
make Scotland independent of imported oil. The same processing
plants will in general produce gas and coke as well as oil. Peat resources
should also be scientifically developed. The only other minerals *at
present* of economic importance are fireclay and barytes, but as part of
a national economic policy the State should encourage search for
economically workable deposits of other minerals.

C. Water Power

Electricity should be readily and cheaply available in both town and
country in Scotland for domestic use as well as for power. In this
respect Scotland is far behind the average European country. A far-
sighted policy of general development is therefore required to make
full use of natural resources of water power and to ensure that the
resultant hydro-electric schemes are designed to serve the community
and not to become the instrument of further depopulation and desola-
tion of rural areas.

(1) The needs of the rural area from which the power is derived must
come first. This will necessitate the installation of numerous small-
scale generators and power distribution throughout the immediate
area of water power at a reasonable cost, in contrast with the present
arrangements.

(2) The use of electric power will stimulate not only the introduction of new light industries in more sparsely populated districts, but also the development of the staple pursuits of agriculture and fishing.

(3) Flat rate charges for electricity (as for goods transport) will prove of great value in the economic revival of the Highlands in particular and of the rural areas generally.

(4) Current which cannot be utilized locally will be available for urban industry and thus relieve the burden on the coal fields.

(5) Railway electrification in and around the main cities is long overdue. Electrification of railway lines in Highland areas should also be thoroughly considered in conjunction with the provision of electric power throughout the areas served by the railways.

2. Agriculture

The fullest development of the home production of food must be a fundamental of national policy in order to provide a sure basis for the physical health of the people and to achieve a wise balance economically between town and country.

(1) Farmers and crofters must therefore have security of tenure, stable prices, and assured markets for their products.

(2) In return the community will insist on a high standard of husbandry as a necessary condition of ownership or tenancy of the land.

(3) Where the right of the State to specify what crops shall be grown in the national interest is exercised, the farmer must, when necessary, be adequately recompensed if required to grow a new or less suitable crop.

(4) Research, technical and scientific, must be conducted in an ncreasing scale with State assistance to maintain Scottish farming in the van of progress and ensure a ready market for surplus production.

(5) Model and experimental farms should be run throughout the country under local or national auspices as appropriate and used as educational centres (technical and non-technical) for both town and country.

(6) Every encouragement should be given to farmers and crofters to organize co-operative associations for bulk purchase, marketing, provision of credit facilities, mechanization and research.

(7) Farm workers must enjoy social and economic conditions and prospects of advancement as favourable as those in any other industry, including reasonable opportunities to establish themselves in farms of their own.

(8) Full provision must be made in all rural areas for the development and establishment of community centres which form the nucleus of an active, well balanced and enriched social life.

3. Forestry

Systematic afforestation presents great possibilities for the rehabilitation of isolated and derelict areas. The establishment of State forests will not only provide employment on an increasing scale as the timber becomes marketable but also lead to the development of local industries of varied character.

(1) The National Land Survey will determine the areas most suitable for planting and detailed schemes will then be prepared under the direction of the State Forestry Department.

(2) Research facilities must be provided to experiment with the introduction and acclimatization of foreign trees, to develop new forestry methods and to extend and improve the use of home-grown timber.

(3) State assistance will be provided where necessary for the development of subsidiary industries.

(4) Individuals and local authorities will be encouraged by means of grants or otherwise to co-operate with the Forestry Department in the development of land suitable for afforestation.

(5) Close co-ordination of afforestation with agricultural policy is essential to prevent encroachment on good arable and grazing land.

(6) Forestry schemes should be planned in crofting areas to ensure steady seasonal employment for crofters and at the same time to provide shelter for stock and arrest soil erosion.

(7) National Forest Parks should be created in suitable localities with facilities for holiday making and recreation.

4. Fishing

Fishing is a vital national industry. On it depends the continued existence of a large number of self-contained communities characterized by independence and hardihood that have lived by the sea for generations and have made a special contribution to the national life. But the industry has declined steadily, even catastrophically, since the Scottish people, unlike the Norwegians, for example, have lacked the real power to develop and encourage it both at home and in the foreign market. The first step to revival must therefore be the organization of the industry on a national basis both in catching and marketing in order to provide high-quality fish at reasonable prices.

A. White Fishing. To ensure the efficient working of the trawling fleet as a whole the formation of larger economic working units is required. The formation of such units should be encouraged, if necessary by interest-free loans, ensuring the purchase of larger and better trawling fleets.

(1) As many young people as possible should be attracted to the industry by practical training schemes, and satisfactory working conditions and fixed minimum wages provided for crews in consultation with the trade unions.

(2) Expansion of the industry demands speedier and cheaper transport services to districts at present poorly served. These are essential in order to increase consumption in the home market upon which the trawling industry depends.

(3) Foreign landings of white fish should be controlled.

(4) Scottish territorial waters should be protected from illegal fishing by adequate air and sea patrols.

B. Herring Fishing. To ensure a prosperous herring fishing industry a long-term policy not of restriction but of expansion is required. The establishment of a Herring Board for Scotland is necessary with the following objects:—

(1) To provide training for people desirous of entering the industry and to furnish interest-free loans to suitable applicants for the purchase of new boats and gear.

(2) To encourage the development of co-operative methods.

(3) To promote new markets abroad and to expand the home market for herring, fresh, cured, or tinned, and to negotiate sales for the export market.

(4) To extend research on canning, dehydration, cold storage and package of fish and to make the results available in the commercial sphere. Modern freezing plants and refrigerator transport must be made available and flat rates introduced as an aid to distribution.

(5) To establish meal and oil factories with a view to supplying Scottish requirements of these commodities. The sale of surplus herring unsuitable for preservation for use in these factories and elsewhere must not affect the price of the normal catch.

5. Industry

In the past circumstances mainly outwith her control have forced on

Scotland an undue dependence on the heavy industries—coal, iron and steel, shipbuilding and engineering—and this factor in conjunction with the progressive transfer of ownership outwith Scotland has had a disastrous effect on the economic structure of the country. It is essential therefore not only to secure the development of a more balanced industrial fabric both by the encouragement of new light industries and the more widespread distribution of existing industries but also to make certain that the control of industry, financial no less than managerial, remains in Scotland.

(1) The State must therefore exercise, through the medium of the Regional Planning bodies, an overriding control over the industrial structure of the country. Subject to such control, however, individuals and corporate bodies will have full freedom to engage in and promote industrial and commercial enterprise.

(2) A national survey is required to ensure the fullest development of natural resources and scientific and technical research must be undertaken on an adequate scale with State assistance in order that industry may benefit from new developments.

(3) As a principle the export of raw materials for processing abroad will not be permitted save in exceptional circumstances recognized by the State.

(4) Legislation will be necessary to ensure that effective majority ownership and control of all industrial enterprises in Scotland remains in Scottish hands.

6. Trade

Every community has the right to retain the benefits derived from trading facilities exercised in its own area. Failure to limit the undue encroachment of outside trading concerns will result in loss of employment and wealth and in the inadequate development of natural resources.

A. Internal

(1) Chain stores, co-operative societies not under immediate local control, multiple firms and similar bodies, must be restricted in operation in the interests of local communities. Those under alien control will not be permitted in Scotland.

(2) Individuals, firms and corporations outside Scotland desirous of trading within Scotland will require to comply with the protecting regulations issued by the State.

(3) Combines and private monopolies will be prohibited by legislation, except where permitted to operate in the public interest under adequate safeguards.

(4) No company will be permitted to own assets in Scotland unless the majority of shares are held and control exercised, by Scots domiciled in Scotland or special permission has been granted by the State.

(5) The development of the home market to absorb home production will have priority and as a general rule only the surplus of home-produced goods over home requirements will be available for export.

B. External

(1) Direct trade with other countries—including the direct loading and unloading of goods at Scottish ports—will be encouraged, and up-to-date port, harbour and airport facilities developed.

(2) Trade agreements with other countries will be negotiated under national auspices. Trading or industrial agreements between individuals or companies in Scotland and in other countries will be subject to regulation. Full disclosure of all material facts will be required and restrictive cartel arrangements prohibited.

(3) Trade Commissioners will be appointed abroad and a general export association established under Government auspices to promote trade by means of advertising, the use of display centres, and the provision of assistance, financial or otherwise, to individuals and corporations.

(4) Practical encouragement will be given to the development of the tourist trade by the provision of satisfactory reception, travelling and catering facilities in Scotland and of adequate publicity services abroad.

7. Labour

Labour is a fundamental factor in production and the efforts of the worker should result in the full satisfaction of his needs. It will be a primary aim in a self-governing Scotland to secure and safeguard the basic right of all workers to stable employment at adequate rates of pay, to full opportunities for advancement, and to the highest possible level of working and living conditions, and a share in the ownership and management of the industries in which they work.

(1) The risk of neglect of the special needs of particular groups of workers in Scotland who have little influence on the central organizations of the present Trade Unions must be obviated by the emergence

P   225

of purely Scottish Trade Unions with a powerful Scottish Trade Union Congress which will play a leading and effective part in the new Scotland and take its proper place in international labour affairs.

(2) The right of the worker to protect his interests by the withdrawal of his labour must be maintained and there must be no compulsory direction of labour. The compulsory direction of labour into Trade Unions must also be prohibited.

(3) Personal direct relationship between organized Labour and Management must be maintained and encouraged without undue interference by the State.

(4) Adequate facilities for the protection, employment and technical education of disabled persons must be provided by regulations requiring the employment of a proportion of such persons in different and suitable occupations.

8. Transport and Communications

Increased productive activity, the development of natural resources, the repopulation of rural areas, and the more balanced distribution of work, wealth and people throughout Scotland largely depend upon access in all areas, to convenient means of communication at reasonable cost. There is a national duty to provide such communications as there was and is to provide cheap postage facilities.

The principles underlying the practice of affording to Government Departments, large industrial and other concerns a flat rate to cover all points of delivery should be extended to every individual. A flat rate for each class of goods to cover combined delivery by rail, road and coastwise shipping to all points in Scotland must therefore be instituted, except where delivery is to be made to a distance of less than, say, twelve miles, or where there are exceptional circumstances. To ensure the provision of these facilities the Ministry of Transport would issue co-ordinating regulations and approve all combined flat rates.

There will be no State monopoly of transport but the State may require to operate essential services where private enterprise is unable to provide the necessary facilities even with the assistance of subsidies.

(1) *Rail.* Railways in Scotland will be nationally owned and similar working arrangements made with the English Railways as operate between adjoining countries in Europe. Main-line railways should be electrified where the volume of traffic justifies the change over and consideration should also be given to the extension of the present system to rural areas by the construction of electric light railways.

(2) *Road.* Road transport, goods and passenger, will be regulated by the Ministry to ensure in general regular services at reasonable rates and to promote in particular adequate services to outlying districts. There will be an extension of national roads including the necessary bridges or ferries, particularly from East to West, under State auspices. Local Authorities will receive every encouragement by means of generous grants to provide adequate roads, including bridges, ferries and piers, for local purposes especially in outlying districts.

(3) *Sea.* The State may require to operate coastwise shipping services particularly between the Islands and the Mainland where adequate and regular facilities are not available.

(4) *Air.* All Scottish and foreign air lines and organizations shall be encouraged to use Scottish air-fields with complete freedom apart from adequate safety regulations.

(5) *Posts and Telephones.* All postal and telephone services will be operated on a national basis and extended to all areas.

9. Finance

The Scottish banking system formed the basis for world modern commercial banking and, until the centralization of financial control in London, played an outstanding part in the development of industry and commerce in Scotland. The Scottish banks can still play an important part in the national economy provided that they regain independence from outside control. Financial policy must however be based on the real wealth of the country. The criterion of whether any particular work should be undertaken must be not 'Have we the money?' but 'Have we the resources and is the work desirable or necessary?'

(1) A Central State Bank will be established to act as the banker for the Government and for the independent Scottish Banks and to control finance, currency and credit under the direction of the Government.

(2) Private banks will be permitted to operate but not to carry on business other than banking or to assume control of industry. Local Authorities will receive legislative facilities to establish municipal banks.

3) Individuals, companies, financial institutions and others operating in Scotland will require to conduct banking transactions through a Scottish bank unless with the express approval of the Central Bank.

(4) A Joint Commission will be set up by the Scottish and English Governments in order to determine the equitable apportionment of

the public debt between the two countries and any other relevant questions.

IV. Social

1. Health

The health of the people of any country depends on the adequate provision and equitable distribution of good food, clothing and housing. It is the duty of the State to ensure a general level of prosperity within which these things are available to all.

(1) Medical and other health services must be provided, free if necessary, by the State where they do not exist or do not reach a reasonable standard.

(2) Such services will be available to all but State intervention must not limit the freedom of choice of services or control the certification of fitness, or otherwise, of any person for work through transforming the medical profession as a whole into a State monopoly or Civil Service.

2. Housing

The problem of housing is one of the most urgent that faces the Scottish people not only on account of its intrinsic magnitude but also because it is bound up with so many other factors such as health, transport, location of industry, and rural repopulation. Only by planning on a national scale can conditions which have for long been a disgrace to a civilized nation be remedied and modern homes embodying all the labour saving devices of scientific research provided for all.

(1) To ensure proper standards of lay-out, accommodation and design, related to the conditions, requirements and resources of the different regions, local housing authorities (cities, burghs and counties —with devolution to districts in large scattered counties) should submit their schemes to a Regional Housing Authority, rather than a Central Office in Edinburgh. Particular attention should be paid to the density of housing desirable, the retention of open spaces and the reconditioning of old houses where of value architecturally or as potential accommodation.

(2) Due priority must be give in labour, in sites, in materials, and in products for housing purposes. The use of local building materials and the development of local techniques and designs, should be encouraged where agreed to by the Regional Research Station.

(3) Deliberate encouragement should be given to Rural and Small burgh housing in order to facilitate the gradual redistribution of the population.

(4) Housing requirements in crofting communities should receive special consideration in view of their peculiar circumstances.

3. Education

Education is not simply a transient process for those of school age but a continuing experience for all. It should be national in inspiration, international in scope, aiming at producing enlightened citizens of the world by stages in which local lore and national tradition play their essential part in broadening outlook and opening new horizons. Educational reform is therefore a most vital element in the national resurgence and the stimulus to new methods and a new outlook can be derived solely from a renaissance in thought and spirit on a truly national scale.

(1) Ad hoc Education Authorities should again be set up. The cost of education should be wholly a charge on central funds and no part of it should fall on local rates since this tends to make the provision of educational services depend too much on local circumstances quite unconnected with the needs of the schools.

(2) The salaries and conditions of teachers should be comparable to those offered in other professions open to men and women of like qualifications and attainments.

In particular, steps should be taken to increase the number of men entrants to the profession. In general it should be the rule that every school should have a reasonable proportion of men teachers on its staff.

(3) Centralization of services should be kept to the minimum. Wherever possible multilateral schools should be developed with a strong territorial connection and providing a full education of every type for the boys and girls of the town or district.

(4) Until the present shortage of teachers has been overcome the reduction of the size of classes should come before the raising of the school age or other extension of educational provision.

(5) Fully-equipped technical schools and colleges for both day and evening tuition should be established throughout Scotland in order to provide a thorough technical training for young people entering industry and commerce.

(6) In view of the desirability of increased facilities for higher

studies in Scotland, and in the absence of private or municipal founders, the Scottish State will endow four additional Universities, in one of which the Gaelic language will be the medium of instruction and examination.

(7) The Scottish State will adopt all appropriate methods to foster the native language, games, music, dancing, arts and crafts, and will establish radio and television services and a cinema-film industry suitable to the Scottish ethos.

4. Social Security

Social Security implies not merely the protection of the individual against want but the guarantee of a decent standard of living to everyone whether able to work or not, and a personal freedom to choose one's home and job. Scotland possesses the natural wealth and her people the ability of hand and head to render such a guarantee effective.

(1) The full development of the country's resources is therefore the first step to social security.

(2) An economic policy which will provide those who produce with the purchasing power to consume and thus ensure to the Scottish people the maximum enjoyment of the products of their own labour is the next essential.

(3) These policies mean jobs for all who can work at wages which will give them the maximum standard of living which their efforts will support. They also entail the highest standards of efficiency in the use of the national resources and hence a drastic reduction in the numbers of non-productive workers and officials.

(4) In a society where all who are able to work have their own opportunity to win social security, provision for those who are unable to work by reason of old age, infirmity, youth or misfortune must be made on the basis of a decent standard of living and not of a bare subsistence level. Scotland has the basic resources to make this goal attainable.

(5) The levy on the country's resources for this purpose can best be effected by a contributory scheme of Social Insurance. But it must be a real insurance scheme where undiminished benefits will be payable in terms of the scheme without recourse to the humiliation of means tests.

SCOTTISH NATIONALIST VOTE
AT GENERAL ELECTIONS

	Candidates	Forfeited deposits	Total votes	Poll percentage
1929	2	2	3,313	·46
1931	5	2	20,954	·96
1935	8	5	29,517	1·26
1945	9*	7*	30,827	1·27
1950	9†	9†	13,301	·49
1951	2	1	7,299	·26
1955	2	1	12,112	·48
1959	5	3	21,738	·81
1964	15	12	64,044	2·43
1966	23	10	128,476	5·03

* Includes one independent.
† Includes two independents, one Irish Anti-Partitionist and Independent Scottish Nationalist, and three Home Rule Candidates.

Scottish Nationalist Members of Parliament

Dr. R. D. McIntyre (Lanark, Motherwell) April–June 1945
Mrs. Winifred Ewing (Lanark, Hamilton) November 1967–

A Note on Sources

The main sources for the study of modern Scottish nationalism are the publications of the various Home Rule and nationalist organizations that have appeared since 1853, the nationalist periodicals, and a considerable number of newspaper articles and pamphlets. There is also one collection of manuscripts, that of R. E. Muirhead, in the National Library of Scotland. This book is based on an extensive reading of these sources and of related materials elsewhere. To list every pamphlet used would be tedious for readers and would needlessly duplicate the list given by Kenneth C. Fraser in his *Bibliography of the Scottish National Movement 1928–1958* (Strathclyde University Scottish Nationalist Club, Glasgow, 1968). Many pamphlets published before 1928 are to be found in two collections in the National Library of Scotland, one relating chiefly to the 1850s (NE.20.f.13–14) and the other to the period of the Scottish Home Rule Association (3.2820 and 3.2820*). The National Library of Scotland also has a wide range of more recent nationalist pamphlets.

Much valuable background information about Scottish nationalism is to be found in the Rosebery papers in the National Library of Scotland, the records of the Scottish Liberal Association in Edinburgh University Library, the Minutes of the Convention of Royal Burghs in Edinburgh Public Library, and the reports of the Scottish Trade Union Congress at the S.T.U.C. offices in Glasgow. I have also made some use of the Gladstone papers in the British Museum, the Blackie papers in the National Library of Scotland, and the Cabinet Papers in the Public Record Office. A number of general periodicals and newspapers have also been quoted in the text, namely the *Celtic Magazine*, the *Daily Bulletin* (Glasgow), *Forward*, *Gairm*, the *Glasgow Herald*, the *Highlander*, the *Jacobite*, *North British Daily Mail*, *North British Review*, *Scots Pictorial*, *The Scotsman*, the *Scottish Highlander*, *The Times* and *The Witness*.

A Note on Sources

The first periodical to carry regular Home Rule articles was the *Scots Magazine* (1885–1900) which began life as the *Scottish Church* in 1885. From May 1891 it carried contributions by 'Harry Gow', the pseudonym of William Mitchell, and from December 1893 it was published along with a Home Rule supplement called the *British Federalist*, with the result that the title page for Volume XIV read 'The Scots Magazine Edited by the Rev. J. C. Carrick, B.D., and British Federalist Edited by A. P. Melville'. The *British Federalist* ceased publication in November 1894. The *Fiery Cross*, published by Theodore Napier from his home in Edinburgh irregularly from 1901 to 1912, was soon overshadowed by a number of more ambitious journals. Charles Waddie issued the *Scottish Nationalist* in Edinburgh in 1903, John Wilson published *The Scottish Patriot* in Glasgow from 1903 to 1906, the Young Scots Society published *The Young Scot* in Edinburgh from 1903 to 1905, the St. Andrew Society of Edinburgh published *Scotia* from 1907 to 1911, the International Scots Home Rule Association published the *Scottish Nation* from 1913 to 1917, and T. D. Wanliss published *The Thistle* in Edinburgh from 1909 to 1918. Longer lived and more interesting was *Guth na Bliadhna: the Voice of the Year*, with articles in either English or Gaelic, published by the Hon. Ruaraidh Erskine of Marr at various places between 1904 and 1925 and its Gaelic stable mates, *An Sgeulaiche*, 1909–11, and *Alba* (edited by Douglas MacEanruig), Stirling, 1920–1. Erskine of Marr was also responsible for producing that most valuable of all nationalist journals the *Scottish Review*, from 1914 to 1920.

After the First World War there was a spate of short-lived journals of a markedly nationalist character, several of them associated with the name of Hugh MacDiarmid (C. M. Grieve), all of which were primarily interested in the development of Scottish letters. Of these the best was the *Modern Scot*, Edinburgh, 1930–6, continued as *The Outlook*, 1936–7. The main stream of political nationalism, however, was represented by a rather different type of paper. First there were the news-sheets of the Scottish Home Rule Association published from 1919 to 1929, which settled down in 1922 under the title *Scottish Home Rule*. Secondly, there were the publications of the Scots National League, which gave way in 1926 to that longest lived of all nationalist periodicals the *Scots Independent*. Started originally as the organ of the Scots National League, the *Scots Independent* was transferred in 1928 to the National Party of Scotland and then in turn to the Scottish National Party. It ceased publication briefly in 1935, then reappeared under the imprint of the Scottish Secretariat, and was restored to the Scottish National Party in 1939. It has remained ever since the organ of the S.N.P. and has been a weekly since 1954.

Those who were not altogether happy with the emphasis of the *Scots Independent* found outlets in a number of short-lived journals. Of these the most important are the periodicals listed below. Others are listed in Fraser's bibliography. The *Pictish Review*, 1927–8, was the product of an alliance between Erskine of Marr and Hugh MacDiarmid. *The Free Man*, Edinburgh, 1932–4, continued briefly in Glasgow as *New Scotland*, 1935, combined libertarianism, support for social credit, and articles by Hugh MacDiarmid. *Forward Scotland*, Glasgow, 1957–64, was a reversion by R. E. Muirhead to the themes of *Scottish Home Rule* thirty years before. And *Scottish Vanguard*, the organ of the Workers Party of Scotland (Edinburgh, 1967+), is an attempt to re-create John Maclean's *Vanguard* of the early twenties. *Catalyst* (Glasgow, 1967+) is a glossy nationalist magazine independent of the influence of the Scottish National Party.

WORKS CITED IN THE TEXT

ALDRED, Guy A. *Dogmas Discarded . . .*, Part II, Glasgow, 1940.

ARNOT, R. Page. *A History of the Scottish Miners from the Earliest Times*, London, 1955.

ATTLEE, C. R. *The Labour Party in Perspective*, London, 1937.

BARR, James. *Lang Syne: Memoirs of the Rev. James Barr, B.D.*, Glasgow, 1949.

BEGG, James. *National Education for Scotland Practically Considered*, Edinburgh, 1850.

—— *A Violation of the Treaty of Union the Main Origin of our Ecclesiastical Divisions and other Evils*, Edinburgh, 1871.

BELL, Tom. *John Maclean: a Fighter for Freedom*, Glasgow, 1944.

BLACKIE, J. S. *The Union of 1707 and its Results: a Plea for Scottish Home Rule*, Glasgow, 1892.

BLAKE, George. *Barrie and the Kailyard School*, London, 1951.

BROWN, Oliver. *The Anglo-Scottish Union of 1707: Then and Now*, Stirling, n.d.

BUCHAN, John. *Andrew Jameson, Lord Ardwall*, Edinburgh and London, 1913.

BUCKLE, H. T. *History of Civilization in England*, new edn., 3 vols., 1902.

BUDGE, Ian and URWIN, D. W. *Scottish Political Behaviour: a Case Study in British Homogeneity*, London, 1966.

BURNET, John. *Higher Education and the War*, London, 1917.

BURNS, William. *'England' versus 'Great Britain'* . . ., Glasgow, 1865.

—— *Scottish Rights and Honour Vindicated* . . ., Glasgow, 1854.

BUTTER, P. H. *Edwin Muir: Man and Poet*, Edinburgh and London, 1966.

The Campaign Guide, 1900: a Handbook for Unionist Speakers, 8th edn., Edinburgh, 1900.

CAMPBELL, R. H. *Scotland since 1707: the Rise of an Industrial Society*, Oxford, 1965.

CARSWELL, Donald. *Brother Scots*, London, 1927.

CENSUS OF GREAT BRITAIN, 1851. *Religious Worship, and Education, Scotland*, [1764], H.C. (1854), LIX, 301.

Central Scotland: a Programme for Development and Growth. Cmd. 2188. 1963.

CHRIMES, S. B., ed. *The General Election in Glasgow, February, 1950*, Glasgow, 1950.

COCKBURN, Henry. *Memorials of his Time*, Edinburgh, 1910.

COMMUNIST PARTY OF GREAT BRITAIN. *The British Road to Socialism*, London, 1951.

Conference on Devolution: Letter from Mr. Speaker to the Prime Minister, [Cmd. 692] H.C. (1920). XIII, 1151–88.

A Constitution for Scotland, Scottish Secretariat, Glasgow, 1964.

Convention of the Royal Burghs of Scotland. *Local Self-Government for Scotland: Report, 11th March 1914*, Edinburgh, 1914.

COUPLAND, Sir Reginald. *Welsh and Scottish Nationalism: a Study*, London, 1954.

COWAN, Charles. *Reminiscences*, Privately printed, Edinburgh, 1878.

DAVIDSON, John Morrison. *Leaves from the Book of Scots*, Glasgow, [1914].

—— *Scotia Rediviva: Home Rule for Scotland with the Lives of Sir William Wallace, George Buchanan, Fletcher of Saltoun and Thomas Spence*, Bellamy Library No. 6, London, 1890.

—— *Scotland for the Scots: Scotland Revisited*, London, 1902.

DAVIE, George Elder. 'Anglophobe and Anglophil', *Scottish Journal of Political Economy*, 14 (1967), 291–302.

—— *The Democratic Intellect: Scotland and her Universities in the Nineteenth Century*, 2nd edn., Edinburgh, 1964.

DICKINSON, W. C., DONALDSON, Gordon and MILNE, Isabel A. *A Source Book of Scottish History*, Volume I, London and Edinburgh, 1952.

DODDS, Andrew. *The Lothian Land*, Aberdeen, 1918.

ERSKINE, The Hon. Stuart Ruadri. *The Kilt and How to Wear It*, Inverness, 1901.

ESCOTT, Harry. *A History of Scottish Congregationalism*, Glasgow, 1960.

EWING, Winifred. *Scotland v Whitehall No. 1: Winifred Ewing's Black Book*, Scottish National Party, 1968.

FERGUSON, William. *Scotland: 1689 to the Present*, Edinburgh, 1968.

FLINN, M. W. 'The Overseas Trade of Scottish Ports, 1900–1960', *Scottish Journal of Political Economy*, 13 (1966), 220–37.

FORBES, W. *An Account of the Life and Writings of James Beattie, LL.D.*, new ed., 2 vols., London, 1824.

GALLACHER, William. *Revolt on the Clyde: an Autobiography*, London, 1936.

GEDDES, Patrick. *Scottish University Needs and Aims: closing address at University College, Dundee, reprinted from 'Scots Magazine' for August 1890*, Perth, 1890.

—— 'The Scots Renascence', *The Evergreen*, Spring 1895, pp. 131–9.

GLADSTONE, W. E. *The Irish Question: I The History of an Idea, II Lessons of the Election*, London, 1886.

GLEN, Duncan. *Hugh MacDiarmid (Christopher Murray Grieve) and the Scottish Renaissance*, Edinburgh and London, 1964.

GRAY, John M., ed. *Memoirs of the Life of Sir John Clerk of Penicuik*, Scottish Text Society, Edinburgh, 1892.

GRIEVE, C. M. *Contemporary Scottish Studies: First Series*, London, 1926.

HAMILTON, Ian R. *No Stone Unturned: the Story of the Stone of Destiny*, London, 1952.

HANDLEY, J. E. *The Irish in Modern Scotland*, Cork, 1947.

HANHAM, H. J. 'The Creation of the Scottish Office, 1881–87', *Juridical Review*, 1965, pp. 205–44.

—— 'Mid-Century Scottish Nationalism, Romantic and Radical', in Robert Robson, ed., *Ideas and Institutions of Victorian Britain:*

Essays in Honour of George Kitson Clark, pp. 143–79, London, 1967.

—— *The Nineteenth Century Constitution, 1815–1914: Documents and Commentary*, Cambridge, 1969.

JOHNSTON, James. *The Ecclesiastical and Religious Statistics of Scotland . . .*, Glasgow, 1874.

JOHNSTON, Thomas. *Memories*, London, 1952.

KELLAS, James G. *The Liberal Party in Scotland, 1885–1895*, Unpublished Ph.D. thesis, London, 1962.

—— *Modern Scotland: the Nation since 1870*, London, 1968.

KENDLE, J. E. 'The Round Table Movement and "Home Rule All Round" ', *Historical Journal*, XI (1968), 332–53.

KYD, J. G. 'Scotland's Population', *Scottish Historical Review*, 28 (1949), 97–107.

LABOUR PARTY (SCOTTISH COUNCIL). *Report of Fifth Annual Conference . . .*, Glasgow, 1919.

LAMONT, Archibald. *Buy Scottish Goods: How to Reduce Unemployment . . .*, Glasgow, [1954].

—— *Scotland: the Wealthy Nation*, Glasgow, 1952.

LAWRENCE, R. J. *The Government of Northern Ireland: Public Finance and Public Services, 1921–1964*, Oxford, 1965.

V. I. Lenin on Britain, Moscow, 1959.

Life and Literature of the Working Class: Essays in Honour of William Gallacher, Berlin, 1966.

LOWE, David. *Souvenirs of Scottish Labour*, Glasgow, 1919.

LUTZOW, Count. 'The Revival of the Czech or Bohemian Language', *Guth na Bliadhna*, VIII (1911), 147–52.

MCCALLUM, R. B. and READMAN, Alison. *The British General Election of 1945*, London, 1947.

MCCLELLAND, V. A. 'The Irish Clergy and Archbishop Manning's Visitation of the Western District of Scotland, 1867', *Catholic Historical Review*, LIII (1967–68), 1–27, 229–50.

MACCORMICK, J. M. *The Flag in the Wind: the Story of the National Movement in Scotland*, London, 1955.

MCCRONE, Gavin. *Scotland's Economic Progress, 1951–60*, London, 1965.

MACDIARMID, Hugh. *Collected Poems of Hugh MacDiarmid*, ed. John C. Weston, 2nd edn., New York, 1967.

MCINTYRE, Robert D. *Some Principles for Scottish Reconstruction*, Scottish National Party, Glasgow, 1944.

MACKENZIE, Agnes Muir. *On the Declaration of Arbroath*, Saltire Society, Edinburgh, 1951.

MACKENZIE, Sir Compton. *My Life and Times: Octave Six*, London, 1967, *Octave Seven*, London, 1968.

MACKIE, J. B. *The Life and Work of Duncan McLaren*, 2 vols., Edinburgh, 1888.

MACKINNON, James. *The Union of England and Scotland* . . ., London, 1896.

MACLEAN, Norman. *The Years of Fulfilment*, London, 1953.

McLENNAN, Gordon. *Demand a Future for Scotland*, Communist Party (Glasgow Committee), Glasgow, n.d.

McMILLAN, William and STEWART, John A. *The Story of the Scottish Flag*, Glasgow, 1925.

MACNEACAIL, H. C. 'The Starving of Scottish Science', *Scottish Review*, 40 (1917), 118–24.

Memoirs and Portraits of One Hundred Glasgow Men, Glasgow, 1886.

MILLAR, J. H. *A Literary History of Scotland*, London, 1903.

MILLER, Hugh. *My Schools and Schoolmasters*, 14th edn., Edinburgh, 1869.

MILNE, Sir David. *The Scottish Office and other Scottish Government Departments*, London, 1957.

NAMIER, Sir Lewis and BROOKE, John. *The History of Parliament: the House of Commons, 1754–1790*, 3 vols., London, 1964.

PATON, H. J. *The Claim of Scotland*, London, 1968.

PHILLIPSON, N. T. *The Scottish Whigs and the Reform of the Court of Session, 1785–1830*, unpublished Ph.D. thesis, Cambridge, 1967.

PIKE, W. T. and EDDINGTON, A. *Edinburgh and the Lothians* . . ., Pike's New Century Series No. 12, Brighton and Edinburgh, 1904.

POTTLE, F. A., ed. *Boswell's London Journal, 1762–1763*, London, 1950.

POWER, William. *Should Auld Acquaintance* . . ., London, 1937.

Prospectus of the Scottish Home Rule Association, Edinburgh, 1892.

Protest of the Scottish Home Rule Association against the Present Policy of Official Liberals towards Scotland, Edinburgh, [1890].

RAMSAY, Mary P. *The Freedom of the Scots from Early Times till its Eclipse in 1707: Displayed in Statements of our Forefathers who Loved and Served Scotland*, Edinburgh, 1945.

REID, Andrew, ed. *Why I am a Liberal*, London, [1885].

RIDDELL, William. *Towards Scottish Home Rule*, Vanguard Publication No. 2, Scottish Liberal Party, Edinburgh, 1968.

ROBERTSON, William. *The History of Scotland* . . ., 12th edn., 2 vols., London, 1791.

ROMANS, John. *Home Rule for Scotland*, Edinburgh, 1893.

THE SCOTSMAN. *How Scotland should be governed: The Scotsman states its Policy on Self-Government*, Edinburgh, 1968.

[SCOTT, Walter]. A Second Letter . . . from Malachi Malagrowther, Esq., on the Proposed Charge of Currency . . ., Edinburgh, 1826.

SCOTTISH COUNCIL (Development and Industry). *Inquiry into the Scottish Economy 1960–1961: Report of a Committee . . . under the Chairmanship of J. N. Toothill*, Edinburgh [1962].

The Scottish Economy, 1965 to 1970: a Plan for Expansion, [Cmnd. 2864], 1966.

SCOTTISH LIBERAL PARTY. *Scottish Self-Government*, Edinburgh, 1962, 3rd edn., 1964.

SCOTTISH NATIONAL CONVENTION. *Draft Resolutions* . . ., Glasgow, 1939.

SCOTTISH NATIONAL PARTY. *Action Now: Coal and Power*, Glasgow, 1968.

—— *No Voice No Entry*, Glasgow, 1967.

—— *SNP & You: Aims & Policy of the Scottish National Party*, 3rd ed., Glasgow, 1968.

SCOTTISH OFFICE. *Scottish Administration: a Handbook prepared by the Scottish Office*, rev. ed., Edinburgh, 1967.

SMITH, Thomas. *Memoirs of James Begg, D.D.*, 2 vols., Edinburgh, 1888.

SOMERVILLE, Thomas. *My Own Life and Times, 1741–1814*, Edinburgh, 1861.

SPENCE, Lewis. 'The National Party of Scotland', *Edinburgh Review*, CCXLVIII (1928), 70–87.

—— 'The Scottish Literary Renaissance', *Nineteenth Century and After*, C (1926), 123–33.

STEEL, David. *Out of Control: a Critical Examination of the Government of Scotland*, Vanguard Publication No. 3, Scottish Liberal Party, Edinburgh, 1968.

STEUART, Sir James. *An Inquiry into the Principles of Political Oeconomy*, ed. by Andrew S. Skinner, 2 vols., Edinburgh, 1966.

STEWART, William. *J. Keir Hardie: a Biography*, London, 1921.

STODDART, Anna M. *John Stuart Blackie: a Biography*, 2 vols., Edinburgh, 1895.

The Thistle Group, pamphlet No. 1, Edinburgh, 1967.

THOMSON, Charles W. *Scotland's Work and Worth* . . ., 2 vols., Edinburgh, 1910.

THOMSON, D. C., ed. *Scotland in Quest of Her Youth: a Scrutiny,* Edinburgh and London, 1932.

THOMSON, George Malcolm. *Caledonia: or, the Future of the Scots,* London, [1927].

The Treaty of Union between Scotland and England, 1707, Scottish Secretariat No. 62, Glasgow, 1955.

WADDIE, Charles. *Dunbar: the King's Advocate: a Tragic Episode in the Reformation in Scotland,* 2nd edn., Edinburgh, 1893.

—— *How Scotland Lost Her Parliament and What Came of it,* Edinburgh, 1891, 3rd edn., 1902.

—— *The Religion of a Layman* . . ., Edinburgh, 1907.

—— *Scotia's Darling Seat: a Home Rule Sermon, and other Poems,* Edinburgh, 1890.

—— *Wallace: or, the Battle of Stirling,* Edinburgh, 1859.

WANLISS, T. D. *Bars to British Unity: or, a Plea for National Sentiment,* Edinburgh, 1885.

—— *The Muckrake in Scottish History: or, Mr. Andrew Lang Re-Criticised* . . ., Edinburgh, 1906.

—— *Scotland and Presbyterianism Vindicated,* Edinburgh, 1905.

—— *Scottish Honour versus English Vanity: being the Report of a Speech by Rev. David Macrae at the Dundee School Board on 'The Misuse of our National Names', with an Introduction by Mr. T. D. Wanliss,* Dundee, 1886.

YOUNG, Douglas C. C. *An Appeal to Scots Honour by Douglas Young: a Vindication of the Right of the Scottish People to Freedom from Industrial Conscription and Bureaucratic Despotism under the Treaty of Union with England,* Glasgow, 1944.

—— *British Invasion of Scottish Rights—Douglas Young's Trial in Paisley Sheriff-Court on June 12, 1944,* Glasgow, 1944.

—— *The Free Minded Scot: Trial of Douglas C. C. Young in the High Court, Edinburgh,* Glasgow, 1942.

—— *Labour Record on Scotland, 1945–1949,* Glasgow, [1949].

—— *A Scot's Free Fight: Statement Delivered in Glasgow Sheriff-Court on April 13, 1942* . . ., Glasgow, [1942].

Index

Abbey Craig (Wallace Monument on), 78, 80

Abercromby, James (Lord Dunfermline), 60

Aberdeen, 16, 18, 95, 99, 105, 135, 168, 187

Aberdeenshire, 98, 125, 184, 192n.

Adams, Francis Lauderdale, 79

Addison, Joseph, 36

Administration, Scottish, 15, 31, 50–63, 213–15

Advocates, Faculty of, 52–5, 57; *See also* Lawyers

Africa, 10, 74, 197

Alba, 123n., 140

Aldred, Guy, 87

Alison, Sir Archibald, 81

Aluminium, 198, 201

Alva, 177

Amalgamated Society of Woodworkers, 199

Amsterdam, 206

Anglicization, 34–49, 56, 67

Annals of the Parish, 26

Arbroath, Declaration of, 65–6, 209

Architecture, Celtic, 135

Argyll, 167

Asquith, H. H., 97, 98, 99, 141, 146

Association for the Promotion of Scottish History in Schools and Universities, 128

Association of County Councils, 215

Atlantic Charter, 9

Attlee, Clement, 115

Australia, 18, 25, 79, 85, 104, 122, 197, 205

Austrian Empire, 9, 10

Auvergne, 68

Avonside, Lord, 54, 197

Ayr, 134

Baldwin, Stanley, 152 and n.

Balfour, A. J., 103

Ballarat, Victoria, 79, 122

Bank, suggested state, 174, 207, 227

Banking, Scottish, 15, 30–1, 34, 227

Bannockburn, Battle of, 34, 79, 109

Bannockburn Day celebrations, 126–7, 130–1, 152

Barbour, John, 64–5, 69, 88

Barr, Rev. James, 115, 117–18, 166

Barra, 20

Barrie, James, 146

Barron, T., 199

Beattie, James, 36

Beaverbrook, Lord, 153, 157, 159

Begg, James, 74–6, 77, 82, 83

Belgium, 10, 45, 202

Belhaven, Lord, 76

Bell, Charles, 135

Belloc, Hilaire, 151

Berlin, 45

Bevin, Ernest, 116

Biafra, 9

Birmingham, 206

Blackie, J. S., 40, 119

Blackwood's Magazine, 53, 71, 78

Blind Harry, 64–5, 69, 88

Board of Trade, 30

Board of Trustees for Improving Fisheries and Manufactures, 52

Boards, Scottish, 61–2

Bochel, J. M., 188

Boer War, 121

Bohemia, *see* Czechoslovakia

Bookman, The, 146

Boots the Chemists, 47

Borders, 16, 181

Boswell, James, 34
Boyne, battle of the, 109
British Broadcasting Corporation (B.B.C.), 157
British Empire, 9
British Weekly, 146, 147
Brown, Oliver, 157, 210
Bruce, King Robert the, 21, 25, 64, 65, 66, 70, 89
Bryce Conference, 107
Bryce, James, 92
Buchan, John, 55, 148
Buchanan, George, 115
Burnet, John, 43, 44
Burns, Robert, 17, 25, 69, 70, 80, 109, 129, 147, 149, 194
Burns societies, 18
Burns, William, 81–2, 83, 88
Bute, 3rd Earl of, 67
Bute, 3rd Marquess of, on Home Rule, 83–5, 88

Caithness, 15
Caithness and Sutherland, 192
Caledonian societies, 18
Cambridge, 37, 38, 43, 44
Campaign Guide (Conservative), 103–4
Campbell, Archbishop, 20
Campbell, Elma, 157
Campbell, Sir George, 55
Campbell, Thomas, 69, 81
Campbell-Bannerman, Sir Henry, 146
Canada, 18, 31, 85, 96, 100, 104, 173, 175, 180
Canna, 20
Canning, George, 71
Carlingford, Lord, 57
Carlyle, Thomas, 148
Carnegie, Andrew, 83
Carswell, Catherine, 149
Carswell, Donald, 149
Catalonia, 68
Catalyst, 209
Catholic Directory, 20
Catholicism, Roman, 19–21, 26, 57, 83, 137, 154, 156
Celtic life and culture, 15–18, 40, 46, 67, 123–6, 135, 136, 137, 140, 144, 162
Celtic Magazine, 123
Chain stores, 47, 224
Chamberlain, Joseph, 91, 93
Chapple, Dr. W. A., 98, 99

Chartists, 72
Chesterton, G. K., 151
China, 194
Christian Socialism, 175
Church of England Prayer Book 29
Church of Scotland, 20, 25, 29, 33–4, 51, 54, 72, 100, 109, 149–50, 170, 176, 178; *see also* Presbyterianism
Churchill, Winston, 97–8
Civil Service examinations, 38
Clans, 25
Clark, Angus, 142, 160
Clark, G. B., 93, 94
Clergy, Scottish, 80
Clerk of Penicuik, Sir John, 36
Clydeside, 110, 114, 116, 140
Clynes, J. R., 141
Coal, 21, 193, 200, 207, 219–20
Coatbridge, 117
Cockburn, Henry (Lord Cockburn), 37, 53
Communism, Scottish, 139–40, 145, 184, 192–4
Comunn Gaidhealach, An, 124
Comunn nan Albannach (Scots National League), 125
Congregational Union, Scottish, 28
Connolly, James, 138, 194
Conscription, industrial and military, 167–9
Conservatives, Scottish, 22, 27, 54, 72, 103–7, 153, 159, 170, 171–2, 181–3, 185–9, 195–8, 205, 210
Constitution for Scotland, A, 178
Convention of the Royal Burghs of Scotland, 52, 54, 77, 82, 96, 127, 170, 215
Convention, Scottish National: suggested by Lord Bute, 1881, 84; of S.H.R.A. held in Glasgow, 118, 143, 150, 151; of S.N.P. not held in Glasgow, 166; Scottish Convention movement, 12, 169–72, 179, 189, 204
Copenhagen, 206
Cotton, 21
Court of Session, 52, 55, 102, 215
Covenant: of National Party of Scotland, 158; of Scottish Convention, 12, 171–2, 179, 189
Cowan, Sir (William) Henry, 102–3; Speech on Home Rule 1913, 98–102
Craik, Sir Henry, 46, 57; on Home Rule, 104–6

Crimean War, 78
Crofters, 100, 221
Cromarty, 64
Cromarty, Earl of, 129
Crossthwaite, Mr., 131
Crosthwaite, Mrs., 117
Culloden, battle of, 42, 85
Cumbernauld, 24, 187
Cumin, Patrick, 57
Cunninghame Graham, R. B., 93, 148, 151, 152 and n., 163
Czechoslovakia, 9; Czech (Bohemian) national movement, 124, 136, 148

Daily Express, 157
Daily Record, 157, 159
Dalziel, Sir Henry, 98, 99
Davidson, J. Morrison, 87–8
Davie, Dr. G. E., 13, 39
Defence, policy of the S.N.P. on, 208, 211
Defence of the Realm Act, 138
Democracy, Scottish, 25–7
Denmark, 201, 202
Devolution, *see* Home Rule All Round
Diack, William, 115–16, 135, 138
Disraeli, B., 83
Disruption, The (1843), 54, 72
Dobbie, Joseph, 134
Donaldson, Arthur, 180
Donaldson, Principal Sir James, 43, 96
Dott, George and Mary, 175
Douglas, The Black, 89
Douglas, Major C. H., 144, 175
Dounreay, 48, 201
Dove, P. E., 81, 87
Dover House, 61
Dress, Celtic *versus* Saxon, 130
Drucker, Peter, 175
Dublin rising (1916), 136, 139
Dumfries, 184
Dunbar, battle of, 42
Dunbartonshire, 157, 164, 184
Duncan, Joseph F., 140
Dundas, Henry (1st Viscount Melville), 71
Dundas, Robert (2nd Viscount Melville), 59, 71
Dundee, 16, 21, 23, 85, 97, 102, 126, 152, 175, 187, 188–9
Dyer, Iain, 185–6

East Kilbride, 24, 187

Eastwood School Board, 117
Edinburgh, 16, 21–2, 24, 37, 39, 40, 53, 61, 68, 73, 78, 80, 84, 86, 94n., 96, 132, 134, 142, 143, 150, 157, 160, 172, 178, 184, 187, 191, 194, 205, 206, 209
Edinburgh, University of, 43, 128, 132, 133, 173n.
Edinburgh Academy, The, 37, 38
Edinburgh Review, 35, 53, 69, 71, 152
Education, Scottish, 15, 25–6, 37–45, 56–8, 80, 101, 175, 209
Edward VII and I, title of, 126, 131
Eigg, 20
Electronics industry, 48
Emigration from Scotland, 17–18, 30, 49, 61, 100, 190
Empire Free Trade, 157
Employers' organizations, 28, 31
'England' *versus* 'Britain', 81–2, 128, 129, 130
English, Scottish use of, 34–6
English- and Welsh-born persons living in Scotland, 48–9
English ministers and Scotland, 51–9
Erskine of Marr, Hon. Ruaraidh Stuart, 110, 121, 123, 124, 125, 128, 136–45, 148, 155, 160, 162
Estimates, Scottish, 101
Eton, 36
European Economic Community, 196, 208
Evergreen, The, 43
Ewing, Mrs. Winifred, 185–6
Expositor, 146
Eyre-Todd, George, 128

Farm Servants' Union, 140
Federal Government Bill, proposed 1968, 191
Ferguson, William, 13
Fiery Cross, 85, 121–3, 128, 133
Fife, 157, 168, 184
Finance houses, 30
First Book of Discipline, 25
Fisheries, 142, 174, 208, 222–3
Flags, Scottish complaints about, 77, 131 and n.
Fletcher of Saltoun, Andrew, 66, 83
Flodden, battle of, 42
Forestry, 222
Forth Road Bridge, 181
Forward, 108, 140

243

Index

Forward Scotland, 177
Fotheringay Castle, 85
Foundry Workers' Union, 200
France, 10, 16, 21, 24, 39, 43, 45, 48, 56, 67, 69, 135, 145, 154; French Revolution, 53, 71
Fraser, A. Campbell, 39
Fraser, Thomas, 186
Fraser-Mackintosh, Charles, 93
Free Church of Scotland, 72–3, 74–6, 119, 173
Free Man, 174, 175
Fyfe, Peter, 117

Gaelic, Scottish, 11, 15, 18, 46, 123–6, 136, 137, 144, 154, 160, 178
Gaelic Society of Inverness, 123
Gallacher, William (of the Communist Party), 139 and n., 192
Gallacher, William (of the S.C.W.S.), 117, 171
Galt, John, 26
Geddes, Sir Patrick, 42–4, 46, 47
Geneva, 68
George IV, 70
George, Henry, 175
Germany, 39, 40, 42–5, 48, 122, 166, 192
Gibb, Andrew Dewar, 159, 163, 165
Gibson, Thomas H., 142, 152
Gilfillan Memorial Church, 126
Gillies, Iain, 142
Gillies, William, 142, 143, 156
Gladstone, W. E., 56, 60, 82, 89, 91, 93, 99; on national question (1886), 91–2
Glasgow, 16, 17, 18, 21, 22, 23, 24, 73, 78, 81, 105, 117, 118, 130, 131, 139, 160, 166, 167, 185, 186, 187, 194, 201, 206; University, 118, 132, 143, 151–2, 153, 156–7, 158, 172; parliamentary constituencies, 27, 139, 152, 157, 158, 159, 167, 177, 184, 185
Glasgow and Aberdeen Universities, 104
Glasgow Herald, 46, 49, 82, 147, 162, 194
Glasgow University Scottish Nationalist Association, 118, 143, 150–2, 172
Glen-Coats, Sir Thomas and Lady, 166
Glenrothes, 24, 187
Gollan, John, 193
Graham, D. M., 141n.

Graham, R. B. Cunninghame, 93, 148, 151, 152 and n., 163
Graham, William, 140
Grant, James, 76–7, 78, 85, 88
Grant, John, 77
Gray, Robert, 170
Greek, 37, 40
Greenock, 16, 128, 130, 157, 164, 192
Grieve, C. M., *see* MacDiarmid, Hugh
Grimond, Jo, 212
Guild socialism, 175
Gulland, J. W., 95
Guth na Bliadhna, 123, 124, 125, 126, 135, 136, 169

Hailes, Lord, 65
Haldane Committee, 107
Halifax, Viscount, 107
Hamilton by-election (1967), 182, 185–187, 200
Hamilton, Duke of, 186
Hapsburg empires, 10
Harcourt, Sir William, 57–9
Hardie, J. Keir, 93, 94 and n., 114
Hawick, 93
Heath, Edward, 196, 198
Hebrides, 105, 109
Hepburn, R. R., 37
Heraldry, 77, 80, 128
Highland games, 18
Highland Land League, 124, 137, 140, 141–2
Highlander, The, 123
Highlanders' Institute, 16
Highlands of Scotland, 15–16, 17–19, 40, 60, 61, 67, 93, 123–5, 137, 140, 181
Highlands and Islands Development Board, 185
History, teaching of Scottish, 21, 44, 126–8, 130, 132–3
Hogge, J. M., 95, 135, 141
Holland, 10, 38, 45, 56, 109
Home Office, 60
Home Rule All Round, 11, 92–3, 97–8, 103, 106–7, 118, 191
Home Rule Bills, 95–106, 117–18
Home Secretary, 60
Hope, Lord Justice-Clerk, 54
Horne, Sir Robert, 156n.
Horner, Leonard, 37
Housing, Scottish, 23–4, 190
Hughes, Emrys, 194

Index

Hume, David, 36, 67, 68
Hungary, 10, 136
Hunter, W. A., 94

Imperial federation, 95, 106
Imperial War Council, 110
Incomes, Scottish, 23, 29, 32, 190
Independent Labour Party (I.L.P.), 108, 135, 177
India, 31, 76, 78
Indian Civil Service, 38
Industries, Scottish, 21, 31, 47, 48–9, 174, 202–3, 223–4
Inglis, Lord President, 54
Inland Revenue, 62
Innes Review, 21
International Scots Home Rule Association, 96
Invergordon, 198, 201
Inverness, 105, 157, 165, 192n.
Inverness-shire, 105
Ireland, 10, 19, 45, 80, 91, 124, 199, 201, 202, 210; Gaelic movement, 11, 124, 136, 138, 162; Labour movement, 138, 139; Home Rule for, 11, 19, 21, 82, 85, 87, 91, 93, 94, 95, 97, 98, 99, 102, 103, 104, 107, 119, 121, 148
Irish Anti-Partition League, 177
Irish immigrants in Scotland, 15, 16, 18–21, 48, 49, 105
Irish Republican Army (I.R.A.), 19
Iron, 21
Israel, 208
Italy, 10, 192

Jacobitism, 67–8, 76, 85, 121, 154
James VI and I, 10, 67
Johnson, Samuel, 35, 42, 67
Johnston, John, 194
Johnston, Russell, 191
Johnston, Thomas, 108–10, 140, 156n.
Jokes, English, about Scotland, 73–4, 130
Journalism, 146–8
Judges, Scottish, 52–4, 71, 102, 132, 215
Judicial Committee of the Privy Council, 102
Jute, 21

Kailyard school, 146, 147, 155, 162
Kellas, James G., 13, 14

Kelso, 146
Kennedy, T. F., 60
Kilmarnock, 157, 164
Kipling, R., 109
Kirkcaldy, 98, 99, 168, 173
Kirkwood, David, 140
Kossuth, L., 11

Labour exchanges, 102
Labour, Ministry of, 62, 169
Labour Party, 11, 103, 114–15, 138, 166, 167, 170–1, 182–9, 198–204, 205
Labour Party (Scottish Council), 110–14, 138
Lallans, 46
Lanarkshire, 16, 81, 94, 105, 148, 186
Land law, 22
Latin, 35, 37
Lauder, Harry, 146
Law, Andrew Bonar, 103
Law, Scottish, 15, 22, 51–6, 215
Law Officers, Scottish, 52–5
Lawyers, Scottish, 34–5, 37, 42–3, 49, 52–6, 71, 197, 204
League of Nations, 9
Leask, William Keith, 122, 126
Legitimist Jacobite League of Great Britain and Ireland, 85
Leipzig, 43
Leishman, Treasurer, 39
Liberals, Scottish, 11, 71–2, 91, 92–6, 153, 166, 167, 170, 182–4, 189–92
Liberal Unionists, 91
Liberia, 10
Limousin, 68
Lindsay, Colin, 14
Linklater, Eric, 148
Liverpool, 21, 104
Lloyd George, David, 103, 106, 107, 136
Local Government Board for Scotland, 61
Local Government (Scotland) Act, 1929, 156
Lochaber, 20, 68
Lockhart, J. G., 71
Lockhart of Carnworth, 135–6
Lodge, Richard, 128
London, City of, 30, 31
Lord Advocate for Scotland, 52–5, 57, 59, 60, 61, 96, 100
Lord High Commissioner, 101, 102

Index

Lord Lyon King of Arms, 77
Lords, House of, 35, 51, 102
Lorimer, James, 39
Lothair, 83
Lowther, Speaker, 107
Luxembourg, 209
Lynch, Arthur, 45
Lyon, Hugh, 113
Lyttelton, Lord, 36

M'Clounie, J. M., 199
MacCormick, John, 151, 152, 153, 155–9, 161–72, 179
McCrone, Gavin, 202
MacDiarmid, Hugh (C. M. Grieve), 45, 46, 108, 135, 136, 140, 143, 144–5, 148, 151, 152, 159, 161–2, 176, 192, 193, 194, 210
MacDonald, Angus, 140, 141
Macdonald, John, 170
Macdonald, J. A. M., 107
MacDonald, Ramsay, 93, 114–15
McDowall, Kevan, 159
MacEanruig, Aonghas, 140
MacEwen, Sir Alexander, 159, 163, 164, 165, 167
McInnes, Myles, 93
McIntyre, Dr. Robert D., 172–6, 183
Mackenzie, Alexander, 93, 123
Mackenzie, Compton, 148, 151, 153, 156
Mackintosh, John P., 200
McLaren, Duncan, 77, 82
Maclean, John, 138–40, 148, 192, 194
MacLean, John D., 178
MacLean, Neil, 141n.
Maclean, Norman, 33–4, 146
Maclean, Surgeon-General, 93
Macleod, clan, 15
MacLeod, George (Lord MacLeod of Fuinary), 194
Macleod, John, 93
MacNeacail, H. C., 135, 142
McNicol, J. M., 157
Macrae, Rev. David, 126–8
Magna Carta, 25
Magyars, 10
Man, Isle of, 85
'Manager', Scottish, 70–1, 73
Manchester, 105
Mar, John, Earl of, 125
Marriage laws, Scottish, 34
Marx, Karl, 137, 138

Marxist arguments against Home Rule, 116
Mary, Queen of Scots, 85
Masson, David, 72
Mathematics, 45
Maxton, James, 110, 135, 140
Maxwell, Sir Herbert, 132
Mazzini, G., 11
Melbourne, Viscount, 70
Melville, Henry Dundas, 1st Viscount, 71
Melville, Robert Dundas, 2nd Viscount, 59, 71
Members of Parliament, Scottish, 28–9, 36–7, 51, 54–5, 57–9, 67, 72, 75, 100, 101, 131, 171–2, 206, 213–14
Midlothian, 184
Midlothian campaign, 56
Midlothian and Peebles, North, by-election 1929, 152, 153–4, 156–7, 168, 184
Millar, John Hepburn, 132, 162
Miller, Hugh, 64–5, 76
Milner, Lord, 106, 159
Miners, Scottish, 110, 140, 148, 186, 192, 193, 200, 204, 207, 219
Mitchell, E. Rosslyn, 29, 152n.
Mitchell, William, 119, 121
Mitchell Library, Glasgow, 151
Moderates, The, *see* Scottish Party
Modern Scot, 145, 158
Moffatt, Abe, 194
Montpellier, 43
Montrose, 157
Montrose, 6th Duke of, 153, 159, 163
Moore, Tom, 148
Morar, 20
Morley, John, 89, 92, 94
Mosley, Sir Oswald, 156n.
Motherwell, 16, 117, 173, 183
Motor industry, 48, 201
Muir, Edwin, 46, 161–2
Muirhead, Roland Eugene, 108, 117–18, 121, 143, 150–2, 157, 165, 169, 177–8
Mull, 138
Mundella, A. J., 57
Municipal elections, 1968, 187
Munro, Neil, 147
Munro Ferguson, R. C., 95
Murdoch, John, 123
Murdoch, W. G. Blaikie, 142
Murison, David, 14

246

Murray, Charles, 148
Murray, Gilbert, 156n.

N.A.L.G.O., 200
Napier, Theodore, 85, 87, 121–2, 125, 126, 129, 131, 134
National Association for the Vindication of Scottish Rights, 77–8, 119
National Committee (formed by Hon. R. Erskine, 1919), 139, 140–2
National Gallery of Modern Art, 63
National Gallery of Scotland, 63
National insurance, 102
National Library of Scotland, 63
National Museum of Antiquities of Scotland, 63
National names, 81–2, 128, 129, 130
National Party of Scotland (1928–34), 115, 118, 143–5, 149, 150, 152–60, 161–5
National plan, 185
National Seamen's and Firemen's Union, 116
National Union of Mineworkers, *see* Miners
National Union of Railwaymen, 116, 199
Nationalism as a world phenomenon, 9–11
Naval bases, 48, 76
Naval chaplains, 131
Naval flags, 131
New Age, 175
New Towns, 24, 187
New Zealand, 18, 25, 175, 205, 212
Newbattle, 119
Newcastle-on-Tyne, 105
Newcastle Programme, 95
Nicoll, William Robertson, 146–7
Nineteenth Century and After, 147
North British Daily Mail, 82
North British Review, 72
North Briton, 67
Northern Ireland, 19, 31, 197
Norway, 10, 15, 202, 208, 222

O'Connell, Daniel, 11
Old age pensions, 102
Orange Lodges, 19
Orkney, 105, 161; Orkney and Shetland constituency, 192n.
Oslo, 206

Outfitter, The, 129
Oxford, 37, 38, 43, 44, 132
Oxford Book of Scottish Verse, 79

Paisley, 170
Palmerston, Viscount, 70, 81
Paris, 45, 110–11, 114, 138
Parliament Act (1911), 95
Parliament House, 55
Parnell, C. S., 11, 82
Paterson, Hugh, 142, 143, 159
Paton, Professor H. J., 13
Patronage, church, 33, 51
Peace Conference at Paris (1919), 110–11, 114, 138
Pearse, P. H., 124
Peel, Sir Robert, 59
Peers, Scottish, 84–5
P.E.N., Scottish centre, 149, 161
Perth, 122, 183
Perthshire, 183, 184
Peterhead Harbour, 131
Phillips, T., 116
Phillipson, Dr. N. T., 14
Philosophy, Scottish, 45, 80
Pictish Review, 140, 144
Picts, 15, 65
Pirie, Duncan Vernon, 95, 96, 99
Playfair, Sir Lyon, 40–1, 104
Poor law, Scottish, 26
Population of Scotland, 15–21
Post Office, 62, 102, 106, 201, 204
Power, William, 147, 148, 149, 167, 168
Power, fuel and, 174, 207, 219–21
Presbyterianism, Scottish, 18, 21, 25–8, 39, 149–50, 154, 158, 173–4
Prestwick, 201
Privy Council, Scottish, 51, 77, 101, 102, 214
Progressive party, 195
Punch, 73, 130

Quarterly Review, 71
Queen's and Lord Treasurers' Remembrancer, 59

Railway companies, Scottish, disappearance of, 116, 199
Railways, 207, 226
Rait, Robert, 135
Redmond, John, 145

Reform Act of 1832, 54, 71–2
Reformation, Scottish, 42
Renaissance, the idea of a new Scottish, 43, 45, 147–8, 209
Renfrewshire, 152, 157, 165
Richmond, 6th Duke of, 60–1
Riddell, William, 189
Robertson, F. J., 96
Robertson, John, 141n.
Robertson, William, 35, 36, 44
Robroyston, 85
Romans, John, 119 and n., 120–1
Romantic movement, 10
Rome, 20
Rosebery, 5th Earl of, 54, 56, 58, 60, 83, 92
Rosebery Burns Club (Glasgow), 130
Ross, J. McGilchrist, 93
Ross, W. Stewart, 87
Ross, William, 198
Ross and Cromarty, 192n.
Round Table movement, 106
Roxburgh, Selkirk and Peebles, 183 and n., 191, 192n.
Royal Commission on Scottish Affairs (Balfour Commission), 172
Royal Scottish Museum, 63
Russell, Lord John, 70
Russia, 9, 45
Russian Revolution, 136–7
Rutherglen, 184

St. Andrew Society of Edinburgh, 121, 123, 127
St. Andrew Society of Glasgow, 127–8
St. Andrew's House, 62, 212
St. Andrew's Societies, 18
St. Andrews, University of, 43, 44, 96
Salisbury, 3rd Marquess of, 12, 57, 58–9, 60
Samuel, Sir Herbert, 152n., 153
Sandford, Lord, 57
Saskatchewan, 180
Saurat, Denis, 45
Scandinavia, 15, 45, 161, 175
Scanlan, Archbishop, 20
School boards, 57, 126, 127
'Scotch' *versus* 'Scottish', 81–2
Scotia, 123
Scotland—national characteristics, 24–9
Scots colleges abroad, 20, 43

Scots Independent, 142, 143, 144, 155, 156, 160, 164, 165 and n., 167, 169, 170, 173, 231
Scots Magazine, 83, 230
Scots National League (Comunn nan Albannach), 125
Scots National League (1921–8), 118, 142–4, 148, 150, 152, 160, 169; Policy, 142–3
Scots Observer, 147, 149
Scots overseas, 18
Scotsman, The, 25, 46, 48, 57, 77, 133, 147, 162, 182, 188–9
Scott, F. G., 45
Scott, Sir Walter, 18, 37, 53, 68, 69, 70–1, 149
Scott Moncrieff, George, 149–50
Scotticisms, 34–6
Scottish American, 18
Scottish Board of Agriculture, 62
Scottish Board of Health, 61–2
Scottish Catholic Herald, 21
Scottish Certificate of Education, 41–2
Scottish Convention, 12, 169–72, 179, 189, 204
Scottish Co-operative Wholesale Society (S.C.W.S.), 117
Scottish Council (Development and Industry), 28, 31, 47, 181
Scottish Country Life, 128
Scottish (formerly Scotch) Education Department, 40, 56–8, 61, 101, 104, 131–2
Scottish Field, 128
Scottish Grand Committee, 101, 191, 201
Scottish Highlander, 123
Scottish Home Department, 62
Scottish Home Rule Association (1886–1914), 40, 83, 86, 88, 92, 93–4, 108, 119–21, 123; policy, 120
Scottish Home Rule Association (1918–28), 108, 114, 115, 117–18, 121, 143, 150, 169
Scottish Home Rule Council, 96
Scottish Horse and Motormen's Union, 113, 199
Scottish Labour College, 138
Scottish Liberal Association (Federation), 92–3, 94–6, 153, 155
Scottish Nation, 96
Scottish National Assembly (1947–9), 170–1

Scottish National Association for the Promotion of National Ideals and the Defence of Scottish Rights (1905), 134
Scottish National Association of Victoria, 79
Scottish National Committee, 95
Scottish National Congress, 177–9
Scottish National Development Council, 149
Scottish National League (1904), 133–134
Scottish National Movement, 118, 148, 150
Scottish National Party, early use of the term, 133
Scottish National Party (1934+), 24, 47, 48, 152, 160, 163–9, 172–7, 179–80, 183–9, 192, 194, 195, 196, 198, 201, 204–12; 1934 Policy, 163–4; 1936 Policy, 174–5; 1946 Policy, 175–6, 213 ff.; 1968 Policy, 205–27
Scottish National Portrait Gallery, 63
Scottish National Rights Association (Dundee), 126
Scottish National Song Society, 129
Scottish Nationalist, early use of the term, 133, 134
Scottish Nationalist, 120, 133
Scottish Office, 27, 31, 51, 56–63, 91, 99–100, 191, 211
Scottish Parliamentary Labour Party, 94
Scottish Party, 159–60, 163, 165
Scottish Patriot, 122–3, 128, 133, 134
Scottish Patriotic Association (Glasgow), 126–8
Scottish Patriots, 178, 179
Scottish Provisional Constituent Assembly, 178
Scottish Review, 115–16, 126, 135–8, 141, 142, 158, 169
Scottish Rights Association (Greenock), 128
Scottish Rights Society, *alternative title of* National Association for the Vindication of Scottish Rights
Scottish Secretariat, 108, 165n., 168
Scottish Self Government Bill (1966), 191
Scottish Trades Union Congress, 14, 15, 110–11, 114, 115–17, 138, 199–200, 226

Scottish Union, 169
Scottish Vanguard, 194
Scottish War of Independence, 21, 81
Secretary for Scotland (1885–1926), 11, 51, 56–9, 59–63, 82, 109, 112; Secretary of State for Scotland (1926+), 59, 62; proposals for a Secretary of State, 75–7
Security, Act of (1707), 51
Selective employment tax, 198
Sgeulaiche, An, 123
Shakespeare, W., 25
Sheridan, Thomas, 35
Shetland, 15, 105, 162
Shinty, 123
Shinwell, Emanuel, 194
Shipping and shipbuilding, 21, 207
Shop Assistants' Union, 116
Sinn Féin, 19, 124, 139
Smillie, Robert, 114, 140
Smith, Adam, 36, 68, 69
Smith, Dr. F. Barry, 14
Snodgrass, Catherine P., 178
Social Credit, 145, 174
Social Security, Ministry of, 62
Social Structure, Scottish, 21–4, 39
Society of Improvers in the Knowledge of Agriculture in Scotland, 52
Solicitor General for Scotland, 52
Somerville, Matthew F., 178
South Uist, 20
Soviet Union, *see* Russia
Speaker's Conference on Devolution, 103, 107, 117
Spence, Lewis, 135, 147, 148, 150, 152–155, 168, 184, 210; on Scottish literary men, 154–5
Steel, David, 191, 212
Steill, John, 78
Steuart, Sir James, 68
Stevenson, Robert Louis, 109
Stewart, Dugald, 69
Stewart, John Alexander, 131 and n.
Stirling, 78, 143, 152, 158, 172, 176
Stirlingshire, 98, 99, 184
Stockholm, 206
Stone of Scone, 172
Strachey, Lytton, 149
Strasbourg, 43
Stuart, James, 171–2
Suburban life, 22–4
Sunday Post, 175
Swabia, 68

Sweden, 10
Switzerland, 10

Taylor, Wilfred, 147
Temperance reform, 100
Texas, 66
1320 Club, 178–9, 209–10
Thistle, The, 96, 122, 123, 126, 127, 128, 129, 130, 131, 132
Thistle Group, 195, 197
Thomson, Charles William, 127, 128
Thomson, George Malcolm, 149
Thorpe, Jeremy, 191
Times, The, 79–80, 130, 145
Toothill Report, 181
Trades Unions, 22, 28, 115–16, 138, 170, 199–200, 204, 225–6; *see also* Scottish Trades Union Congress
Transport, 174, 198–9, 207
Transport Act (1968), 198–9
Transport and General Workers' Union, 116
Treason law, 51
Treasury, 59–60; Scottish Lord, 60
Trevelyan, Sir George, 51

Ulster, 135, 197
Under Secretaries at Scottish Office, 61–2
Unemployment, 28, 29–30, 139, 190, 206
Union of the Crowns (1603), 10, 67, 73
Union of 1707, 10, 34, 50–2, 56, 66–7, 72, 75, 77, 82, 84, 86, 105, 111, 129, 138, 156, 197, 200
Union of Picts and Scots, 144
Unionist Party, *see* Conservatives, Scottish
United Nations, 9, 211, 216
United Presbyterian Church, 126
United States of America, 10, 18, 19, 31, 45, 66, 81, 96, 173, 175, 180, 196, 197, 201
Universities, Scottish, 25–6, 28, 37–40, 44, 46, 57, 61, 70, 80, 128, 132, 204, 209

University Grants Commission, 49
Ure, Alexander (Lord Advocate), 100

Victoria, Queen, 26, 85, 121

Waddie, Charles, 86–7, 88–90, 119 and n., 120–2, 133, 134
Wales, 11, 91, 93, 94, 97, 98, 108, 193, 197
Wallace, Sir William, 21, 25, 64, 65, 70, 85, 89, 109, 132, 194; Monument at Abbey Craig, 78–9, 80; Monument at Ballarat, 79
Wanliss, T. D., 44, 85, 96, 121, 122, 126, 129, 133, 162
War, S.N.P. policy on, 166, 168–9
Weimar, 43
Welsh, James C., 148
West Lothian, 183, 184, 187
Western Isles, 15, 165
Westminster Review, 71
Whisky, 47
Whitelocke, Bulstrode, 74
Wilkes, John, 67
Wilkie, Alexander, 141n.
Wilson, Alexander, 185–6
Wilson, Harold, 182, 200
Wilson, John, 121, 122–3, 126, 128, 129, 133–4
Wilson, Woodrow, 138
Winstanley the Digger, 87
Wishaw, 16
Witness, The, 76, 78
Wood, Hon. Edward, 107
Wood, Wendy, 47, 148, 178, 210
Woodburn, Arthur, 171
Workers' Party of Scotland, 140, 193–194, 210
Writers to the Signet, Society of, 52–3

Young, Douglas, 14, 166, 167, 168–9, 173, 174, 176, 210
Young Conservatives, 195
Young Ireland, 73, 148
Young Scots Society, 95, 108
Younger, George, 27 and n.